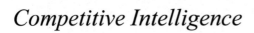

Competitive Intelligence

Competitive Intelligence

Gathering, Analysing and Putting it to Work

CHRISTOPHER MURPHY

GOWER

Published by
Gower Publishing Limited
Gower House
Croft Road
Aldershot
Hants GU11 3HR
England

Gower Publishing Company
Suite 420
101 Cherry Street
Burlington
VT 05401-4405
USA

Christopher Murphy has asserted his right under the Copyright, Designs and Patents Act 1988 to be identified as the author of this work.

British Library Cataloguing in Publication Data
Murphy, Christopher
    Competitive intelligence: gathering, analysing and putting
    it to work
    1. Business intelligence
    I. Title
    658.4'72

0 566 08537 2

Library of Congress Control Number: 2005929611

Printed and bound in Great Britain by TJ International Ltd, Padstow, Cornwall.

Contents

List of Figures

List of Tables

Foreword by Michael Ridpath

In business, as in war, politics or games, you cannot operate effectively unless you know what everyone else is doing. A general can never win a battle if he doesn't know the location and strength of his enemy. Political elections are about choice, how can a party provide the most attractive manifesto if it doesn't know the policies to which it will be compared? Imagine playing a game of chess as black when the white pieces are invisible. It would be a short game.

So too with business. Many businesses are inward looking, with managers spending most of their time discussing budgets, year-on-year forecasts and inter-departmental squabbles as if the outside world does not exist. In fact, there is a tendency for *all* businesses to slump towards this bureaucratic state unless someone at the top forces them to do otherwise.

It is the process of looking outwards that Mr Murphy discusses in this excellent book. He shows how to gain a total understanding of the market in which a company operates and the competitors within it. As Mr Murphy demonstrates, this is much more than a question of gathering facts and figures. It involves understanding the strategy and motivations of competitors and customers, assessing the factors that make a market what it is today and how these are likely to develop in the future. In business, unlike in games, the rules change all the time. These changes are not formally announced, you have to find out about them for yourself. Mr Murphy shows us how.

My novels[*] are firmly set in the milieu of business and finance. Whether writing about biotechnology or virtual reality, hedge funds or emerging markets, dot.coms or newspapers, I am aiming not just to provide authentic detail, but more importantly to try to convey how a section of the business world *works*. One of the things that has always fascinated me about businesses and markets is the way they represent the interaction of hundreds, thousands, or even millions of human beings, each with their own agenda, pursuing profit, power, security or just a quiet life.

To give a true picture of the real world I don't want numbers, I want opinions and prejudices, motivation and emotion, conflict and change. Over the past ten years Mr Murphy has provided invaluable help in these research efforts, as much through the width of his knowledge as the depth. I've often wondered, how on earth did Chris come up with that answer? Now I've read this book, I know.

---

[*] The works of Michael Ridpath, the world's leading financial thriller writer, are not only supremely entertaining and enjoyable novels, but also contain much informative and instructional material for anyone interested in business: www.michaelridpath.com

Acknowledgements

Although this book appears under the name of a single author many people have contributed to its publication.

Ingmar Folksman initially commissioned the work. His persuasiveness was decisive in getting me to undertake this project at all – a daunting task for someone who has never written anything as lengthy and complicated as a monograph. Ingmar's urbane and insightful guidance also ensured that my efforts were pointed in the right direction from the very beginning.

During the subsequent evolution of the text I was fortunate to have the support and advice of two outstanding Gower Publishing editors, Jonathan Norman and Guy Loft. Their expertise, motivating influence and patience were crucial in encouraging me to press forwards when I was feeling less than enthusiastic. The book has also benefited hugely from the detailed and most helpful criticism made by them and Gower's external editors, which has assisted me powerfully in improving upon my first draft. I know how heavy their other duties are so their generous commitment of so much time and hard graft is much appreciated.

Jonathan and Guy have stayed on board throughout the development of this book, but Fiona Martin of Gower had the arduous task of piloting the text to harbour in the form of proof pages. Her consistently imperturbable and amiable approach to this complex and often frustrating part of the project was cheering and professionally impressive. Nikki Dines subsequently took up the baton in handling proof corrections and other difficult production matters with considerable skill and charm. On the marketing side Luigi Fort has been splendidly enthusiastic and imaginative, while his colleagues Donna Hamer and Gemma Court also deserve my thanks for their ready support.

The genesis of a book of this sort is to be found, of course, in activities far earlier than my commissioning editor's invitation to discuss such a project. So I must express special gratitude to Margery Hyde, who asked me to deliver a course on 'Competitive Intelligence' (CI) at a time when the subject was much less well-known in Europe than in it was to become in later years. Having to present this course forced me to sharpen hitherto hazily formed ideas, place them within a coherent structure and dig deeper into the rich seams of knowledge, techniques and opinion that had been contributed by practitioners and scholars working in the CI field. As well as being the ultimate inspiration of this book, Margery has been a source of consistently sound counsel and a generator of a flow of creative ideas from those early days to the present.

I also have been blessed with huge good fortune in enjoying the help of many other talented people. They have given so generously of their time, knowledge, skill and uplifting encouragement in assisting me before and during this project and I now wish to repay a little of what I owe them by expressing my admiration and affection for them and my gratitude for their support.

First, my post-graduate tutors: Alan Beattie, formerly of the Department of Government, London School of Economics; Professor Roderick Floud, former Vice-Chancellor and now President of London Metropolitan University; and Leslie Hannah, Professor of Economics,

University of Tokyo, formerly Dean of the Sir John Cass Business School and Chief Executive of Ashridge Management College.

Next Charles Handy, whose ideas so heavily influenced me in searching for and discovering a new and far happier working life and whose kindly words have been of significant value to me at two decisive moments in my career.

My thanks is naturally due to my legal and accounting editorial colleagues on international corporate procedures: Len Sealy, S.J. Berwin Professor Emeritus of Corporate Law, University of Cambridge; Peter Xuereb, Professor of European and Comparative Law, University of Malta; Bob Drury, Senior Lecturer in Law, University of Exeter; Clive Emmanuel, Professor of Accounting, University of Glasgow; Sid Grey, Professor of International Business and Head of the School of Business, University of Sydney, as well as Chris Nobes, PricewaterhouseCoopers Professor of Accounting, University of Reading.

I have also benefited from the stimulating insights and alternative standpoints provided by academic friends working in fields seemingly unrelated to business: Alistair Black, Professor of Library and Information History at Leeds Metropolitan University; Dr. Werner Heinz, archaeologist; Dr. Teresa Fuentes Peris, Department of Spanish and Portuguese, University of Leeds, and Gareth L. Schmeling, Professor of Classics, University of Florida.

Profound thanks needs to be extended to the many excellent colleagues I have been privileged to work with and from whom I learned so many valuable lessons. For reasons of confidentiality many I would like to praise cannot be named, but they can be assured their contribution is not forgotten.

My public gratitude is thus due to: Martin Ainsworth, Fatma Ali, Karol Bains, MarySusan Barry, Amit Ben-Haim, Jacky Berry, Paola Binelli, Jude Bissett, Nick Blaker, Antoine Bordelais, Wendy Brooke, Nick Brown, Tim Buckley Owen, Garry Campbell, Rachel Charles, Lynne Clitheroe, Laurence Collins, Dr Roger Cordery, Desmond Crone, Charlotte Dominguos, Gill Dwyer, Anne Diepman-O'Grady, Sue Edgar, Ann Folksman, Sian Gough-Roberts, Tony Hay, Stephen Hume, Kevin Jewell, Ben Johnston, Catherine Kelly, Veronica Kennard, Sharon Lake, Laila Luff, Mike McKinley, James McLaughlin, Hasmita Makwana, Tim Marriott, Mario Mesilio, Frieda Midgley, Christine O'Hare, Sean O'Neill, Christiana Outu, Kim Pearce, Paul Pedley, Daniel Pipe, Vanessa Potts, Brian Reed, Elaine Reid, Jenny Robertson, Tony Rook, David Rose, Pete Savage, Cheryl Schuster, Luke Simonds, Val Skelton, Adrian Stacey, Helen Stranding, Kerrie Stubbs, Jeanne Underwood, Dr Ben Van Den Assem, Rennie Walker, Mary Walwyn, David Wardrop, Sue Watt, Carl Wiper and Adonis Zanettos.

I would particularly like to acknowledge how much I gained from my association with present and former colleagues at Apax Partners, to name just a few: Michael Chalfen, Sir Ronald Cohen, Anne Dillon, Andrew Fischer, Ian Fisher, Anne Glover, Rupert Hill, Shelley Jenkins, Antonia Jenkinson, Helen Kilsby, Charles McIntyre, Jackie Meeks, Charles Montanaro, Shu Ling Ng, David Sykes and Valerie Varcoe.

Exceptional thanks are due to three people whose ever-stimulating company, breadth of knowledge and variety of experience have done so much over many years to widen my horizons and alert me to new possibilities: Andrew Bram Chapman, Richard Ford and Dot Smith.

I am obviously hugely flattered that Michael Ridpath, the world's finest writer of novels set in a corporate environment, should have graced this book with a foreword. His works display superbly the drama, passion and ingenuity that make business a sometimes dangerous vocation, but also so gloriously exciting and rewarding.

Finally, my wife Sheila deserves special recognition for cheerfully taking on the hard graft of reading the entire text and correcting my textual or interpretive mistakes. Her sharp eye for linguistic infelicities and vigorous dismissal of weakly formulated ideas were of enormous benefit in improving my initial manuscript. My debts to Sheila – in so many different ways – are immense.

All those named above have helped realize the publication of this book, but naturally the responsibility for any errors or misjudgements within it is solely mine.

CM, 2005.

Introduction

Intelligence – and the terrifying consequences of failures in it – has overshadowed the first years of the new millennium. Government security services and law enforcement agencies received bitter criticism for not detecting and foiling the horrific '9/11' atrocities in the US. Even more ferocious condemnation was unleashed when the shockingly dire quality of intelligence regarding Iraq's weapons of mass destruction was revealed by official enquiries in America and the UK. In both cases key principles of successful intelligence were violated: in the first example, by failing to assemble an accurate picture of a situation by fitting together many small, often seemingly trivial, pieces of information and using the power of imagination to project the possible shape of things to come; in the second, by sliding into 'group-think' where shared assumptions went unchallenged and evidence was used to buttress rather than test them.

Intelligence failures in business, as opposed to those in the political and military spheres, do not entail death, mutilation or physical devastation. Yet they can still bring great psychological and financial pain in terms of lost aspirations, reputations and jobs.

Good military intelligence can mean the difference between life and death for those having to cope with the terrors of war. In a corporate context it may be the factor that determines success, prosperity and security as against failure, penury and fear. Every business manager needs intelligence to find suppliers, mobilize capital, win customers and fend off rivals. However, obtaining this is often an unplanned, instinctive process. In contrast the executive who has a conscious, systematic approach to acquiring intelligence will be better placed to carry away the most desirable prizes, while safeguarding their firm against the most menacing perils. Such a person, regardless of their professional background, job title or corporate role is a practitioner of 'competitive intelligence' (CI).

Gathering information – and turning this raw data into intelligence by the exercise of judgement – is a permanent and fundamental aspect of business. However, over the last couple of decades competitive intelligence has also emerged as a distinct, recognizable occupational category and evolved into a fully fledged corporate discipline with formal education programmes and a global professional association boasting members in over 50 countries. So the vast number of people in business engaging in some form of this work now have a substantial cadre of vocational specialists they can call upon to provide intelligence services, advice and training.

The purpose of this book

Everyone working in business needs to appreciate the great benefits to personal and corporate performance that purposefully directed competitive intelligence can deliver. While only a proportion will be heavily directly involved in the mechanics of creating it, they still need to understand its value and something of the means through which it is fashioned. Those specializing in this field will naturally wish to possess a thorough awareness of the breadth of its concerns and the wealth of techniques at their disposal.

This book is intended to meet the needs of both parties.

It assumes no previous knowledge and ranges across the whole span of the discipline. The work should thus be a good starting point for anyone coming new to the subject.

However, I also hope it will be of help to more experienced readers by:

- providing a fully developed framework for organizing their existing knowledge;
- bringing together into a single volume – albeit in highly condensed form – a considerable portion of the treasure of wisdom, advice and exhortation amassed by fellow professionals and scholars, which is presently scattered among scores of books and hundreds of journal articles. It thus supplies a launch pad for more searching exploration.

The book is structured so as to cater for a variety of reader requirements and can be used in several ways. Some readers may prefer to start at the beginning and read to the end (particularly when coming to the subject with little previous knowledge of it). Others will like to first study the sections that are of especial interest to them and peruse the others later. More experienced users might just skim or even skip some of the earlier scene-setting chapters. As well as being a textbook this is also a work of reference. It can be used to refresh readers' memories about topics they deal with only occasionally and to enable them to start to come to grips with new ones. Casually browsing through its pages may also prove rewarding and less taxing than attempting to digest it in one go. Finally, the book serves as a thematically organized initial introduction to other works and resources that will provide far greater depth of treatment for the manifold aspects of the discipline that are discussed in it.

What it contains

'Integration' is the keynote of this work. It addresses the academic aspect of competitive intelligence by delineating the theoretical foundations upon which the discipline rests. At the same time I have sought to meet the needs of practitioners for practical advice on how to achieve even greater success in their work. *Competitive Intelligence* combines the teaching I have delivered in business schools and universities with my experience as a practitioner. It thus embraces:

- the theory of business competition – understanding the ways in which companies try to get ahead of rivals in the competitive struggle;
- methods of research and sources of information that generate the raw material for creating intelligence, and
- analytical techniques which transform a mass of inchoate facts and opinions – 'data' – into a guide to making better business decisions – 'intelligence'.

While this work provides a synoptic view of the discipline, it is very far from being an 'encyclopedia of competitive intelligence'. Indeed, many of the individual themes covered – financial analysis or interview techniques for instance – obviously merit a book on their own. So I have concentrated on the vital elements of each topic, sprinkled a generous selection of practical tips and listed other key resources for readers to explore them further.

Competitive intelligence makes considerable demands upon its practitioners. Obtaining it is intellectually challenging and tests their knowledge, ingenuity and resilience. It also has a moral dimension, with them having to gather their material in a scrupulously legal and ethical manner. Furthermore it takes courage for an analyst to not flinch from delivering unwelcome news to a sceptical senior executive or client when this is necessary.

However, it also offers much in the way of compensations. Undertaking research and generating intelligence is a stimulating and creative task. Furthermore studying the competitive landscape ultimately means trying to understand the people involved in the various market players and this human aspect is always a fascinating pursuit. Far from being a dull and dreary discipline, I strongly contend that business intelligence work is fun and the satisfaction to be gained from knowing one's efforts have made a positive difference to management decision taking is very great.

In the course of this book I have tried to convey some of its fascination by recalling some of my own experiences during the many years I have spent as a practitioner. To preserve the confidentiality of clients and sources I have been obliged to omit most of the most interesting ones or alter incidental details of those included, but I hope the ones recounted conjure up something of its variety and appeal. A recurring theme is that successful practitioners should not confine themselves to the study of business in any kind of narrow way, but need to draw on many other disciplines. This includes some, such as literary criticism or anthropology, that may superficially appear very far removed from the world of balance sheets and board meetings. In accord with this aim of enlarging the analyst's horizons, I have not hesitated to include examples from beyond the field of business.

Neither have I shrunk from allowing a dash of humour. Apart from providing a little light relief in what might otherwise be a too stolidly didactic text, this also has a serious purpose. Observing and laughing at the absurd opinions and actions of others gives us a chance to become aware of our own folly – before we pay the price for it. Furthermore, humour is one way of sparking the sort of creative response to solving difficulties and identifying new opportunities that breaks the bonds of thought confined by a excessive (and virtually always solemn) regard for what is familiar, habitual and conventionally accepted.

Audiences this book will benefit

The nature of this subject means that it should be of interest across all sectors.
Specific groups likely to find it of help are:

- those specialist members of staff charged with monitoring competitive developments
- managers in many other functional roles (strategy and corporate planning, marketing, sales, production and research and development) who are also involved in tracking competitive trends within their spheres. They need to know what questions to ask and how they might be answered
- information professionals carrying out research or running knowledge management operations
- senior management striving to systematize or enhance their company's competitive analysis
- management consultants, corporate financiers, commercial lawyers and financial public relations executives who need to understand the competitive environment in order to provide the best advice to clients
- managers of smaller businesses, who recognize their need for CI, but lack the financial resources to employ specialist staff or engage consultants

- investment analysts for whom an appreciation of the competitive situation in the sector they cover is a fundamental requirement
- investment professionals in asset management and private equity houses
- financial and business journalists
- teachers and students involved in business studies courses
- officials in trade associations and chambers of commerce
- public servants in the Civil Service, local government and regulatory bodies who need to understand the world of business and are obliged to undertake research on industries and individual companies in order to discharge their duties with full effectiveness
- employees involved in corporate research on behalf not-for-profit organizations such as charities, lobbying groups or trade unions.

Despite its primarily commercial orientation, many of the approaches and techniques outlined in the book can be applied to the study of other types of organization. They will naturally have to be adapted to suit the rather different circumstances of, say, a school or hospital, but should still be of value to those managing such non-commercial bodies.

Structure of this book

Part I lays out the background to the practice of competitive intelligence:

- Chapter 1 argues that merely obtaining information on competitors – while vital – is not sufficient. The study of competitors is ultimately motivated by a desire for *self*-understanding, finding answers to the question: 'How can we improve the way we do business?' So competitive intelligence must embrace all aspects of the commercial environment.
- Chapter 2 looks at how the function is actually performed at present (drawing on the evidence of two major surveys) and offers some reflections on obtaining better results from it.
- Chapter 3 provides a theoretical framework for understanding how companies compete and the forces shaping the competitive environment.
- Chapter 4 offers a scheme for describing a firm's resources and operations, the internal drivers of its performance.
- Chapter 5 reviews the external drivers influencing its fortunes that a company must monitor.
- Chapter 6 considers the legal and ethical dimension of the discipline.

Part II focuses on data gathering:

- Chapter 7 examines planning research and creating a knowledge base.
- Chapter 8 outlines a scheme for understanding industry sectors and exploiting the many sources of sectoral information.
- Chapter 9 is devoted to refining research strategies in the light of the results initially achieved, testing of hypotheses and deciding when to terminate a still-uncompleted research project.
- Chapter 10 reviews the regular document filings firms incorporated in Britain must submit to Companies House that are available to researchers.
- Chapter 11 discusses ad hoc public domain filings by UK companies.

- Chapter 12 switches from the UK business scene to examine approaches to researching industries and companies in other countries.
- Chapter 13 is concerned with ways in which researchers make best use of human sources – as distinct from the documentary ones reviewed earlier – of information and enlightenment.
- Chapter 14 considers how researchers can exploit voluntary public information disclosure by enterprises and ways in which direct observation of a company may add to their knowledge of it.
- Chapter 15 is concerned with the creative aspects of CI both in terms of finding information which systematic sources have failed to supply and using creative techniques to tackle difficult problems encountered when undertaking research and analysis. It also offers some thoughts on the craft of analysis.

Part III is devoted to the interpretation of the data collected and the presentation of conclusions derived from this. Its focus moves from gathering information to the process of analyzing this material to create intelligence. The first three chapters provide a grounding in understanding and interpreting a company's report and accounts:

- Chapter 16 outlines the structure and content of financial statements.
- Chapter 17 shows how they can be analyzed to evaluate a firm's financial health and performance.
- Chapter 18 explores the non-financial sections of corporate reports and suggests ways in which they can be sifted to yield further insights.
- Chapter 19 focuses on the crucial issue of 'How trustworthy is our information?', setting out a hierarchy of data reliability and the application of source criticism to appraise its quality.

The following three chapters look at different modes of CI analysis:

- Chapter 20 discusses corporate description. Apart from providing a checklist of the items that may be included in a company profile, it also considers several approaches to delineating corporate culture and assessing the relative influence of individuals within firms.
- Chapter 21 is concerned with making comparisons between companies and determining their relative positions in terms of various competitive strengths and deficiencies.
- Chapter 22 peers in the future. It considers how analysts can hone the personal qualities and apply the forecasting techniques and alternative methods of anticipating what lies ahead that will enable them to make good judgements as to how to best cope with it.
- Chapter 23 is devoted to the final part of the intelligence process – testing and then disseminating the analyst's findings.
- Chapter 24 reverses the focus of the book from obtaining competitive intelligence to ways of shielding one's organization from prying rivals.

A discipline for all times and places

Systematically gathering and assessing information is a human activity stretching back to far beyond the start of historical records. The quest for business intelligence is as old as any form of economic activity.

My initial intention was to use only the most current examples to illustrate the points made in this book. However, I later realized that this reinforced the view (surprisingly often encountered) that CI is in some way a new, untried and perhaps even shallow discipline. By including examples throughout from over 15 years of my professional involvement with the subject (and a number of even earlier ones) I hope to dispel this misconception. I also believe this approach will give the text a more enduring value than one focused on the perhaps transitory and unrepresentative events of the very recent past.

In a similar vein, readers should note that while descriptions of the institutional, legal and technological context are up to date at the time of writing, all of these factors are changing and the pace of change in many of their aspects is accelerating. This also applies to the organizations, publications and websites referred to. I have thus listed (see Appendix 1) some resources that will enable them to stay abreast of the evolving business environment which forms the framework within which intelligence gathering is conducted.

A final few words of encouragement

The sheer range and diversity of subjects and skills referred to in this work may appear daunting and imply that to be good at their jobs CI analysts must be multi-talented polymaths. This is not the case. Versatility is an essential attribute, but this does not mean universal knowledge or mastering a vast array of skills at a high level of adeptness. A chief executive has to possess some measure of understanding of every aspect of their business. They are not expected, however, to have expertise in all areas of it. This also applies to those engaged in CI. They will not perform well if they limit themselves to narrow fields of specialism, so they need a broad sweep of knowledge. The extent of this will vary according to their particular role. In some posts a familiarity with patents may be necessary, in other it will be irrelevant. The crucial point is the analyst should strive to enlarge and deepen their knowledge and extend and hone their skills at every opportunity.

Finally, effective analysts are not vocational hermits, toiling away alone and unaided. They seek the support and advice of both colleagues and people in other organizations, particularly those brought together in various communities of practice. When undertaking CI activities *you are not alone.*

Steps Towards More Effective Competitive Intelligence

Understanding the competitive landscape and contributing to better decision-making

1 *Competitor Intelligence is Not Enough!*

This chapter sets the scene for the rest of the book by arguing that the commonly held view of *competitor intelligence* as merely 'keeping an eye on our competitors' is much too restrictive. In order to realize the full potential of this discipline for protecting and increasing profits its scope must be far wider. The chapter covers the following topics:

- motivation determines actual behaviour so I shall begin by examining some generalized theories about what motivates those involved in business
- the harm that can result from an excessively narrow focus when scanning the competitive environment is then considered. Evidence regarding this, drawn from a major empirical study, is presented together with some business examples
- three major influences on the competitive landscape (technological developments, changes in consumer tastes and the general economic climate) are briefly explored
- CI is shown to be concerned with threats to existing levels of profit and opportunities for increasing them. It also involves the identification of alliance partners (including competitors in some cases)
- the chapter ends with a discussion of terminology – what should this discipline be called?

People engaged in business are often said to have a simple goal – to make as much money as possible. Success or failure is measured by the amount of profit made. This is the classic version of the 'Theory of the Firm' and forms the cornerstone of microeconomic analysis. Compare this clarity of aim with the multiple goals a public administrator has to pursue, trying to balance fairly the interests of different groups and without this single objective measure as the yardstick of performance.

The idea that most of those in business want as much profit as they can get is a valuable analytical fulcrum. While it is an over-simplification of a more complicated reality, it provides us with a good initial point of departure for explaining the behaviour of firms and those managing them. Nevertheless, an awareness that the pursuit of profit does not embrace the whole range of economic motivation and behaviour – and the ability to discern 'non-rational' factors at work – are essential qualities in a good strategist or competitive analyst.

In the real world businesspeople's motives are more complex. The assumption that they are 'rational economic actors' pursuing profit maximization to the exclusion of everything else is flawed. A person who is utterly fixated with a single idea and purpose is surely better described as 'obsessed' rather than 'rational'. All life is a trade-off between various desirable ends. Some business owners prefer to grow their firm to a size that provides them with an acceptable standard of living without the toil, stresses and anxieties that would accompany a bigger scale of operation. In contrast to these 'lifestyle' businesspeople, others may gain greater satisfaction from maximizing the size and growth rate of the enterprise – and hence its economic and social 'presence' – regardless of the effect on profits.

Indeed, William Baumol[1] argues that many firms aim at maximizing sales rather than profits as this led to greater emotional and material rewards for management. This is particularly likely in most large companies, which are run by a cadre of professional managers acting as stewards on behalf of the actual owners. Such an 'agency' relationship offers scope for them abusing their positions and there have been plenty of cases of 'fat cat' executives who were more concerned with ensuring a lavish corporate lifestyle for themselves than looking after the bottom line for shareholders. Similarly, given the notoriously poor record of achieving enhanced profits in the case of numerous mergers and acquisitions, many executives were clearly mesmerized by building corporate size rather than profitability when they set out on the acquisitions trail.

So both owner and hired managers are often motivated by goals other than profit alone. For instance, they may be desperate to damage their rivals (regardless of the effect on their own firm's profits) or may simply end up so focused on the task in hand that they forget why on earth they are doing it. Profit maximization may also be sidelined if its pursuit in a particular situation conflicts with executives' emotional or ethical imperatives. Finally, the best may be the enemy of the good. Aiming to increase profits is an achievable goal; trying to maximize them for a sustained period, as Andrew Ehrenberg has pointed out, is unattainable (because rival firms can undercut the maximizer's prices) and may actually wreck long-term profitability.[2]

Other theorists have proposed a 'behavioural theory of the firm' which views enterprises as a coalition. This eschews any kind of maximizing objective because the groups and individuals within a firm are primarily pursuing their own interests, hence the way a business actually operates is a compromise between these. This model, principally associated with the Carnegie Institute of Technology, also asserts fluid rather than fixed objectives as the goals of these varied interests – or the balance of power between them – change over time.

Competitor intelligence

The discipline I shall be discussing in this book is often termed 'competitor intelligence' and involves observing the other players in our market, comparing their operation with ours and trying to divine their next moves. This approach relies heavily on benchmarking where we make comparisons, using various indicators, between our rivals and us. The result will be something like a school report, flagging up those areas where we enjoy superiority over our competitors and those in which we lag behind them. Strategy will then be guided by efforts to maintain our advantages and close the gaps in areas where our rivals out perform us. One benchmarking study I was involved with concentrated on the client's transport costs. These were found to be considerably higher than those of most other players in their sector. The action conclusion was to eliminate this weakness and the actual means adopted to cut costs was the replacement of the client's expensive dedicated car pool by outsourcing its transport function. Similar exercises trimmed costs without harming performance in other parts of the firm's operations, improved its competitive position relative to other market players and gave a sustained boost to its profits. Learning from others thus allowed the client to gain ground on them.

Yet benchmarking is not enough.

---

1 Baumol, W. (1959), *Business Behaviour, Value, and Growth*, Macmillan.
2 Ehrenberg, A. (2002), 'Marketing: Are you really a realist?', *Strategy and Business*, 27, 25.

In reality, a too narrow view of 'competing' can be a dangerous distraction. Chan Kim and Renée Mauborgne of the Insead business school near Paris carried out an intensive study of some 30 companies across the world to uncover the factors which lead to high growth.[3] They found that the less successful enterprises were the ones who were competitor fixated, devoting their energies to benchmarking themselves against their rivals and making incremental competitive improvements. The winners were those that concerned themselves less with their opponents and their industry's accepted wisdom. Instead they concentrated on 'breaking the mould' by looking at what *customers* wanted, rather than what suppliers were currently giving them, and devising innovations that delivered a radical improvement in value in the eyes of the purchaser.

In the mid-1980s when IBM found that its market share in personal computers was being eroded by Compaq's cheaper, yet good quality machines, the company made beating its rival the centrepiece of its strategy in PCs. The two firms then became locked in a struggle to produce ever-more technologically sophisticated, feature-laden desk computers. They fell into imitating each other's marginal enhancements instead of creating fundamental innovation and were focused on each other's moves rather than shifts in customer preferences. What both companies failed to recognize was that they were offering expensive complexity when what most customers wanted was a cheap and easy to use machine. At the end of the 1980s these deadly rivals saw other, seemingly less well-placed enterprises, trading on low price and user-friendliness, devour their market.

Another case quoted by Kim and Mauborgne – demonstrating the ability of a company to seize a market opportunity by breaking away from the pack – is Callaway's 'Big Bertha' golf club. This was an industry with well-entrenched manufacturers of clubs and thus seemingly unattractive soil in which to nurture market leadership. However, Callaway noted that there was little to distinguish between the products then being sold and found golfers reacted warmly to a club with a bigger head which gave them a more satisfying game.

One major risk is where people in a company have so much industry experience and knowledge that they assume only their accustomed rivals pose competitive danger. They will then fail to detect and respond to an aggressive newcomer. Xerox failed to spot Canon's ability to break into its market because the Japanese company was not perceived as a reprographic equipment manufacturer. Likewise US car makers regarded Honda as a motorcycle producer and woke up too late to the damage it would inflict on them when it began building automobiles.

Attaining pole position in terms of product excellence, a coveted goal for many enterprises, can also leave a firm competitively exposed. Encyclopedia Britannica was proud of its 'best of breed' encyclopedia and had enjoyed a long period of unchallenged pre-eminence. When Microsoft brought out its electronic *Encarta* encyclopedia, Britannica scorned it as far inferior to their product. Just as with IBM and Compaq, the company had lost touch with the market. Encarta was much cheaper and adequately met the needs of many people for an ubiquitous reference source. Britannica then had to make radical and painful adjustments to its offering to stay in business. Market leaders in other sectors have been bruised in a similar way, indeed Clayton Christensen,[4] coined the term 'disruptive technology' to describe situations where a technically inferior offering destabilizes an industry by giving customers most of what they want at a much lower cost.

---

3 Chan Kim, W. and Mauborgne, R. 'Value Innovation: The strategic logic of high growth', *Harvard Business Review* (originally published in 1997, now available as product R0407P from www.harvardbusinessonline.com).
4 Christensen, C. (2003), *The Innovator's Dilemma*, HarperBusiness.

So 'competitor intelligence' is insufficient in itself to enlighten a business to guard against competitive threats or to seize market opportunities. This certainly does not mean ignoring rival firms and what they are up to, but does require a much wider sweep of vision.

Competitive intelligence

Hence this discipline is better described as *competitive intelligence* or CI.

Thus its scope is not limited to researching and assessing other firms and acting to outperform them. It embraces *all* factors that could endanger or enhance a company's revenues and profits. I shall be looking at these in more detail in Chapter 5. For the moment I wish to pave the way by considering the impact of a) technological developments b) changes in consumer tastes c) the general economic climate.

TECHNOLOGY

One of the most influential articles to be published in the *Harvard Business Review* was Theodore Levitt's 'Marketing myopia'.[5] His theme was the dire consequences when an industry failed to see beyond its own limited boundaries. Thus makers of buggy-whips remained blissfully unaware of the implications for their trade posed by the spread of the horseless carriage until their market collapsed. US railway companies were slow to recognize and respond to the competitive threat offered by the nascent automobile and, later, aviation industries. They perceived themselves as operating in the railroad business, whereas they were really providing transport services and their customers would desert in droves once other modes of travelling became more attractive to them.

A more contemporary example of the risks posed by technological development would be Filofax, makers of personal organizers. This product was inspired by the binders filled with technical data and specifications engineers carried with them while on site. The idea of replacing a diary, address book and other reference aids with a single folder whose pages could be added or removed whenever needed proved hugely appealing and the company enjoyed high sales. As electronic miniaturization galloped ahead Filofax found its market under siege. Customers could now access a great deal more information in electronic organizers the size of a cigarette case instead of carrying around a cumbersome volume. They were also able to perform more powerful and faster search and retrieval functions. Filofax had to move from its original business proposition: 'this makes you more efficient', to a greater emphasis on the aesthetics of a fashion accessory that was also useful and easy to use.

CHANGING CONSUMER TASTES

Levitt focused on the capacity of technological change to undermine the competitive foundations of an industry, but other types of shifts in the wider business environment can also cause them to crumble. Consumer tastes may change, devastating a once prosperous sector. Up to about 1960 western men tended to wear hats. A hat was regarded as necessary as a jacket and in old films, when detectives rush out of their office on the way to the scene of a crime, they still grab their hats before leaving. Inside a relatively short period wearing a hat habitually became positively eccentric for all but older men. Some fashion historians trace its sudden decline to Jack

---

5 Levitt, T., 'Marketing myopia', *Harvard Business Review* (originally published in 1960, now available as Product R0407L from www.harvardbusinessonline.com).

Kennedy's inauguration in 1961. On a bitterly cold winter day in Washington, he broke with custom by appearing hatless. The youthful vitality of the handsome, eloquent new president contrasted strongly with his elderly, highly conventional predecessor and is alleged to have inspired men to abandon their hats. This sector of the clothing industry remained in the doldrums until the wearing of baseball caps brought a revival many years later.

GENERAL ECONOMIC CONDITIONS

At first glance it would seem extraordinary that anyone engaged in business would fail to take the general economic climate into account and yet it has happened only too frequently. Examples abound, but I will quote one from my own experience.

CASE OF THE 'FOLLOW THE HERD' FINANCIAL INSTITUTIONS

At the end of the 1980s I was working as a conference producer and we decided to hold a conference on estate agency. Our choice was an obvious one because the sector was going through a period of radical change. A booming house market in Britain had spurred both the number of property transactions and their prices. Estate agents' fees were a percentage of the purchase price, so their income was boosted by both factors. Most agents were highly profitable, small-scale partnerships. Strategists in big financial institutions such as the Prudential saw this as a wonderful opportunity. The market was attractive and they reasoned that buying out partnerships scattered across the country and imposing uniform nationwide branding and exploiting economies of scale would further enhance its profitability. So the financial houses were busily buying up agencies and placing their names over the doors.

In preparing the conference we took soundings from the various players involved and met with a senior executive from one of the acquisitive institutions. My boss and I outlined a counter-scenario to him whereby property prices could not continue rising at such a hectic pace indefinitely, especially as the UK government had adopted a restrictive fiscal and monetary stance to check inflation. We also argued that most of the value of the acquired agencies resided in the local knowledge of the former partners who were now quitting the business and enjoying affluent lives of leisure from the proceeds of selling their firms. On that basis these very expensive acquisitions were a poor investment. In response our adviser said: 'I hear all that you are saying and the points you have made are valid. Yet we simply have to do this.' Puzzled we asked: 'But why?' His answer was concise: 'Because all our rivals are doing it.'

Not so much later the economy slipped into a well-forecast recession, the housing market slumped, estate agency profits evaporated and a number of institutions eventually extricated themselves from the sector with considerable losses in terms of prestige as well as money.

In the light of this experience it is hardly surprising that I was not enamoured of this 'lemming' strategy when it dramatically resurfaced during the more recent dot.com debacle.

So the task of *competitive* intelligence (CI) is to help identify and properly assess *both* business risks and opportunities so that they can either be avoided or taken advantage of. Thus the US buggy-whip makers were oblivious to the danger, the Callaway people correctly detected a genuine market prospect, while in the UK financial institutions buying estate agents misjudged an apparently glittering opportunity.

CI is not limited to competitive issues – the role of *cooperative* intelligence

Much discussion of CI is expressed in the vocabulary of warfare and uses martial examples. Although some military analogies are fruitful in the study of business competition I will avoid employing them too often. The art of war is concerned with convincingly threatening or actually inflicting sufficient death and damage to either persuade an enemy to give us what they would otherwise refuse or, in extreme cases, conquer or even annihilate them. The game of business can sometimes be rough, but the kind of behaviour required in war would be regarded as psychotic in a civilian context. Killing our competitors or burning down their premises, unless we are members of a criminal syndicate, is not an acceptable way to win.

Even in less extreme situations, treating business as a form of warfare may produce inferior returns because it assumes gains only result from success at the expense of competitors and ignores the increased profits created for several of the players through business cooperation. Barry Nalebuff, a leading authority on the theory of games (a branch of mathematics concerned with the strategies players adopt, of considerable interest to both business and military leaders) warns against such distractions from the central goal of growing profit. One result from game theory has entered common parlance, the *zero sum game*, where one party gains and another loses within an unchanging total. Tobacco companies, in resisting curbs on cigarette advertising, portrayed their competitive contests as such a game, arguing that their adverts merely shifted market share from one player to another, but did not increase total demand for tobacco products.

Nalebuff sees business as a game, though generally not with a straightforward 'winner/loser' result. Cooperation can increase the size of the prize on offer, while competition decides the extent of each player's winnings. Only where competitors can be effectively eliminated will the simple outcome occur; in most cases there will be a number of winners and losers. He noted Intel's success in the microchip sector helped Microsoft and the latter's triumphs in the software market benefited Intel, while Apple was left out in the cold. With Nalebuff's approach 'winning' is not about beating one's rivals if this relative superiority does not translate into higher profits. Instead it involves seeking a bigger absolute return even if this means competitors also make more money. Such a mindset is thus more in sympathy with the traditional profit-seeking goal than the non-rational 'we'll do down our hated competitors – regardless of the damage it does us'.

Hence film studios initially tried to fight off competition from video rental stores like Blockbuster, only to find that renting and selling videos was greatly expanding the total market for their films. Drug companies work together in health screening campaigns to extend the market for treatments and then battle for individual shares of the increased sectoral spending. Typical forms of alliance are briefly considered at the end of Chapter 5 of this book, while Nalebuff and Brandenburg give many more examples of collaboration between industry rivals in their *Co-opetition*.[6] The competitive landscape they depict is analogous to the political and military contests in Europe during much of the Middle Ages or for the century or so before the French Revolution. These wars, not being fuelled by ideological or national motives, were far less intense than the ferocious Wars of Religion or those that came after 1789 and involved the various parties forming fairly short-lived alliances and having no reluctance in fighting alongside a rival in one theatre while they were belligerents in others.

---

6   Brandenburg, A.M. and Nalebuff, B. (1977), *Co-opetition: A revolutionary mindset that combines competition and cooperation*, Currency.

Nalebuff believes that business strategists and CI analysts may be playing the competitive game in too crude a fashion with their war stories, war games, war rooms, pre-emptive strikes and counter-attacks. Instead he advocates the discipline should embrace not only 'war' – competitive intelligence – but also 'peace' – *cooperative* intelligence – actively searching for collaborative opportunities that may even involve major rivals. As he points out, unlike in other games, in business one can change the rules and the greatest success often results from tearing up the existing rule book.

(It should be emphasized that the forms of cooperation Nalebuff envisages are not those involving illegal anti-competitive practices such as collusive price-fixing or agreements to carve up markets and shut out new entrants. Instead he is referring to relationships between industry players that benefit the consumer as well as the suppliers. A 'win-win' game for both sides.)

What should this discipline be called?

Andreas Persidis[7] has argued that 'competitive intelligence' is a bad name for the speciality as it is too restrictive and he dislikes the word 'competitive' which 'doesn't focus on the big picture, just when our goal should be exactly that'. This contention is valid as regards the narrower 'competitor' intelligence, but unfounded when the broader 'competitive' concept is employed. He is also uneasy about 'intelligence' which he sees as both provocatively arrogant and carrying implications of 'spying'.

One dictionary meaning[8] of the word 'intelligence' is simply 'news', but an 'intelligence department' is 'one which 'gathers and *interprets* information' (my italics). Practitioners of CI have much in common with journalists. They do not act as wire services disseminating news, instead they place it in context, explain its significance and try and predict its future consequences. I have seen no evidence that other colleagues are offended by 'intelligence' in this context, they know it is just a name for a function and not a boast! Nor do I believe dropping 'intelligence' would avoid those irritating 'so you're a kind of corporate spook' comments.

Names like 'business intelligence' or 'corporate intelligence' (which allows the 'CI' abbreviation to be retained) are indeed preferable as they more accurately capture the breadth of this activity. However, 'competitive intelligence' is the most commonly used term and very well entrenched. Abandoning a long-established brand name is not something to do lightly and is often seen by others as either meaningless or even as a defensive euphemism (the great Swedish entrepreneur, Marcus Wallenberg, created a CI unit misleadingly called the 'Statistical Department' for his conglomerate in 1903[9]). So throughout this book I shall simply refer to 'CI', which can stand for either 'competitive intelligence' or 'corporate intelligence' according to the reader's taste.

While on the subject of acronyms: business and management studies, information science and intelligence work have sired a bewildering array of these, but I shall largely eschew them, employing only those in everyday use. Some guidance as to where to find what they stand for is given in Appendix 2 (CI Terminology) on page 255.

Because CI, once no longer confined to just tracking competitors, is now so catholic in its range of concerns it becomes difficult to know where to fix its boundaries. It is intertwined with functions such as 'market research', 'business information' and 'knowledge management' which

---

7   Persidis, A. (2001), 'SCIP/CI: Where to next?', *Competitive Intelligence Magazine*, 4(4), 27–28.
8   *Chambers Dictionary* (1993), Chambers Harrap Publishers, 870.
9   Dedijer, S. (1998), 'Competitive intelligence in Sweden', *Competitive Intelligence Review*, 9(1), 66.

all feed and support CI. To become 'intelligence', information must be analyzed so that its competitive significance can be understood. CI consequently goes far beyond gathering and disseminating data. Likewise, for it to be of any value to a firm, the CI function must also influence decision making and should be initiated and directed solely by virtue of its contribution to better business judgements. The end product of any worthwhile CI activity is what practitioners term 'actionable intelligence'. ('Actionable' in this context means intelligence that management can act upon, rather than the legal meaning of providing grounds for a lawsuit.) If it fails to do this, the exercise is merely a pointless waste of resources.

Hence true CI can be defined as the transmutation of intelligence into shared learning within an organization that provides an informed basis for its corporate actions.

That alchemy is the theme of this book.

Conclusions

- Although the profit motive is a good starting point for understanding business behaviour, the analyst must always bear in mind that the motivation of managers is more complex than simply maximizing profits.
- While the discipline of competitive intelligence naturally includes a considerable interest in competitors, the range of its concerns are far wider.
- *Any* factor that poses a risk to profitability or an opportunity for its enhancement (including the scope for mutual cooperation) should be the concern of those charged with competitive intelligence activity.
- 'Competitive intelligence' may not be the ideal term for the discipline, but it is so very firmly established that we should be reluctant to replace it.

2 *How is CI being Conducted and How Should it be Performed?*

This chapter is divided into two sections. The first considers the results of two surveys which illuminate management attitudes towards CI and how it is presently practised in European businesses. In the second I offer some reflections on the corporate philosophy that should inform CI activity if it is to yield the most benefit.

How is it being done?

A deeper understanding of the potential scope of CI and how it should be best conducted can be gained by looking at how it is presently carried on. Virtually all studies of the discipline's application have been confined to US companies. However, two interesting academic surveys have been undertaken which throw light on the CI practices of European firms.

Rouach and Santi,[1] who studied companies in the US and Europe in 2001, divide corporate attitudes to CI into five types:

SLEEPERS

Those least interested they term *sleepers*. These companies have no deliberate CI activity and are led by passive managements who believe that they already know all they need to run the business and are blinkered by a dismissive 'not invented here' attitude to learning from the outside world.

REACTIVE

The next category are *reactive* in that they have no regular CI operation, but will be provoked into undertaking some ad hoc CI exercises when faced with an overt competitive challenge. Rouach and Santi, on the evidence of their survey, place many French SMEs (small- and medium-sized enterprises) in this group.

ACTIVE

Companies with an *active* approach have a permanent CI function and try to anticipate opportunities and threats rather than respond to them when they become prominent. Modest resources will be devoted to the activity and there is no consciously developed structure to handle the information obtained. These authors place most American SMEs and many large French companies within this category. If their survey results are an accurate reflection of the French

---

1 Rouach, D. and Santi, P. (2001), 'Competitive intelligence adds value: 5 intelligence attitudes', *European Management Journal*, 19(5), October, 552–59.

corporate sector then it is suffering a competitive disadvantage because of the higher levels of awareness and more vigorous CI activity by smaller US rivals.

ASSAULT AND WARRIOR

There is a big gap between the active group and what Rouach and Santi distinguish as the forceful *assault* and even more aggressive *warrior* corporate attitudes. Such firms take CI very seriously and devote considerable resources to it, including at the top end of the scale (the warrior class) the provision of a dedicated 'war room' for the operation, conducting extensive patent searches, casting a dragnet for counterfeit versions of their products and the playing of war games. The difference between warrior and assault companies looks more a question of degree as compared to the substantive disparities separating them from the other groups. 'Big name' CI users like AT&T, Hoffman Laroche, L'Oréal, Mitsubishi and Shell populate the warrior segment.

Wright, Picton and Callow, who conducted the first empirical study in 2002 of how CI is viewed and conducted in the UK, have also developed a typology of attitudes and practice based upon the results.[2]

They found that the majority of respondent companies regarded CI as confined to traditional 'competitor intelligence', simply knowing about their competitors. Only five companies took a wider perspective, wishing to also understand their market environment, while a mere three firms had an integrated approach, combining this with keeping a watch for new market entrants as well as established ones.

The authors found that most companies relied upon general and specialist publications to provide their research material, with a few others undertaking some primary research. Most of the latter activity was conducted by the three enterprises with the integrated attitude towards CI, with the other firms either believing that the published material was sufficient for their needs or admitting it was insufficient but contending that they lacked the capacity to carry out primary research.

From their survey results, the authors sketched a four-level typology of corporate attitudes:

- *Immune* – these companies were not interested in their competitors, believing themselves too big or too little or too special for it be worth engaging in. They equate to Rouach and Santi's sleepers.
- *Task driven* – ad hoc CI activity, more usually carried out by individual departments than by the company as a whole. Such companies are similar to the reactive category.
- *Operational* – these companies were trying to understand their market environments, although their CI efforts (which are usually under the auspices of senior management) were focused more on the current situation than on taking long-term factors into account. They resemble the active group.
- *Strategic* – akin to the more aggressive players in Rouach and Santis typology. Sponsored both at top management level and by departments, the CI programme is broad in scope and its timeframe extends beyond immediate conditions and concerns.

Both studies support a number of commonly held views as to how CI is viewed and used in companies:

---

2 Wright, S., Picton, D. and Callow, J. (2002), 'Competitive intelligence in UK firms: A typology', *Marketing Intelligence and Planning*, 20(6), October, 349–60.

- First, a lot of firms are either unaware of it or regard it as not worth doing.
- Second, many of the enterprises undertaking CI do so at a very low level of commitment and intensity. It remains a small-scale, sporadic activity inspired, as Wright and colleagues found, by a desire to match the superior practices of competitors or as a 'knee jerk' reaction to sudden events.
- Third, a more developed form of the discipline is seen as the preserve of large, well-resourced businesses (although Roach and Santi found many *big* French companies were making only modest efforts with it). Those firms with dedicated CI units in the British survey had annual revenues in excess of £10 million.
- Fourth, even when a more developed CI programme is in place, it receives meagre resources. Hence about half of the designated CI sections in the Wright and colleagues survey were staffed by only one or two people and the most common complaint from those struggling to perform this function was 'lack of time/too many projects'.

Taking it as axiomatic that informed business decision making is generally superior to that based on intuition and guesswork (while accepting that a well-informed management may still make bad decisions), these are depressing conclusions. They also indicate that European business is lagging behind the US corporate sector in appreciating the value of CI and willingness to devote adequate resources to it.

How it should be done

The studies referred to above show us how CI is defined and delivered in practice. I shall now turn to the question of 'how should it be conducted?' It is impossible to offer more than some advice of a generalized character as individual companies differ so vastly in their lines of business, scale, structure and ways of working. There is no such thing as a 'CI organizational master model', but a number of universally applicable observations can still be made.

CI IS PART OF EVERYONE'S JOB DESCRIPTION

A principle I believe all practitioners of the discipline would subscribe to is that, just as war is too important to be left to generals, 'CI is too important to be left to us alone'. Every member of an organization, whatever their role, should be on the alert for useful intelligence. Ideally, all employees should be contributing to the firm's CI effort.

In reality this is extremely difficult to achieve. For a start open-ended tasks that are everybody's responsibility usually end up being no one's responsibility. Likewise every member of staff should be watching out for sales opportunities, but this does not render a specialist sales function unnecessary. This problem worsens as the size of the organization increases. In a small start-up the team members have (or at least should) have a very clear understanding of the strategy their firm is pursuing and what information is valuable for the success of the business. Lines of communication are short and direct so new data are easily exchanged and can be speedily refined into useful intelligence by the team. This is one of the competitive advantages small companies enjoy. For bigger firms the challenge of promoting shared understanding of goals and the competitive environment, together with the exchange of information and its conversion into intelligence, is far more daunting.

Yet 'elephants can be taught how to dance' and the best giant companies have made considerable efforts to foster strategic awareness throughout their organizations, improve the efficiency of information retrieval and internal communications and employ knowledge management to facilitate shared learning. Part of this push towards restoring competitive nimbleness is a greater emphasis on conscious, formalized, specialized CI.

George Friedman and colleagues naturally advocate that all staff members should be contributing to intelligence gathering, but point to two major obstacles in attaining this ideal state.[3]

First, the significance of the information is not grasped and it consequently fails to get passed on to those who could make use of it. Every CI consultant can recall assignments where this has happened, particularly in hierarchical organizations where the potential contribution of lower ranking staff to intelligence gathering is not understood. Consequently vital information is 'in the hands of a company employee, but light years away from the decision maker'. I would also add that it is also frequently consciously withheld because individuals and departments within a company interpret 'knowledge is power' in terms of their own narrow interests. Indeed this may be a sensible attitude on their part, for only if an organization's culture is such that they regard sharing knowledge as more personally beneficial than keeping it to themselves will they be prepared to do this.

Furthermore, despite my enthusiasm for shared learning, an important caveat must be entered. There are certain situations where knowledge certainly should not be passed on. This may be for many reasons. Client confidentiality, data protection, legislative requirements, security measures to counter fraud or the avoidance of conflicts of interest (such as the 'Chinese Walls' separating the corporate advisory teams from fund managers in an investment bank) are all obvious cases. A more universally applicable axiom is that the greater number of people with access to privileged knowledge the less likely is it to remain secret. Excessive secrecy inhibits the group learning that provides such a strong foundation for corporate success, while excessive openness can be competitively damaging. Those leading the organization have to decide where to strike the balance between protecting secrecy (information is disseminated largely on a 'need to know' basis) and sharing knowledge.

The second stumbling block is that intelligence gets swamped in the numerous, multi-subject conversations taking place every day in a firm. As Friedman and colleagues say: 'Gossip is an extremely efficient method for gathering information, but an extremely inefficient way to distribute it', in the sense of filtering the commercially significant from everyday chat and getting that precious intelligence into the hands of those who can make use of it.

CI AS A DISTINCT BUSINESS FUNCTION

It is because of these limitations that the discipline – while CI awareness should be universal within a business – has to be organized as a special responsibility. There are many ways of arranging this. Some typical approaches to the task of undertaking and delivering CI are:

- it is often given to an employee (probably in the marketing or sales function) as one of several duties or as their sole duty
- less frequently, a discrete CI unit formed
- it commonly assigned in varying degrees to external consultants. These can range from one-off help with specific projects to continuous monitoring of certain subjects through to being wholly outsourced to CI consultants

---

3 Friedman, G. and others (1998), *The Intelligence Edge: How to profit in the information age*, Century Business Books, 87–88.

- a board-level director (as at Proctor & Gamble) takes charge and reports direct to the chief executive officer (CEO). In these organizations CI is given a high priority and substantial resources devoted to the function.

These examples fit well with the typological schemes mentioned earlier in this chapter where the intensity of CI activity ranged from the passive, sporadic, present moment, minimally resourced approach to the active, continuous, future-oriented and well-resourced one.

For CI to contribute effectively to the formulation and evolution of strategy the analyst needs to be capable of thinking as a CEO does. Indeed, as Friedman and colleagues argue,[4] that in some ways the CEO would be the best head of corporate intelligence. One very successful mortgage broker does indeed combine the two roles. With a compact team, a clearly defined product range and a narrow geographical territory there are few administrative decisions to make. Instead, the broker is a voracious reader of announcements of new products from financial institutions, and of reviews of these in the general, and trade press and keeps a careful eye on regulatory changes being mooted. Most of the rest of the time is spent in discussions with clients and groups of other local professionals such as surveyors, lawyers, accountants, planning officials and fellow financial advisers. This web of contacts and the broker's profound knowledge of the locality are used to leverage his lengthy experience in the industry and achieve very healthy profits.

The problem for CEOs in larger firms is that they need this sort of intelligence, but have too much else to do just running the business to obtain it themselves. (They also need an alternative viewpoint to provide a 'reality check' on their own perceptions.) So they have to rely on others to perform this task. This in turn means that the analyst must be privy to the strategic thinking of senior management. As Friedman and colleagues aptly point out: 'an analyst without access to the secrets of the executive suite is like a doctor who can't examine the patient.'

STRATEGIC AND TACTICAL CI

Just as CI is focused on both potential risk and reward, it can be applied in both strategic and tactical contexts. 'Strategy' comes from the Greek words for generalship and the ancient Athenians gave the title 'strategos' to their military commanders. This aspect of command was concerned with the grand plan of a campaign, decided by the leader and long term in perspective. 'Tactics' referred to the arrangement and manoeuvring of forces on the actual field of battle. Rapid adjustments to operational tactics on the spot had to be made in response to the shifting pattern of engagement while the commander's masterplan unfolded.

As to the tactical aspect, Persidis[5] contends CI 'should not address top management alone but, more importantly, include the "fighting units" throughout the company ... Terms such as "strategic" might therefore best be avoided whereas terms such as "operational" might by more suitable if this bottom-up dimension is to be included in the name' and 'as the life expectancy of plans is shortened due to increasingly rapid developments in any business environment, a plan tends towards, at worst, a reaction and, at best, a move ... and so terms such as "strategic" should be avoided.'

---

4   Friedman, G. and others, 192–93.
5   Persidis, A. (2001), 'SCIP/CI: Where to next?', *Competitive Intelligence Magazine*, 4(4), 28. Other contributions to this debate are to be found in Belkine, M. (2001), 'Symposium: Corporate CI – tactical or strategic?', *Competitive Intelligence Magazine*, 4(5), 27–31. John Cain provides advice on providing effective tactical CI in Cain, J. (1998), 'Supporting field sales with competitive intelligence', *Competitive Intelligence Magazine*, 1(1), 26–28, while Bill Fiora discusses achieving this shift in intelligence capability in: Fiora, W. (2001), 'Moving from tactical to strategic CI', *Competitive Intelligence Magazine*, 4(6), 43–44.

While I certainly agree that the benefits of CI should not be confined to senior management, I have to part company with Persidis on this latter point. Any business lacking a strategy, a plan, a programme – whatever we call it – is undertaking a journey without a map. Its actions will be an incoherent series of ad hoc and perhaps mutually conflicting responses to new events. Sensible strategy is not a form of straitjacket imprisoning management and preventing them from adapting to new circumstances. It is a guide and a means of coordinating the various activities of the firm towards the achievement of its goals which can – and should – be modified to take account of changing conditions. Napoleon said that he always worked out how he would fight a battle in his mind first, before engaging the enemy, but this certainly did not mean strategic rigidity in the face of the swift course of events once his troops engaged the enemy.

In a company, as on a battlefield, a vital role for the leadership is to decide strategy and communicate it to their people so that everyone knows what part they must play for it to be realized and acts in harmony with it. 'Fighting units' acting without coordination dissipate the combined strength of an army. I see the prime role of CI as supplying the intelligence needed to craft a winning strategy, which then serves as a lodestone for those carrying out the actual operations. Except in a fairly small-scale partnership, cooperative or a company where everyone has an equal voice in the formation of strategy, this cannot be done 'bottom-up' (although the greater the involvement of everyone in the company in its development the better). Operational units should always have the 'big picture' at the back of their minds, yet will be primarily focused on the more immediate demands and narrower scope of their particular tasks.

Those specializing in CI will often be able to feed useful tactical intelligence – information that might lead to changes in near-term marketing activities or pricing, a potential new customer, an alternative supplier, a promising technological development – to those on the front line. However, if they get too bogged down in drawing up prospects lists for the sales department and similar tactical tasks their primary goal will be neglected. Their complaint of being overburdened with 'too little time/too many projects' argues for sharper focus on what is crucial for the firm as a whole.

The conclusions of the two academic studies referred to in the first part of this chapter might lead one to suppose that effective CI can only be carried on by big companies with deep pockets. I do not draw such a defeatist inference.

All firms – regardless of their size – must undertake some CI. This is frequently done unconsciously and in complete ignorance of the existence of the discipline, but it is nevertheless an unavoidable element in doing business. At the most fundamental level the owner must have some reason to suppose that there is a demand for their products or services. The basis for this belief can range from a 'hunch' through to an elaborate piece of market research, but even an intuitive view is formed as a result of some form of observation of what is going on. Similarly prices are not arbitrarily plucked from the air, they must be set with reference to other prices being charged.

However, much of this is sleep-walking – activity without conscious, explicit aims and the employment of systematic methods to achieve them. It stands in sharp contrast to the purposeful, wide-awake goals and methodical practice of more developed CI.

I believe it is differences in awareness rather than disparities in resources that lead to the pronounced feebleness of much small company CI. Thus the higher level of CI consciousness in the US permits a superior standard of practice among American SMEs compared to their counterparts in France and indeed enables them to match the efforts of large French firms (excluding multinationals). This is not to ignore the fact that much more comprehensive and sophisticated CI operations can be conducted by big companies with larger budgets. Yet when small firms plan their marketing they do not throw their hands up in despair because they cannot afford prime time television advertising like the corporate giants. Neither should they shun CI just because they lack the ampler resources of big corporations.

This contention is supported by the impressive CI record of some smaller European businesses. I know of several firms with a modest headcount who nonetheless are obtaining excellent results within their limited resources thanks to a well-organized and imaginative approach to the discipline. On the other hand some very large concerns are unable to get beyond the blinkered belief that a CI function is limited to monitoring the press for items concerning their obvious competitors and obtaining their financial accounts. The difference lies in some managements placing a high value on what CI activity can yield and giving it a central place in their decision making, while others see it as mildly interesting background.

Conclusions

- Contributing to firm-wide CI should be part of every employee's job. They need to be made aware of the importance of intelligence and given guidance as to the sort of information that might constitute it. Mechanisms should be in place to encourage and facilitate the contribution of CI.
- Despite this there needs to be an individual or group with specific responsibility for CI.
- Those charged with this responsibility need to have the broad strategic outlook of the CEO – and to be entrusted with senior management's strategic thinking.
- CI can contribute in both strategic and tactical contexts, but the strategic one is crucial and must receive priority.
- CI is not just for rich multinationals. Every business has to engage in it, but most firms do it without conscious commitment or deliberate planning.
- The starting points for CI that delivers the maximum impact are, in sequence:
  - awareness that such a well-developed discipline (just like marketing or financial management) exists,
  - appreciation of its potential value and placing it at the heart of the decision-making process rather than on the sidelines, and
  - willingness to devote resources rather than lip-service to it.

3 *How do Companies Compete?*

That a discipline such as CI exists implies that a general theory (that is applicable to all industries and companies) as to how businesses compete underpins it. Analysts need this theoretical framework in order to structure their work, as understanding the basis on which firms compete is essential in explaining their behaviour.

Readers already familiar with this topic can go on to later chapters. However, those coming fresh to it will find an account of the historical evolution of competition theory a suitable starting place and a knowledge of it indispensable for the study of CI.

This chapter reviews how competition theory has progressed:

- beginning with the neo-classical economics view of it taking place in perfectly competitive markets and based on *price*
- its subsequent amendment to include situations where elements of monopoly were present and firms sought to compete by *differentiating* themselves from their rivals
- the later refinement of 'contestable markets' where the influence of potential *new players* as well as existing competitors was taken into account
- Michael Porter's three axes of competition
  - price
  - differentiation
  - customer focus
- his subsequent 'five forces' model of the competitive environment.

Competition in economic theory

The theory of competition in economics is heavily focused on price competition. A company can gain a competitive advantage through charging lower prices than its rivals. Customers will migrate to it from its dearer competitors and the enterprise will make more profit so long as the total additional sales bring in more revenue than is lost through selling at a lower price per item. From this simple premise a very sophisticated body of analysis has been constructed. There is no ambiguity in the data as the prices charged are known and a chain of deductive logic yields a lengthy series of results which can be pleasingly displayed in chart form, just as Euclid's six axioms and six postulates generate a whole corpus of geometry extending over 13 books of theorems.

Competition theory in economics began with the supposition of a perfect market where price is the only factor a would-be customer needs to know when choosing which supplier to buy from. Recognizing that there were times when the buyer did not have a choice, as there was just one supplier in the market, it was also applied to predict what would happen under such monopoly conditions. Some examples of at least near-perfect markets and some of pure monopolies could be found in the real world. Nevertheless, dissatisfaction with the theory's lack of realism led Edward Chamberlain to publish his *Monopolistic Competition* in 1933. Chamberlain's analysis was grounded in the fact that most markets were neither perfect, with the happy buyer skipping from supplier to supplier as their prices altered, nor monopolistic with sullen customers having to accept grudgingly a price laid down by the seller.

In monopolistic competition a few rival companies struggled for business within a market. Not enjoying a monopoly position because of the existence of their competitors they strove to create a quasi-monopoly. Traditional economic theory had assumed that the only distinction between what the various market players offered was in terms of price. This might be largely true for commodities like cotton – bales of the same grade would be of the same quality. However, it was absurd where most business activities were concerned. Firms sought to persuade customers that what they offered was different from what their rivals were selling. This differentiation could be substantive: one supplier offering extra features, longer product life, better after-sales service and so on. It could also be subjective – hence the heavy use of branding, supported by advertising, to establish the difference between products even if this was objectively hard to identify or actually minimal. These companies, while competing in the same line of business, were trying to build a penumbra of monopoly around their brands.

A later refinement of competition theory was Baumol, Willig and Panzer's concept of *contestable markets*. This covered not only the actual players in a market, but also potential entrants. More attractive markets would tempt outsiders to join the contest for a share of them. The extent of contestability was determined by the ease or difficulty of entering a market. If there were high sunk costs (expenses of entry that could not be recovered) such as heavy spending on advertising to build and develop a brand or incurred in creating a distribution network then market contestability would be low. Where sunk costs were low (for example where a factory and its machines could be cheaply converted to other uses if the owner decided to withdrawn from this particular market) then contestability would be high.

Porter's three axes of competition

A decisive advance in understanding competition took place in 1980 with the publication of Michael Porter's *Competitive Strategy*.[1] Porter's model of how companies compete had three dimensions:

- price
- differentiation of the product or service from its competitors
- customer focus – concentrating upon meeting the needs of specific groups of customers.

---

1   Porter, M. (originally published in 1980, now available in a 1998 edition) *Competitive Strategy*, The Free Press.

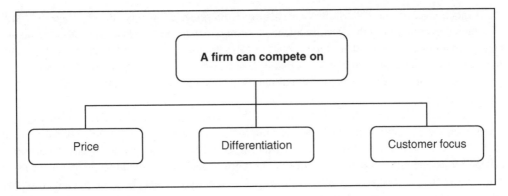

Figure 1   Porter's three axes of competition

Companies are naturally not restricted to employing only one of these modes of competing, shown in diagrammatic form in Figure 1. They may mix a couple or even all three of them and firms with a wide range of products often use a different competitive mode for various parts of their portfolio.

Porter's scheme met with initial resistance (and still does to a slighter extent) from some sections of academia on the grounds that it was too simplistic and failed to cover the full range of ways of competing. This is undoubtedly true, but the Porter model won favour from the business community exactly because it made sense to them in terms how their firms competed. His framework organized the complex numerous elements of competing into an easily grasped summary that nonetheless had considerable explanatory power of how the real world worked. This also accounts for its popularity with CI analysts.

PRICE

As noted earlier, traditional economic theory had largely explained competition in terms of price. It did doff its hat at 'non-price' ways of competing in imperfect markets. However, this never received the same degree of attention or achieved the intellectually pleasing elegance of price theory. Of course a price advantage can be a powerful means of winning business success – people like a bargain or use a low-cost supplier simply because their budget does not stretch to a more expensive offering, even if the latter is better value.

However, even in the nineteenth century it was realized that price was more complicated than assumed when drawing charts of demand and supply. The economist Giffen noted that sales of bread, contrary to theory, did not rise when the price fell. The failure of the price of bread to increase became known as 'Giffen's paradox'. Bread was the 'staff of life' and the first item to be bought. If the price fell, consumers did not buy more loaves, their money went instead on more desirable foods such as vegetables, meat, fish and fruit. A more modern example of this was the Tesco supermarket chain. Sir John Cohen successfully built up a huge business where low prices were the key selling point. His motto was 'pile 'em high and sell 'em cheap'. Later on, as people grew more affluent, Tesco began to lose market share to supermarkets that were dearer, but had a wider range of products (particularly of higher quality foods) and a less Spartan shopping environment. Tesco had to go through a lengthy period of reinvention, moving away from the original 'cheap and cheerful' model, to recover its market position.

For many businesses charging more than their rivals can actually be the path to success. Higher prices often indicate superior quality and hence better value for money for those able to afford them. Even when the difference in quality is marginal or wholly illusory there will still often be a perception of higher quality attached to more expensive goods or services. For luxury items a high price is essential for the product to carry conviction. Hence consumers will usually shun very cheap perfume on the grounds that it must be rubbish, a fake or stolen. High prices also convey a sense of exclusivity. Being able to pay them is a sign of wealth and confers a degree of social cachet.

Actual prices are also more difficult to determine than in economic theory. A straightforward comparison of them is often impossible because varying prices will be charged under different circumstances. Discounts on unit prices will often be given for larger purchases and the terms and conditions of the offer made more appealing by allowing the payment to be made in instalments, financed by interest-free credit, there may be the choice of paying an annual subscription, regular sums or on an 'as you use' basis and so on.

DIFFERENTIATION

The second way for enterprises to compete (recognized in the economic theory of monopolistic competition) is by differentiating their goods and services from those offered by other suppliers. A few examples will show how common this is. Tim Waterstone, working as a manager in WH Smith, realized there was a mismatch between what customers wanted from a bookshop and what they were being offered. Most bookshops were too small and did not offer a wide range of stock. Their opening hours were also inconvenient for those wishing to browse and purchase books. Waterstone's developed a chain of large shops, carrying an extensive stock and open till late in the evenings, which proved very successful. A new way of buying insurance was delivered by Peter Wood in his Direct Line telephone insurer service. Instead of the effort and inconvenience involved in going to an insurance company office, customers merely had to pick up the phone. Ted Turner carved a strong market niche with his CNN, a television channel devoted to news and continually updated. Viewers could catch up with world events without having to wait for the slots dedicated to news bulletins interspersing the other TV programming.

Anita Roddick created a global personal care product retailing empire by giving her stores a 'green' image. The Body Shop laid a heavy emphasis on showing social and environmental concern, so that customers felt that not only were they benefiting from buying its products, but that they were helping the world as well. All of these entrepreneurs established an enduring franchise, despite the fact that others could imitate their concepts. Others are unable to sustain their early lead in the competitive race. Internet service providers (ISPs) used to insist customers paid a subscription to join. Dixon, with their Freeserve ISP, broke the mould by offering internet access without an upfront subscription. Freeserve prospered at first and was given a separate stock market listing from its parent, but could not maintain the large market share it had rapidly seized as other ISPs followed suit and abandoned subscriptions.

CUSTOMER FOCUS

The third mode of competing, well known to those in marketing, is not trying to sell to the world in general, but focusing a company's offering on a specific market. Many companies dream of establishing a global business or brand. Building a worldwide presence is very costly, takes a long time to do and is extremely difficult to achieve. In a lot of cases a higher percentage return on investment may be realized much more quickly and easily if a particular geographical area (which can range down to a small locality) is targeted. Apart from focusing on specific locations, there are many other ways of segmenting markets. Age group is one of them, as exemplified by the success of Club 18–30, offering sun, sex and sangria holidays for younger people, and Saga, providing less hedonistic vacations for the older generation.

A fine example of skilful market segmentation was the Bank of Credit and Commerce International (BCCI). This focused on customers in Britain who had been brought up in the Indian sub-continent. Existing retail banks were failing to meet the needs of these people, who often perceived them as intimidating places and who forced them to discuss complex financial matters in English when their command of the language was limited. BCCI literally 'spoke their language', its staff could speak Hindi, Punjabi, Gujurati and the other languages of the sub-continent and had a better understanding of the culture and financial needs of their clients. The later collapse of the bank, owing to management dishonesty, does not detract from the inspired nature of its original business model and the adroitness with which it was implemented.

'Five forces' model

Professor Porter further enriched the literature of competition by devising his 'five forces' approach to analyzing an industry and the players operating in it. He looks at the balance of bargaining power between a company and, on the one side, its suppliers and, on the other, its customers. Porter also examines the competitive threat posed by new entrants to the market and by substitute products which its customers can use to replace the company's offering. The fifth force (shown as the central box in Figure 2) is the intensity of competition within the industry itself.

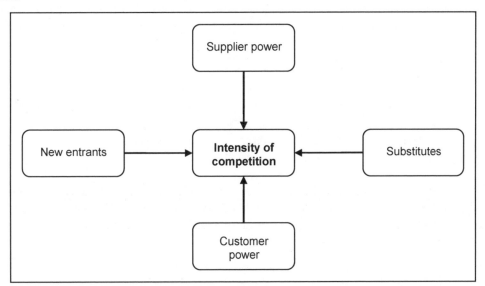

Figure 2   Porter's five forces model

1) Bargaining strength of *suppliers*

   A powerful customer can compel discounts or preferential service, or delay payment, so then the supplier has to partly finance them. Supermarket chains, with their huge, concentrated buying power, enjoy a very strong bargaining position in relation to their suppliers. In other sectors there may be a handful of suppliers, controlling essential raw materials or proprietary technology, who hold the whip hand over the firms dependent on them. The trend towards outsourcing more functions traditionally performed in-house has enhanced the power of many suppliers, especially where they enjoy elements of exclusivity under the partnering agreement.

2) Bargaining strength of *customers*
The other side of the coin, ranging from poorly placed customers who have to accept the terms offered through the spectrum to monopsony situations (where there is only one customer, as opposed to monopoly, where there is only one supplier).

3) Competitive threat posed by *new entrants*
The extent of this depends on the height of barriers to entering the market. It is very difficult for a new pharmaceutical firm or electricity generating company to break into these sectors because the obstacles to entry are so formidable. In contrast, for people-based service sector lines of business there may be no significant barriers to deter new players. Former suppliers frequently decide to extend their operations through forward integration (moving into their customers' business spheres), while ex-customers likewise often do this via backward integration (by invading their suppliers' market territory).

4) Competitive threat posed by *substitutes*
Industry players may be largely insulated from this danger if there are no acceptable substitutes for what they are offering. The threat will become serious if customers are able and willing to switch to other products or services. Many factors can trigger this migration such as a technological breakthrough that creates a new substitute, steep price increases which undermine customer preference for the existing product or changes in consumer tastes as exemplified by young female drinkers turning to alcopops in place of wine.

5) *Strength of competitive rivalry* between market players
The intensity of competition will depend on the structure of the industry. Some sectors are dominated by a handful of giant producers with large individual multinational market shares and rivalry is fierce. In fragmented industries where numerous players hold tiny market shares, inter-firm competition will usually be mild and localized.

Porter's model reduces the myriad of factors influencing a competitive environment into a handful of key determining forces. Once again, despite its simplicity, his framework matched well with how businesspeople actually viewed the competitive landscape and quickly became an indispensable tool for CI practitioners.

Conclusions

- Porter's three axes of competition provide a good place to begin analyzing the basis on which an individual company competes.
- His five forces model offers a starting point for understanding and describing the competitive situation within an industry.
- Both models are heavily used to direct the course of CI research and are frequently included in CI reporting.

4 *Key Internal Business Drivers*

A firm's performance is driven by both internal factors (how it operates) and external ones (which define the context in which it trades). This chapter considers the internal drivers, while the next reviews the external ones.

Porter's three axes of competition (firms can compete on price, differentiation or market focus), described in the previous chapter, show the ways of entering and contesting a market. To assess each player's competitive prowess we also need to know what resources are available to them and how well they make use of these.

The present chapter outlines a classification of:

- organizational resources
- the business processes by which they are converted into products and services, giving examples of each type.

I shall also mention some potential sources of data on them. The various types of source will be treated in much more detail later in the book. However, including them at this point will give an initial idea of the kind of places where researchers can obtain the information they need to assess a company, offering some guidance as to appropriate sources for each of the descriptive categories discussed below.

Like the previous chapter it is primarily for the benefit of those new to CI, but may still be of some value to the more experienced in offering a scheme for describing and assessing firms' resources and operations. It also briefly explores how a firm can amplify its resources and often improve its operational efficiency through alliances with other businesses and organizations.[1]

Critical success factors

A firm's competitive capability depends upon the resources at its disposal and how efficiently they are used. Competing *at all* demands a certain minimum level of resources, while competing successfully requires that the firm's strategic ambitions are appropriately resourced. Insufficient resources will hamper its efforts, but an excessive level of provision will be wasteful and perhaps even a hindrance. As Bhide[2] notes, a lot of start-ups or fairly new companies divert far too much management time and effort trying to win non-essential external funding when they would be

---

1   A very full account of the topics covered in this chapter can be found in Fahey, L. (1999), *Competitors: Outwitting, outmaneuvering and outperforming*, John Wiley & Sons.
2   Bhide, A. (2004), *Bootstrap Finance: The art of start-ups*, Harvard Business School Press.

better advised to grow the business with modest resources until it attained a scale where raising money from outsiders would be beneficial.

So winners in business need to combine a sound strategy with a fitting level of resources. They must also correctly identify the critical success factors (CSFs)[3] for the market sector they choose to compete in.

Ronald Daniel, who later became managing director of the McKinsey management consultancy, enunciated the CSF principle in 1961.[4] He observed that company leaders were being overwhelmed by information overload and were often unable to distinguish the vital elements in their business from the less important. Daniel reasoned that there must be a limited number of features that were crucial for success in a sector. A serious weakness in just one of these threatened potential failure, whereas many defects in other spheres would not prevent a firm still being a winner.

Daniel identified the CSFs for supermarkets, for example, as including offering the right product mix to match customer wants in each store, effective advertising to entice people to visit the shop, attractive prices to persuade them to buy and efficient logistics to avoid products selling out or being left on the shelf. Hence management attention should be concentrated on these. CSFs, he emphasized, would vary considerably between different economic activities so that a winning formula in one sector might be a recipe for disaster in another. They were also likely to change over time.

Resources

Output is determined – in part – by the inputs available to produce it. Economists describe these inputs as the 'factors of production' and much effort has been devoted to trying to understand the relationship between them and the resulting output.

Resources can be:

- tangible (for example, capital and premises)
- intangible (such as the quality of management and workforce).

Figure 3 illustrates the different categories of resources.

---

3   In management literature CSFs may also be called critical success requirements (CSRs), key success factors (KSFs) or key factors for success (KFS). Whatever the name the underlying idea is the same.
4   Daniel, D. (1961), 'Management information crisis', *Harvard Business Review*, 111–21.

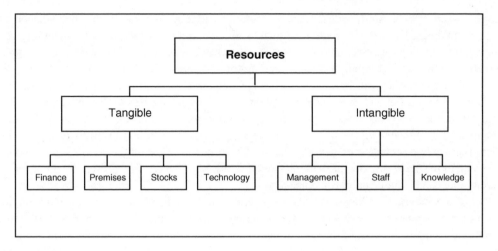

Figure 3   Corporate resources

TANGIBLE RESOURCES

Tangible resources can be subdivided into:

- financial assets (like issued share capital, cash, bank loans or bond issues)
- physical assets (raw materials and machinery, for instance).

Financial assets

'Money talks' asserts the well-known saying. Wisely used it does more than talk, being both a precondition for establishing business success and a decisive factor in sustaining it.

Finance is needed to fund both a company's acquisition of the long-term 'fixed' assets required to produce its output over several years, and the short-run working capital it must have available to meet day-to-day expenses. Balance sheets (which will be considered in detail in Chapter 16) show the allocation between fixed assets and working capital, that is, how company capital is being used.

They also reveal the extent to which this finance is being obtained from either internal or external sources.

Internal financial resources partly consist of the capital contributed by shareholders when they buy the company's shares. While many businesses, particularly smaller ones, are owner-managed, there are a considerable number of firms where many of the shareholders may not actually work in the company. However, as they have a stake in its ownership, their investments are treated as internally sourced capital.

The other type of internal capital is that part of the annual profit which is not distributed to investors in the form of dividends, being instead retained in the business to strengthen its resources.

Although the financial statements show the relative proportions of total capital contributed from internal versus external sources they give no indication as to who the shareholders are. Likewise one often sees descriptions of a company's asset structure that simply reproduce the balance sheet or are a graphical representation of it. For good CI analysis it is helpful to understand the shareholding structure as this will influence the strategy and culture of the business. For instance, the ways of operating and strategic preferences of a firm owned by a single person or by a family will usually be markedly different from one with a wide dispersion of shareholdings. Knowing its pattern of ownership can enrich not only our understanding of a company's development and present state, it can also provide valuable clues as to its future direction. Sources of information on shareholdings are discussed later (pages 86 and 98–99).

External finance can take several guises. Companies usually receive goods and services from their suppliers on credit terms, giving them a breathing space before they have to pay. The flip side of this coin is that customers often expect credit, thus opening a gap between making the sale and receiving payment. However, firms can sell the rights to these debts to finance providers such as invoice discounters or factors, thereby avoiding a squeeze on their cash flow. Another very common source of external working capital is the bank overdraft, representing a borrowing facility that can be drawn upon when needed.

The acquisition of long-term fixed assets, on the other hand, can be financed by buying them on hire purchase or leasing them. While leased assets are still owned by the leasor (the firm supplying them) in the eyes of the law, in reality the lessee (their user) is buying them using the credit extended by the leasing firm. Apart from overdraft facilities, banks also provide long-term loans, where repayment is deferred for a number of years, for the purchase of fixed assets. There is no equivalent to the obligatory list of shareholders to reveal the providers of external finance, although companies often choose to disclose this voluntarily. However, if the company has pledged assets such as its buildings as security for a loan, which banks generally make one of the conditions of longer-term lending, the identity of the bank will be recorded in a filing at Companies House, the official corporate registry (these filings are discussed more fully at pages 94–95). For listed companies there is the further option of borrowing external capital by selling bonds. Most of these are assessed for credit quality by the credit rating agencies and their reports extend the range of research sources available to the analyst.

Financial capital is of crucial importance to a company's existing and future capability. However, the relative ease with which data on it can be obtained, its seeming precision and the speed with which it can be rearranged in so many ways in spreadsheets, inclines analysts to give it disproportionate attention compared to other types of asset.

Physical assets

Physical assets comprise:

- land or premises
- stocks (also called inventories)
- technology and equipment like tools, machinery, fixtures and fittings (recognizing that some technological assets, such as those used under licence from their owners, are classed as intangible assets).

Land

Land in business analysis refers to its property portfolio. The company using it can own it outright (freehold), lease it or rent it. Freehold land can have very significant value even if not built on (farms and golf courses for example) or if the existing buildings are being demolished. Property developers obtain their landbanks for new building from both unbuilt and cleared sites and these are of vital importance to them. Ownership of freehold land and buildings can form a major component of a firm's assets regardless of the main focus of its activities. Thus some retailers, such as Marks and Spencer, own many of the properties they use. Indeed some companies have been bought in order for the acquirer to gain control of their property assets rather than because of an interest in purchasing its actual business. The aggregate cost (or its market value at the date of revaluation if it has been subsequently revalued) of freehold land and buildings is recorded in the balance sheet.

What makes an appropriate property profile for a company varies with its line of business. Retailers will look for prime sites and be willing to pay highly for those exposed to large numbers of the types of shopper they wish to attract. At the other end of the spectrum will be call centres sited well away from customers to take advantage of lower wage rates and property costs. Manufacturing concerns will seek to locate where communications are good, with motorways, rail links and ports close at hand for the transport of raw materials inwards and of finished goods outwards. Another factor is the benefits of *externalities*, where groups of companies in the same industry cluster together. This can be for several reasons, such as wishing to be close to a source of a crucial input or to sell to the same group of customers. Thus the bookshops concentrated along London's Charing Cross Road have found the gains in sales from the convenience this offers book-buyers more than offsets the losses from the close proximity of other booksellers.

Where a company operates from several sites their geographic spread can also be of interest. Examining the distribution of a retail operation's stores, for instance, can help towards a better understanding of the types of customer they are trying to reach. A major shift in this may indicate a strategic move aimed at changing the customer profile (although it might be motivated other reasons such as a drive to trim costs). A geographic realignment also sometimes gives stronger clues to the nature of a change in strategic direction than the vague statements made to outsiders by management. Where a firm has multiple sites these can be usually located through their webpages or in telephone and other directories. Whether it owns these or leases/rents its premises can be ascertained at the Land Registry (see page 101). However, the Registry's records do not identify the sites owned or occupied by an individual firm or person.

Finally, some firms may be able to dispense with dedicated corporate premises altogether by becoming 'virtual companies' where the staff communicate electronically and only need to meet face to face infrequently.

Stocks (also called inventories)

Manufacturers and utilities need to have stocks of raw materials if they are to carry on production.

They will also have some partly processed products which have yet to be finished. In several sectors (like construction, aircraft manufacturing or shipbuilding) where the product will take a long time to complete this work in progress will be a significant asset category.

Last in the production chain are the stocks of finished goods awaiting purchase by customers. Levels of stocks are a key indicator of a firm's efficiency. Running short of raw materials, tardiness in completing work in progress or lack of finished goods to meet customer demand without undue delay are serious corporate deficiencies. Yet excessive levels of inventory are wasteful, while rising levels of unsold finished stocks may reflect a failing sales operation.

The balance sheet provides information on inventory levels.

Technology and equipment

This heading brings together a vast range of different types of items including plant and machinery, IT systems, fixtures and fittings within a company's premises, furniture, tools, vehicles, ships, aircraft and railway rolling stock. The quality of these assets is of prime importance. Superior technology offers substantial potential competitive advantage. This applies not just in cutting edge, hi-tech industries or in manufacturing, but also in the service sector. It can make a powerful contribution even in low-tech activities. A shop with an old-fashioned till can ring up the price, issue a receipt and provide storage for notes and coins. However, with a computerized till using barcode technology sales can be tracked in real time – with important gains in terms of business process efficiency. Accounting data is available far more quickly and easily, the logistical control of stocks and orders is enhanced, valuable information is made instantly available as to which lines are selling well to direct the store's buyers and intelligence on customers is generated to guide marketing.

Both quoted and privately held companies may say something about their technology, particularly when it is cutting edge, on their websites and in their press releases. Quoted companies will also frequently refer to it in their annual report and prospectuses. However, documentary sources at best supply a partial view of this category of asset. A fuller picture can be built up through interviews with technologists within our own firm, others within the industry, equipment suppliers, customers of the company being researched and directly observing its premises.

Attempting to create a comprehensive inventory of an enterprise's technological base if it is of any substantial size would demand a great deal of effort and be extremely difficult. Fortunately, such a level of detail is not required in order to extract actionable intelligence. The aim is to understand the firm's present and potential capabilities and a much narrower research focus can deliver this. Its existing competences can be deduced from its current operations with the help of those with the requisite technical knowledge. Future capabilities may be discerned through watching out for signs such as it ordering new equipment, extending or reorganizing its premises or advertising for certain types of employee. Detecting these will involve using a blend of documentary and interview material, together with direct observation.

INTANGIBLE ASSETS

Management

The quality of top management is crucial in any line of business – even though not shown on the balance sheet as an asset. It is the principal factor that private equity investors focus on when deciding whether or not to invest in a venture. Good leaders will actualize a distant dream into a tangible business reality, poor ones can drag down a once-mighty firm and other suitably gifted ones revive its flagging fortunes. Despite this, individual talent alone is no guarantee of success, balance in a management team is also vital. The board of Rolls-Royce at the end of the 1960s was dominated by engineers. These included some of the most brilliant members of their profession, but there was a decided lack of financial expertise. With senior management fixated by the superb engineering quality of the company's products, they did not understand that its finances were deteriorating alarmingly and the firm collapsed financially in 1971.

Human resources

I have seen the use of the term 'human resources' condemned on the grounds that we are not talking about inanimate units of production, but people. I sympathize with this outlook in that its employment can imply – and may even encourage – a callous attitude where human beings are regarded from a solely instrumental perspective. However, in a business analysis context, where we are pursuing the limited goal of trying to understand the key influences on how companies operate and compete, I do not believe that it is objectionable. The term also has the merit of reminding us that human assets have monetary value, that they should not be wasted, but be carefully looked after and their potential maximized. Many generals in history would have been less willing to casually squander the lives of their men through neglect or reckless frontal assaults if they had viewed them as a resource to be husbanded and used prudently.

The total number of staff will depend on the size of an enterprise, whether it is in a labour or capital-intensive sector and the availability and cost of the type of labour sought in those places where it operates. An average figure for the company's accounting year will appear as a note to the annual accounts.

From an analytical perspective a more detailed understanding of its staff profile would be desirable, although the data may be difficult to obtain.

For example, it would be interesting to know how the employees are distributed within the company in terms of functional area, grade and location. A demographic profile of the staff (analyzed in terms of sex and age group) can provide insights into both the culture of a firm and sometimes its strategic situation. The extent of home working, absence at external locations (like the offices of clients or building sites) and teleworking and will also affect the scale and nature of other resource categories such as premises and technology. Outsourcing has become massively important as companies concentrate on their core competences and transfer responsibility for the delivery of functions such as security, IT services and training to external contractors. The adoption of outsourcing has significant implications for a company's capabilities, business processes and strategic options.

Ideally we would like to know more about the levels of educational attainment, experience and skills these numbers represent. We should be able to find some information on directors of quoted companies (those whose shares are traded on a stock market, see page 174) in their annual reports and prospectuses (including, in the latter type of document, perhaps some senior staff who are not members of the board). Company promotional material can provide some evidence as to qualifications and experience, as may general biographical, industry directories and those covering the alumni of universities or business schools – although there is considerable unevenness in the amount of detail given. Fuller information on a firm's personnel, extending beyond the top echelon of management, will tend to be supplied where the key competitive advantage of a firm lies in its portfolio of people (consultancies and private equity providers[5] being obvious examples).

It is also very enlightening to have information as to the state of morale within a firm. This is one instance in which a military metaphor is highly appropriate. Any general knows that the state of morale is vital in determining victory or defeat – this equally applies to business. Are the staff committed to their company or are they emotionally detached, perhaps even alienated from it?

Information on these issues has to be sought through the firm's published material (including press releases when new senior staff are appointed and its job advertising), but mainly through human sources. The latter include:

- our own company's senior executives, human resources and sales staff
- suppliers, customers and industry rivals of the enterprise being researched
- other parties having dealings with it such as ex-employees, contractors and those who have had job interviews with the firm.

Company literature and statements by chief executives routinely state that 'our people are our prime asset'. For some firms this may be a slogan devoid of real belief or commitment, but

---

5   A good example is the annual directory of European private equity executives: *Who's Who in Private Equity*, Initiative Europe.

for people-based industries such advertising, public relations and fashion houses it is clearly true. Such businesses have relatively little in the way of other assets if they lose their key creatives, account managers and designers and this dependency is linked to the vexed question of *corporate knowledge* as an asset, which shall be considered next.

Corporate knowledge

Academic management discourse has shifted strongly towards embracing the concept of the *knowledge economy* as the successor to the agricultural and industrial ones prevalent in early periods of history. Within such an economy a company's knowledge is, in turn, viewed as its principal asset and source of competitive advantage. Major efforts are being made in major corporations and consultancies to capture this elusive butterfly, preserve it for the future and to develop it further. *Knowledge management* (KM) has gained a leading part on the corporate stage, costly systems have been put in place to record, store, organize and retrieve it and the contribution of individual employees to enhancing the stock of company knowledge even made one of the factors taken into account in appraisals of their performance. By the end of the 1990s there were calls for it to be included as a balance sheet item in the same way as brands had been added to the traditional categories of assets in earlier years.

These approaches are surely right in principle, as it is self-evident that knowledge is crucial for a company to compete at all and that superior corporate knowledge, provided it is of an appropriate kind and properly applied, strengthens the competitive position of its possessor. Regrettably, there is no generally agreed definition of what 'knowledge' consists of, never mind a consensus as to how to place a numerical value upon it. Furthermore, the accounting scandals after the turn of the millennium have provoked a severe distrust of attempts to extend the scope of the intangible assets entered in balance sheets.

There are also some practical difficulties in applying the concept. An obvious form of corporate knowledge is the 'know how' of its people, often described as *tacit knowledge*. This represents an operational resource for the company employing them, yet while it can make use of this knowledge it cannot be said to own it, because the employees are free to leave, taking it with them. KM systems are an attempt to establish proprietary rights by firms over at least some of this knowledge in a form separate from the individuals in whose head it is held. They can certainly preserve facts, informed opinions, advice and other valuable material. The sterner challenge is their inability to transfer the ownership from employees to the company of the skills and judgement needed to convert knowledge into profitable action. Furthermore, because there is generally no copyright on ideas (as opposed to written texts or tangible inventions for instance) it is virtually impossible to prevent many of a firm's most prized original concepts, ways of working and solutions to problems being adopted by rivals.

We are on firmer ground where intellectual property rights can be asserted, exercised and defended in law. These assets include patents, trade names, trade marks, copyright and internet domain names. Although these are intangible assets (unlike physical assets they cannot be touched or seen) they are often immensely valuable. The monopoly right to use, or to license the use by others, of an original invention during the period of patent protection is given under well-defined conditions and can be valued in monetary terms using accepted accounting rules. In sectors such as pharmaceuticals, high technology industries, publishing and consumer goods they assume a particular importance.

Companies with well-developed knowledge management systems are proud of them and thus often refer to them in public sources such as their websites, KM conferences and journal articles. A firm's intellectual property assets, having a formal status in law, can be researched through public registries in the form of national and international patent offices (see page 99).

Reputation (an unusual category as it's outside the firm's direct control)

Finally, *reputational* assets need to be taken into account. These relate to a company's image, standing and esteem in the eyes of outsiders. The accounting concept of *goodwill* allows (to an extent) corporate reputation to be expressed in monetary terms. It is defined as the extra amount paid on top of the fair value of the company's total assets when a business is purchased (see also page 141) and is supposed to reflect intangible advantages like the favourable opinion of customers and suppliers towards the firm, the esteem its management and employees are held in and a beneficial location. There is, however, no attempt in accounting to place a value on the goodwill of a company until it is sold to new owners.

Some trade journals will name the firms, based upon surveys of those involved in the business, who are best-regarded in their sector. A feel for how a company is perceived can sometimes be gathered from the press (although this data should be treated with care, as explained on page 188). Less penetrating analysis only considers the attitude of customers (and perhaps 'the public' in general), but the opinion of other external groups can also count. These include a firm's suppliers, distributors, potential customers who have not bought its goods and services, competitors and regulatory bodies. Probably most of the evidence concerning reputation will be gathered through interviews with members of the groups mentioned above.

Business processes

These represent the second category of internal drivers, involving activities such as research and development (R&D), production and marketing.

The more efficient these operations the greater the firm's success in achieving higher returns from its resources. Significant weaknesses in any of them can undermine excellence in the others. A company may have a strong product range and a superb sales operation, but be hobbled by poor post-sales service. It achieves great early success, only to suffer low repeat sales and an increased difficulty in finding new customers. Some others are good in most respects, yet suffer because of poor billing control. Customers are not sufficiently vetted for credit-worthiness, invoices are slow to be sent out or outstanding invoices are not chased promptly enough. One client encountered cash flow and customer relations problems simply because of over-elaborate invoicing. Its customers were irritated by these daunting documents (including trivial sums itemized for a few 'pages photocopied') and slow to pay them. Some big professional services firms have absurdly complicated billing systems and internal cost charge-backs. The waste of staff time involved in completing such very detailed records and the 'can't see the wood for the trees' type of information they yield heavily outweighs any benefits.

One of Michael Porter's most important later contributions to the study of business competition[6] is the concept of a value chain. This separates the various activities a business must undertake to create the goods or services it offers and get them into the hands of the customer. It is shown in Figure 4. The links in the conventional value chain, which aligns well with *manufacturing*, are as follows:

---

6   Porter, M. (1985), *Competitive Advantage*, The Free Press, especially Chapters 2 and 3. Now available in a 1998 edition.

1) Inbound logistics. This link relates to the purchasing, delivery and storage of the raw materials and other supplies needed for production.
2) Operations. These processes convert the raw materials into finished products.
3) Outbound logistics. Preparing the finished goods for despatch and transporting them to customers through distribution channels.
4) Marketing. Developing, promoting and advertising products and brands.
5) Sales. Taking and processing customer orders.
6) Service. Providing product support to customers before and after the sale.

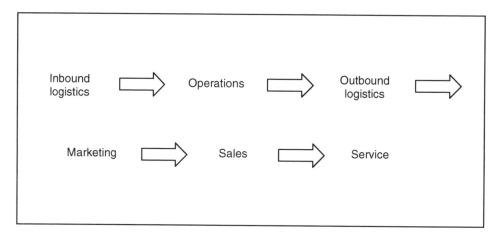

Figure 4   Porter's value chain

A chain more appropriate for analyzing a *service* sector activity is depicted in Figure 5 and contains the following links: design, produce, market, deliver, support.

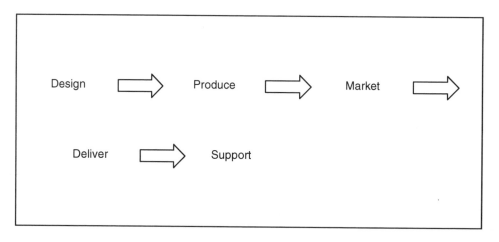

Figure 5   Service sector value chain

A third view of the chain is taken from the *customer* perspective. Its links are:

1) determining customer needs or desires
2) developing products or services to meet these
3) create a prototype or test version
4) testing with customers
5) production. Adjust product or service in the light of test results and produce the final version
6) sales
7) delivery and installation
8) service.

There are companies such as software developers or advertising agencies where the producers must have a close partnership with the user in devising and developing solutions to match their requirements. A good example of this is the second stage *beta testing* of software with selected clients (following the initial in-house alpha testing), before the final version is released.

These links are the primary activities of a firm in bringing their offerings to the customer. There are also some functions such as personnel or human resources, R&D and other 'infrastructure' tasks (telephone switchboards, plant maintenance, regulatory compliance and so forth) that are vital to support the primary activities. In a number of sectors, like pharmaceuticals or hi-tech industries, R&D has to prime the product pipeline and so is treated as a primary link.

Value chains are a useful way of categorizing the numerous tasks involved in producing goods and services and can be applied across vastly differing industries. The chain metaphor is also helpful in highlighting the need for these activities to be well coordinated, with the chain only being as strong as its weakest link. Measuring the efficiency of these operations and the extent of their coordination involves both an assessment of internal strengths and weaknesses, as well as comparisons using benchmarking between firms in the same line of business – and those in other industries. Benchmarking will be looked at in more detail in Chapter 21.

In assessing the efficiency of business processes, researchers will once again make use of a mixture of published information and material garnered from both their own company's internal sources and external parties with knowledge of the operational characteristics of the company under review.

Alliances

It is important to note that a firm's corporate reach in terms of resources may extend far beyond those assets it actually owns. Alliances enable an enterprise to use those held by other parties. Likewise operational efficiency can be enhanced by a well-judged structuring of which parts of the value chain are undertaken in-house and those performed externally.

Cooperation between companies can take many forms starting with one merely acting as a supplier to another. Outsourcing may deliver superior performance, lower costs or both for certain activities. Closer forms of cooperation include:

- companies entering into licensing agreements to make or distribute certain products created by other firms
- joint research and development
- joint production.

The strongest types of alliance are those conferring ownership rights, as with joint ventures or the acquisition of minority shareholdings in other companies or, taking the concept to its ultimate extent, by completely acquiring them.

Alliances, as Fahey notes, 'are typically highly visible'[7] and thus generally straightforward to research (although not necessarily to interpret accurately). Most are described in publicly released material issued by the partners such as press releases, stock exchange announcements, circulars to shareholders and annual reports.

Conclusions

- Assessing the resources available to a company is a crucial element in understanding its behaviour and future potentialities.
- A similar appraisal of the efficiency, strengths and weaknesses of its operational performance is also a vital analytical requirement. Value chain analysis is a helpful tool for conducting this.
- Analysts should not restrict themselves to only considering the assets owned by a firm, or to the study of its in-house operations, but must also take into account those available to it through alliances.

---

7   Fahey, 210.

5 *Key External Business Drivers*

The previous chapter set out a scheme for analyzing a company's internal drivers. A similar framework is needed to place the huge number of external factors influencing its fortunes – but over which it has no direct control – into broad, readily comprehensible categories. Of course these elements frequently interact, so that an environmental issue such as pollution from vehicles may translate into political action to reduce emissions in the form of changes to taxes on petrol, which in turn may stimulate shifts in motorists' behaviour and encourage the development of new automotive technologies. However, a framework provides a convenient way of separating them for the purpose of carrying out analysis.

Various handy acronyms are available to remember the components of such business context monitoring. For example:

- PEST analysis, standing for the 'political, economic, social and technological' factors.

This is sometimes rearranged as:

- STEP – social, technological, economic, political
- STEEP adds a second 'E' for issues relating to the *environment* (in an ecological sense)
- PESTLE contributes a 'L' to cover *legal* matters.

In this chapter I shall use the STEEP approach and give a few illustrative examples for each category.

Social and cultural drivers

Some social developments are on a grand scale, taking place over a lengthy period of time and becoming part of the familiar landscape of life. These are the easiest both to discern and to project forward as they are built in a series of (mainly) one-way steps. The rising social, political and economic status of women is a clear example. When females over 30 years of age received the vote in Britain in 1918 it would have been fairly safe to predict the extension of the franchise to younger women (men then being able to vote from 21 years) in the reasonably near future. And, despite the furious opposition of the *Daily Mail* to allowing 'flappers' to vote, this indeed happened a decade later.

Other shifts in social attitudes, behaviour and institutions are subtler, less visible and present more of a challenge in predictive terms. If perhaps rather ethereal, they can still be of considerable significance to a business. Some new features in society may acquire sudden prominence and be regarded as the 'wave of the future', only to fizzle out in a short time. Thus the hippy phenomenon and student protests of the 1960s died away after a few years. Nevertheless, they did make a contribution to a far longer-running, wider and more enduring movement towards a reduction in deference, less formality and a greater openness about sexual relationships and social acceptance of those not abiding by traditional sexual mores.

If sifting out the transitory social phenomena from the enduring one is a key skill for any business, it is an acute issue in those consumer businesses (notably clothing and leisure) heavily exposed to the vagaries of fashion. Heavy investment in a 'nine day wonder' will be an expensive mistake. On the other hand a short but intense burst of spending on a briefly popular product can prove extremely profitable for those companies nimble enough to take advantage of it.

While the 'big picture' social developments are fairly easy to identify, project and allow management time to make appropriate strategic readjustments, the other kind can rush up unawares on a company, leaving it struggling to re-adjust to the new circumstances. As a systematic, focused approach cannot pinpoint them, analysts and strategists need to adopt an open-ended one. This means being on the alert for all and any potentially interesting social or cultural signal whether this is something said, published or observed. Further analysis is then required as to likely strength, longevity and strategic implications of the phenomenon. This involves drawing upon industry experience (although being careful not to allow this to overwhelm receptivity to unfamiliar ideas and being readily prepared to use analogies drawn from other spheres) against which to test the new development.

DEMOGRAPHIC DRIVERS

Demographic issues deserve a reference on their own. It could be argued that they are a subset of economic drivers rather than social ones, but I shall include them under the latter.

Businesses have to tailor strategy to evolving population patterns. Changes in the relative numbers of each sex can have important implications for many companies, as can shifts in the comparative size of the different age groups. The 'greying' of most of the richer countries presents major issues for firms both in terms of labour inputs ('where will we get workers as the supply of younger people decreases?') and the markets they are selling to. Strategic repositioning will be required to anticipate a market environment with proportionately more older people and fewer young ones. Changes over time in the geographical distribution of population will also need to be taken into account in many companies' production, distribution and marketing plans. Likewise a changing ethnic mix can have a marked effect on the marketing front. The increased proportion of Hispanics in the US (the Bureau of the Census predicts they will grow from some 13 per cent of the total in 2000 to over 24 per cent by 2050) is a striking case in point.

Household structures, as well as total numbers of people, are another major market determinant. The rising number of households and their declining average size induces significant changes in demand patterns, with an obvious impact on firms building residential property and manufacturers of consumer durables.

Technological drivers

Some management writers treat technology and knowledge as indistinguishable. However, it is helpful to differentiate the two, regarding *technology* as knowledge physically embedded in inanimate objects whereas *knowledge* resides in human minds. The first is the 'means of doing', the second the 'how to do'. A CD-drive in a personal computer represents technology, while knowledge is using it to read and write CDs.

Developments in technology extend the range of possibilities available to a company – provided it is aware they exist, is allowed to acquire them (export bans on technologies with potential military applications may prevent this) and has the wherewithal to pay for their purchase. Many companies contribute to the onward advance of technology through developing it themselves and yet all depend on outsiders for most of the technological solutions they use. Hence I place it among the external drivers even though it can be created inside a firm.

Two very broad types of technological change can be discerned. The first covers those small, frequent, incremental improvements to techniques, capital equipment and products. Devising or adopting these confers an initial competitive advantage or eliminates a disadvantage. Because their use incurs costs (in initial financial investment, perhaps disruption of production, retraining, revised marketing and other expenses) companies may choose to ignore some of them. A strategic decision may be taken to eschew buying a slightly improved release of a software package and only replace the older version when a more markedly better edition is available. Terotechnology – from the Greek 'terein' ('to watch') – is the managerial discipline whereby a careful watch is kept on a firm's technology to ensure its most efficient exploitation and replacement when appropriate.

The second group of innovations are those which radically transform technological capabilities such as steam power in the classic Industrial Revolution, the development of the internal combustion engine or the IT revolution of more recent time. These are rarer, have far more powerful and profound effects and impose a heavy competitive disadvantage on those who fail to or cannot adopt them. Such path-breaking innovations often seem to be clustered together (perhaps because one of them enables the others to happen and/or because their interactions are symbiotic and partly because of the influence of arms races and wars as technology forcing-houses). Once each wave of innovation slackens a period of consolidation follows. Most recently developments in IT, telecommunications, biotechnology and genetic engineering have been the principal engines propelling technical progress.

Forecasting the source and direction of technological change is extremely hard and the accelerating pace of innovation adds to the difficulty. Judgements have to be made as to which new technologies are going to win long-run acceptance – as opposed to those that will merely end up as historical curiosities. Meanwhile strategy has to be crafted in an environment in which products can be developed and brought to market more quickly than in the past. The analyst has to be alert to promising lines of research, assess their likelihood of mass adoption, see the potential for applying developments in another industry or context to their own sector and try to foresee technological responses to changing social needs.

Economic drivers

Business strategists cannot complain that they lack economic data, commentary and forecasts. The difficulty rather lies in making sense of a welter of information generated in the forms of economic indicators, news, analysis and prediction. Fortunately changes in the economy are usually gradual, fairly small in extent and take quite a time to manifest themselves fully (recognizing that certain rare events, the great slump in the early 1930s, the slide into a world war at the end of that decade or the hike in oil prices following the Arab-Israeli war of 1973, can precipitate radical and pretty rapid shifts in economic direction). Once an economic trend has gained momentum it will not be quickly reversed.

Although this reduces the scope for short-run change, economic forecasting remains a hazardous occupation. One reason for its limited reliability is that data on the state of the economy include a margin of error and, owing to delays between collection and release, are always somewhat out of date. Economists are forced to base their advice on newly published figures that may be revised (sometimes substantially) at a later date. Changes in underlying conditions or data collection arrangements can undermine the validity of economic time series or the seasonal adjustments imposed on them. Another difficulty (as members of the Bank of England's Monetary Policy Committee can testify) is that economic indicators rarely all point in the same direction – if they do the circumstances will be of a boom or bust so pronounced that there is no need to consult statistical data to be aware of it. The evidence from each indicator has to be weighed and an overall assessment reached, especially when these signs contradict each other.

It should also be remembered that forecasts, policy changes and actual outcomes are linked together in an iterative relationship. Forecasts generally assume the continuation of present trends and policies (though some try to factor in some switch in the government and central bank's policy stance). In reality the authorities respond to assessments of the economic outlook with policy changes, thereby altering the predicted outcome.

Most strategists and analysts do not have to produce in-house economic forecasts from scratch, but they still have to choose whose standpoint is the most convincing. Some will have a favourite academic or commercial forecaster, many simply use the consensus forecast. The latter provides safety in numbers. However, it must be remembered that the consensus view can be, and has been, wrong and that there are occasions where a business leader or analyst has to go against the prevailing wisdom. It is also worth noting that statements by finance ministers and heads of central banks are generally over-optimistic. This is understandable as one of their roles is to maintain public confidence and avoid negative outlooks proving self-fulfilling, but reduces the value of their predictions. One particularly notorious example was the former British Chancellor of the Exchequer Norman Lamont. During the recession of the early 1990s the Treasury never produced a forecast indicating a shrinking economy, each quarter's downturn being assumed to be the last, and Lamont's cheerful vision of the 'green shoots of economic spring' breaking through became increasingly mocked as they failed to materialize. Attempts to predict turning points in the economic cycle are seldom crowned with success.

Strategists cannot content themselves with merely tracking actual and forecast changes in gross domestic product, as other factors in economic life have to be included in their assessment. Levels of consumer spending, saving and confidence are crucial for sectors such as retailing, leisure, consumer goods manufacturers and financial services providers. Corporate expenditure and confidence are of similar interest to those involved in business-to-business markets. Price movements affect a company's costs, its pricing policy and perhaps its general strategic posture. Labour market trends such as the participation rate (proportion of the population who are economically active by either working or seeking work), level of unemployment, productivity and employee earnings will have an impact on the availability of workers and wage costs per unit of output. Interest rate changes raise or cut the cost of obtaining finance. Swings in the exchange rate have a profound impact on firms buying from foreign suppliers or who are involved in exporting. Government plans for public spending and alterations to tax rates and the taxation regime can have a powerful effect on individual industries and the companies operating in them.

Exporters have to monitor and forecast economic conditions in their major geographical markets as well as their own. Likewise firms whose sales are concentrated on certain regions or cities will need data on regional or sub-regional trends.

Having a good knowledge of the macroeconomic context is helpful when trying to understand specific industries or markets. An analyst possessing it will be able to scrutinize the macro assumptions made by those producing market research and, if these appear questionable, make appropriate adjustments to published sales forecasts resting upon them.

Environmental drivers

These assume more importance in industries producing a significant environmental impact such as the energy-producing sector (and heavy energy consumers), chemical and detergent manufacturers, car makers and packaging firms.

Because of its all-pervading influence, it is worth noting a few implications for businesses of weather patterns. Although, like fundamental shifts in demographic patterns, secular climatic change is slow it has a profound influence on patterns of expenditure and production and commodity prices. Sectors such as food and agriculture, the energy industries and insurance are clearly directly affected by phenomena such as global warming and the seeming increase in the general volatility of the weather, but these also hold implications for many other parts of the economy.

A shorter-run climatic event with powerful effects is the periodic heating of the sea along the western coast of South America called El Niño. This occurs roughly every five years and lasts for some 18 months, while there are fears that it is increasing in frequency and severity. This might appear a far-off phenomenon with little relevance for European analysts. However, it exercises a major impact on climate not only in South America, but also North America, Africa and Asia. Given the high level of global economic interdependence this meant European companies were not unscathed by the last El Niño, particularly those dealing in agricultural products and those insurers exposed to claims following the natural disasters that it triggered.

The immense complexity of the earth's climate makes short-term forecasting prone to a high level of inaccuracy. Retailers, clothes manufacturers and beverage makers and vendors, to name just a few sectors, would be delighted to be reasonably confident as to whether the summer will be sunny, hot and dry – or cloudy, merely moderately warm and wet. So important is this factor to them that a number of companies pay for weather forecasting tailored to their specific needs. However, although Meteorological Office research reveals unexpected weather conditions have noticeably dented the profits of a large majority of businesses across virtually every sector at some time, only about a quarter of those surveyed carried out a consciously planned and sustained monitoring of these.

Political, regulatory and legal drivers

In some industries – utilities, pharmaceuticals, transport, financial services – regulatory issues are massively important. In others they will be a background concern. Regulation has an impact on participant's costs, operational freedom and their prices and profit margins. The extra resources required to comply with a tighter, more detailed, more intrusive regulatory regime adds to a firm's expenses.

Restrictions on things a company in a regulated industry is permitted to do and how it should do them inhibit the range of what the firm can offer customers and the ways in which it may lawfully conduct its business.

Legal constraints as to shop opening hours in the retail sector are a highly visible example of a limitation on competitive strategy. For many years most British stores were unable to open on Sundays. Once liberalization of this law became a real prospect, retailers had to make a strategic judgement on whether Sunday trading would boost sales sufficiently to justify the extra cost of opening then or merely redistribute an unchanged total revenue across seven days. In some countries, notably Germany, there are still considerable restrictions not only on Sunday trading, but also on the permitted opening hours during the rest of the week. Other British examples of the impact of regulation are where planning permission was once readily granted to build out-of-town superstores and now has becomes far harder to obtain or the reluctance to grant licences to open a pharmacy (a policy now being relaxed, triggering new competitive moves in the market for pharmaceutical goods).

In the sphere of financial services a prominent example of regulatory constraint is the 'polarization' regime covering retail financial advisers introduced in 1987. Under this advisers had to be either fully independent and offer products such as insurance or pensions from the whole range of providers or else were obliged to restrict themselves to those offered by a single provider. When proposals to liberalize polarization were announced in 2002, advisers could start to envisage introducing new approaches, hitherto prohibited, to selling financial services.

Unusually, utilities (owing to their natural monopoly market position) in most countries can be subject to a variety of controls relating to their prices, profits or dividends. They (and other sectors like chemicals or waste disposal) will also be strongly affected by changes in environmental legislation and enforcement. In this sphere CI intertwines with lobbying. Companies in regulated industries have to anticipate possible changes in the authorities' regulatory stance. Depending upon the nature of these proposals they may encourage their adoption, seek to modify them or even try and head them off. Once a proposal has reached a certain point in the authorities' decision-making process it may be impossible to prevent its realization, while reversing it will be extremely difficult. Achieving such anticipation involves an awareness of the views of other pressure groups, ministers, legislators and regulators.

It should also be noted that regulatory or legal developments can have a major effect even when not emanating from government. Hence a new Accounting Standard on the treatment of retirement benefits (FRS 17) had a significant impact on some companies running pension schemes for their employees.

The potential implications of lawsuits also need to be gauged. A dramatic example was the debacle at Britain's venerable and highly respected Equitable Life Assurance Society when it lost a court case brought by some of its members in 2000. The enterprise had guaranteed attractive levels of annual income to one group of its policyholders during a period of high interest rates. These became unsustainable in the subsequent low interest rate environment and the directors reduced these payouts. The policyholders affected successfully sued for enforcement of the guarantee, financially crippling the firm. The Equitable had to close to new business and its assets were sold to the Halifax in the following year.

Conclusions

- CI analysts need to be aware of a myriad of external factors that may affect a company.
- Their broad scans of the total business environment make them well placed to identify potential risks and opportunities.
- The choice of information sources regularly scanned by them will depend upon the particular circumstances they operate under. The BBC provides an excellent service of breaking news and in-depth analysis on a huge diversity of subjects free of charge (www.bbc.co.uk) while other organizations like the Economist Intelligence Unit offer a rich range of alerting, briefing and forecasting products on a paid basis (www.eiu.com).
- Easily remembered organizing schemes such as STEEP can help in structuring both research activity on external drivers and the reporting of its findings.

6 *For Goodness' Sake! – Legal and Ethical Aspects of CI*

CI, by its very nature, raises serious issues of legality and business ethics. Before commencing intelligence gathering the practitioner must be aware that certain methods are unacceptable and have a clear understanding of what constitutes lawful and ethical conduct in this field.

This chapter is concerned with:

- examples of illicit intelligence gathering
- the United States Industrial Espionage Act 1996 as a legislative response to this kind of activity
- the efforts of CI professionals to raise ethical standards within the sector through a Code of Ethics
- interpreting the practical effects of the Code for those engaged in CI.

Illicit means of gathering intelligence

Like any form of competitive endeavour, business has its rules of conduct, its prizes and its temptations. Because the potential rewards for success in business are so great, not only in terms of material wealth, but also in the prestige and influence arising from it, the incentive to bend or break the rules is extremely powerful. On the push side, growing competitive pressure generated by globalization, the liberalization of markets and related factors adds to this temptation.

Respectable CI practitioners wince at the often 'sleazy' reputation of their discipline. They hate being branded corporate spies who spend their time crawling through air conditioning ducts in their target's offices and microfilming precious secrets purloined from its filing cabinets. They are also professionally contemptuous of those engaged in the 'James Bond without a dinner jacket' sphere of CI gathering, arguing that resorting to illicit or unethical practices demonstrates a lack of skill and/or intellectual and creative laziness. It often asserted that 90 per cent of intelligence can be obtained by legitimate research and the other ten per cent by analysis. I have strong sympathy with the honourable feelings underlying this outlook and there are clearly many instances where the intelligence sought could have been obtained using purely legitimate means if enough talent and imagination had been employed.

Granting this is often the case, and wishing that it were always true, I fear that such an optimistic and idealistic assessment is sometimes not justified. If a rival's secrets can be unearthed using publicly available information and good analysis, why do they take such care to safeguard them and others go to such lengths to expose them? There is also the drawback that the unethical approach may be a far faster or cheaper way of obtaining intelligence than the ethical one, even when the latter succeeds.

CRIMINAL CI ACTIVITIES

The most extreme forms of aggressive CI involve illegal acts as well as unethical ones. Breaking into the offices of a rival or the homes of their senior executives is clearly beyond the pale on both counts. Likewise the tapping of phones or intercepting emails would breach criminal law. The special skills required, plus the serious consequences if a burglar or telephone tapper gets caught, act as powerful deterrents to resorting to such acute measures. Nevertheless, they have been employed, the classic example being the Watergate scandal of the early 1970s.

MOLES

More subtle and insidious is the planting of moles within a rival company. The most valuable mole will become a permanent employee, though this is obviously more difficult to arrange. An easy and likelier approach is to infiltrate a temporary worker or a contract cleaner. A fine fictional example of this was depicted in the film *Wall Street* where the unscrupulous Gordon Gekko inveigles Budd Fox to microfilm sensitive documents while ostensibly doing an office cleaning round. There is also the possibility of insider information from a corrupt or disgruntled employee, who is prepared to take bribes or acts simply out of malice. Another aggressive approach from a rival is to try and suborn otherwise unwilling employees by tailing them and similar methods of prying into their private lives in the hope of being able to uncover a basis upon which to blackmail them into giving secrets in return for not being exposed.

Rogue executives

A rogue senior executive poses an even greater danger. Membership of the top management team places such a person close to the highest level of strategic decision-making, gives them access to the fullest range of internal company information and exempts them from scrutiny by a line manager, while enabling them to exploit the firm's resources for their own ends.

Roy Lazzyman headed Britain's Davy International, a major division of the quoted construction company Trafalgar House. Davy's parent was eventually bought by Kvaerner, a Norwegian engineering firm and Lazzyman obtained a new job at their competitors, Voest-Alpine Technologie of Austria. Kvaerner became suspicious that some of the success their rivals were enjoying arose from inside information and hired private detectives to investigate. A search of Lazzyman's dustbin revealed faxes showing that he had taken copies of sensitive paper and electronic documents with him when he left Davy.

Even more spectacular was the case of motor industry executive José Ignacio Lopez de Arriorutua, who had achieved a stellar reputation while working for General Motors. Volkswagen were delighted when they persuaded this much-admired manager to join them in 1993. Unfortunately, Lopez brought not only his inspirational skills to his new company. According to GM he had also taken more than 20 boxes of their documents, the majority of them plans for a state-of-the-art factory specializing in building small cars, with which the American automakers intended to challenge VW's market leadership in attractive emerging markets such as Eastern Europe and China. Although he took more care than Lazzyman, shredding the documents after they had been digitized, Lopez was still found out and an irate GM launched the world's largest international corporate espionage suit against the German company. The case was finally settled out of court in 1997 when VW agreed to make an ex gratia payment of $100 million to the Americans and buy $1 billion worth of GM components over the next seven years.

The United States Industrial Espionage Act 1996

The sheer scale and pervasiveness of industrial espionage prompted the US legislature and government to take special measures to combat it. In February 1996 Louis Franks, Director of the Federal Bureau of Investigation (FBI), testified as to the extent of commercial spying and theft of trade secrets before a Congressional inquiry. Companies had reported some $1.5 billion losses to the FBI, a figure the Bureau regarded as significantly lower than the actual incidence of these crimes. Many firms were reluctant to concede that they had been victims of such malpractice or feared bad publicity if they admitted to being damaged by it. A large number of others were simply unaware that corporate spies had targeted them.

Given that reported commercial spying and information theft had increased by 300 per cent in just four years, the American authorities decided that tough action was needed to tackle this growing corporate plague. The 1996 Industrial Espionage Act made the theft of trade secrets a federal offence for the first time (a number of individual states of the Union already had legislation in place directed against it), demonstrating the gravity now attached to such conduct. The Act laid down stiff penalties for breaches of its terms, with fines as high as $10 million and prison sentences of up to 15 years being placed at the discretion of judges when defendants were convicted.

The draconian punishments now available to the courts in such cases were a natural source of anxiety to American CI professionals. They also held implications for the many foreign and multinational firms – and for those of their employees undertaking intelligence gathering – with US relationships. In addition, the case law evolving from this statute will influence the judicial treatment of industrial espionage cases in other countries.

However, the lawmakers were at pains to emphasize that the severe new statute was not intended to inhibit ethical CI activity, but was instead directed at the kinds of abusive behaviour referred to above. Several features of the legislation demonstrated this concern. The statute laid a duty upon those alleging industrial espionage to show that they had taken 'reasonable measures' to protect their secrets. The exemption from its ambit for 'publicly available information' included not only published material, but also the results of interviews and surveys that had been conducted ethically. The definition of 'confidential information' was restricted to that which was not 'readily ascertainable through proper means', allowing plenty of legitimate scope for analysts, using their skill and experience, to make deductions about matters that remained unpublished.

The SCIP Code of Ethics

A significant indication that a profession has 'come of age' is when an association is created to advance the interests of its practitioners. For CI this occurred in 1986 when the Society of Competitive Intelligence Professionals (SCIP) was founded in the US. SCIP has enjoyed explosive growth in numbers since then. CI practitioners in other countries were quick to see the advantages of a professional association, with SCIP Europe being established in 1990 and similar bodies springing up across the world (www.scip.org).

Another sign of professional maturity is the adoption of a code of conduct binding upon its members. One of SCIP's principal achievements is to have devised a code of ethics to govern CI activity that goes beyond merely obeying the law.

The SCIP Code of Ethics contains the eight principles set out below. I should emphasize that the commentary I have provided on each item in the code is a personal interpretation and has no official sanction from SCIP. I nevertheless hope the amplification offered regarding these principles will make them better understood and less likely to be breached inadvertently:

1) To continually strive to increase recognition and respect for the profession.
   A fairly standard provision in professional codes. SCIP members should advance the interests of the CI profession by trying to demonstrate the value and importance of the role it plays – and has the *potential* to play. The quality of an individual member's work and standards of professional integrity should also contribute to the good reputation and standing of the profession as a whole.

2) To comply with all applicable laws, domestic and international.
   It is fair to assume that someone active in CI who *knowingly* breaks the law will not be fretting too much as whether it is unethical. However, I do believe that the sheer volume and complexity of legislation makes full compliance genuinely rather difficult, even if one has no intention of violating the law's requirements. There are also 'grey areas' such as interviewing former employees of a company being studied. If confined to general matters such as the firm's corporate culture this is probably permissible. On the other hand, asking for trade secrets like the names of clients or details of technical processes has been ruled illegal in judgements given by courts in both the US and Britain. However, the dividing line separating questions about 'what is your company like?' to those soliciting trade secrets is far from clearly defined. New technological possibilities, such as satellite observation,[1] can also lead to uncertainty as to what the law actually prohibits.
   Clearly wise practitioners will seek professional legal advice before commencing any intelligence activity that they feel may be legally questionable.
   However, an observation worth making here is that the 'we'll do whatever will get past the lawyers' approach is highly subversive of moral sensitivity. Attention switches from the principles motivating and underpinning legal ordinances to how to remain within their letter. There is a serious risk of sliding from this into a completely cynical, indifferent attitude ('but everyone else is doing it!') or regarding the Eleventh Commandment ('thou shalt not get caught') as one's ethical lodestar.

3) To accurately disclose all relevant information, including one's identity and organization, prior to all interviews.
   I fear that this is probably the principle violated most frequently by otherwise upright and honest people operating in this sphere. When giving my competitive intelligence courses I always emphasize that SCIP members are not permitted to assume false identities, or pretend they are students or would-be customers. They have to give their real names and correctly state who is employing them (although *not*, as noted in the commentary on the next principle, the identity of their client if they are operating on a consultancy basis).

4) To fully respect all requests for confidentiality of information.

---

1   See Ehrlich, C.P. (1999), 'The propriety of commercial remote sensing', *Competitive Intelligence Review*, 10(1), 18–33. Also Gilmore, J.F. (2003), 'Satellite imagery as a primary source in CI analysis', *Competitive Intelligence*, 6(2), 18–24.

CI analysts working on behalf of a client should not reveal that client's identity unless this has been explicitly authorized. Like journalists they are also obliged to protect the anonymity of their sources of information except where these unambiguously agree to be publicly cited.

5) To avoid conflicts of interest in fulfilling one's duties.

CI professionals must abstain from misusing the information entrusted to them. An obvious instance of abuse (which would also fall foul of the law) would be to try and profit, through trading securities, from inside information gained in the course of their duties. Consultants providing CI services to clients likewise must not take advantage of data supplied in confidence during earlier projects. Although it is clearly impossible for those who have worked on an assignment to erase their memories regarding it, care should be taken to limit access to such data on a 'need to know' basis and to store only non-proprietary information for use in future projects.

6) To provide honest and realistic recommendations and conclusions in the execution of one's duties.

This must be one of the toughest SCIP guidelines to follow scrupulously. People do not like to hear bad news or findings that conflict with their entrenched views – and they do not warm to the bearers of these unwelcome tidings! Yet they all like to believe that they are hard-headed realists who want to be 'told it as it is' and who have no difficulty in revising their opinions when made aware of new evidence. While there are such clear-sighted and open-minded people around, there are many others who possess these admirable qualities to only a modest extent. Analysts and consultants are often under unspoken (or even overt) pressure to come up with the answer expected. It takes courage to resist this. Leading CI authority Ben Gilad describes one of the key roles of practitioners of the discipline as that of 'china breaker', shattering complacency, comfortable assumptions and cherished beliefs. Those playing it have to possess the nerve to drop the plate and steadfastness in justifying their seeming vandalism.

7) To promote this code of ethics within one's company, with third-party contractors, and within the entire profession.

I think this translates as 'not only should we comply with the SCIP guidelines, but we should try and get colleagues to follow them, even if they are not SCIP members'. Problems can arise when other employees who are not members engage in some CI activity. Insistence on acceptance of the SCIP code should also form part of any contract signed with external consultants and all reasonable steps taken to monitor compliance with its obligations. Apart from our moral responsibility for what contractors do in our name we may also be found responsible in law, with potentially disastrous consequences. Additional protection may be gained through establishing a formal company policy regarding its CI activities. SCIP's *Navigating through the Gray Zone: A collection of corporate codes of conduct and ethical guidelines* contains examples of CI policies from firms like DuPont which can serve as models for developing a set of in-house guidelines.

8) To faithfully adhere to and abide by one's company policies, objectives and guidelines.

One way of gaining kudos, a bigger bonus and promotion within our organizations is by getting results that our colleagues are unable to achieve. This creates a strong incentive to side-step or simply ignore the internal rules made to prevent unethical conduct on the part of employees.

This principle has been criticized as confusing in situations where a CI consultant is working on behalf of a client rather than as their employee. Which 'policies, objectives and guidelines' should be followed in this case, those promulgated by our own organization or those set by the client? In fact I believe the answer is straightforward, although it may place an ethical CI consulting firm at a disadvantage when competing for clients. Essentially we should abide by the sterner of these internal rules. Thus if our standards are higher than those of a client we should refuse to compromise these, and if the client places extra restrictions upon what methods we can employ we should abide by these. Proper consultant/client communication is needed here. Potential clients should be aware of the rules we impose on ourselves before we agree to act for them and we should ensure that colleagues working on a project are familiar with the client's policies in this area and scrupulously comply with them.

Does the SCIP code work?

How effective is the SCIP code in practice? Some people dismiss such formulations as either hot air or mere public relations and point out that the society has no disciplinary machinery. I do not believe these judgements are fair. For a start, unless we actually ponder and debate questions of professional ethics in this kind of collective fashion we are bereft of any guidance except our personal opinions. I have also been impressed, having met a wide range of SCIP members, to see how seriously they take their professional code and strive to uphold it.

Nevertheless, it has to be admitted that there is a gap between ethical theory and actual conduct.

At SCIP's 1997 Annual Conference, those attending the ethics presentation were confronted with a group of hypothetical situations, all them involving a moral dimension, and asked to pick a course of action out of a set of alternatives. Rather surprisingly those attendees who had been in SCIP for less than a year were more likely to plump for the 'ethical' choice than more established members. In fact the relatively poor results of members who had been directly engaged in CI activity (thus excluding students, academics, consultants operating in other fields and the like) for between two and three years were described as 'unquestionably disappointing' by the survey's authors, who expected greater experience would produce higher scores. On the more positive note, those working for firms with either a specific policy on CI practice (such as adopting the SCIP principles) or code of general business ethics gained far better scores than people operating without such guidelines. Likewise those employed in firms with specialized guidance for the conduct of CI activity scored substantially better than where this was absent.

In any profession there will always be some who are willing to cut corners – or worse – and CI work involves obvious temptations The SCIP code provides a framework for ethical CI and anyone abiding by its spirit and actual provisions is unlikely to be tarnished by professional misconduct or endanger the reputation and interests of their employers, partners or clients. Ultimately, though, its observance and effectiveness lies in the hands of individual practitioners.

Conclusions

- CI is not industrial espionage. Genuine CI professionals are scrupulous in conforming with the law.
- If you are unsure that a form of CI activity is lawful take advice from a lawyer before engaging in it.
- The SCIP code demands higher standards of conduct than required by the law. Adhering to these should ensure additional protection against legal claims.
- 'Accurately disclosing one's identity and organization' is probably the defining difference between a true CI professional and those that operate in dubious ethical territory, even if they do not break the law.
- An in-house code of CI conduct based on the SCIP one, but with more detailed examples of acceptable and unacceptable practices, should be created. Any colleague involved in CI-related activities or any third party (such as consultants) engaged to undertake these must be made familiar with it. The seriousness of departing from the code should be emphasized and prompt action taken in the event of it being breached.
- Being aware of the unethical methods that may be used is also helpful when defending one's organization against external CI. This theme is explored further in Chapter 24.

PART II

Collecting Data

7 *Commencing the CI Quest – Planning and Initial Data Gathering*

The process of creating *actionable intelligence* follows a number of stages and borrows the *intelligence cycle* used by those operating in the military and political spheres. This progression traces the steps from the identification of intelligence needs through to their final delivery to the end-users. It is a cyclical activity because the finished product will generate further demands from its recipients and so is both an end and a new beginning. The intelligence cycle offers a readily understood and logical programme for producing CI and I shall be following its course through the bulk of the book. My own version of it is shown in Figure 6.

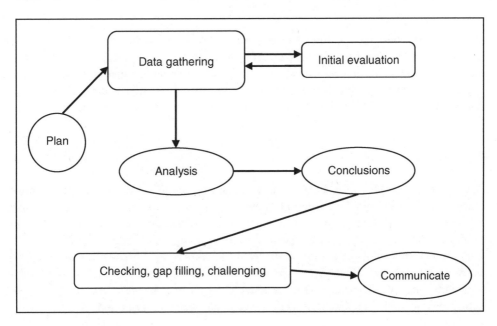

Figure 6   The intelligence cycle

According to the US Central Intelligence Agency (CIA) model[1] there are five steps in the cycle:

1) Planning and direction. This is the management process through which intelligence users table requests for intelligence, strategies for satisfying these are decided and resources for the activity are allocated (dealt with in this chapter).
2) Collection. Raw data are gathered and stored to form a knowledge base (also covered in this chapter).
3) Processing. The inchoate data obtained are sorted into a structured body of information (discussed in Chapter 9).
4) Analysis. This information is assessed, conclusions drawn from it and intelligence products such as briefings or alerts are prepared (most of the chapters in Part III of this book are devoted to the analytical phase of the cycle).
5) Dissemination. Findings reached are presented to end-users (Chapter 23).
6) This chapter is thus concerned with the first two stages in the intelligence cycle:

- *planning* at both the CI functional level in general and for individual projects
- turning to *data gathering* some reflections are offered on how information is created and from them is derived a 'Golden Rule of Research'.

It emphasizes the importance of preparing a framework within which research will be carried out before commencing the search for data and the value of hypotheses in directing the quest. To help encourage a striving for excellence in research, common causes of failures in data collection are then reviewed. This is followed by a discussion of the qualities typically displayed by successful researchers and how these can be acquired and enhanced.

Planning

We have already seen in Chapter 2 that even when some CI activity is taking place its quality and usefulness are depressingly low. Poor planning is a major factor in this failure to reap the discipline's potential rewards. This weakness pervades both the general approach to running the function and also the management of specific projects. Many senior executives regard CI as a comfort blanket rather than as a guide to better decision making. These will tend to ask for a great deal of information, which gives them reassurance that they are alert and well-briefed, but has little influence on their actions. There is also the danger of scarce resources being wasted on collecting 'nice to know' intelligence,[2] while the essential issues are neglected.

FUNCTIONAL LEVEL PLANNING

At this level, for those charged with creating a CI operation from scratch 'where to begin?' is one of the most difficult challenges as there are so many potential areas of interest. Those that are of special concern to an individual organization will also vary hugely, but a helpful method for beginning to organize and prioritize CI needs is to focus on key intelligence topics (KITS).

---

1 Detailed on the agency's website at: www.odci.gov/cia/publications/facttell/intelligence_guide.html.
2 For example, Patrick Marren who was a member of the pioneering NutraSweet CI function in the late 1980s, argues that attempting to obtain figures for a competitor's cost structure is very expensive and usually pointless: Marren, P. (1998), 'Competitor cost structure or, the great white whale', *Competitive Intelligence Magazine*, 1(3), 13–16.

These broad groups consist of:

1) Strategic decisions and actions. These are the moves that will have a significant impact on the performance and value of the business and should be based on a sound understanding of the competitive environment.
2) Early warning topics. Issues that are not presently included in management's assessment of their competitive situation, but which could be of future significance.
3) Description of key players in the market. The traditional role of the more limited 'competitor intelligence'.

This KITS categorization, devised by SCIP founding member Jan Herring, who constructed Motorola's highly regarded intelligence capability,[3] has become widely used. A fourth topic, counterintelligence (which receives detailed consideration in Chapter 24 of this book), has been added to the scheme by Douglas Bernhardt.[4]

PROJECT-LEVEL PLANNING

Turning from the functional dimension to specific projects, the first stage in the intelligence cycle is deciding what should be looked for. Many CI projects are marred by a lack of precision in specifying the problem to be tackled. They then degenerate into misdirected or even completely directionless exercises in gathering data, without a clear idea of what is being sought and why it would be valuable.

Of course the problem for many CI analysts is that they have limited discretion in choosing the topics to be assessed or the priority they should receive. If they are unlucky they may be used as general researchers, set to find information that might be more appropriately sought by a functional unit like the sales department or told to 'get me *everything* on company X'. This is particularly likely in the earlier part of their career. The best way of avoiding this is at the recruitment stage by ensuring that the analyst's true role is properly understood and their duties are adequately defined before accepting a job. Subsequent deviation from these ground rules during the period of employment justifies the analyst in complaining and resisting. There also needs to be an ongoing educational campaign to persuade users that ineptly planned CI projects waste the analyst's time and the organization's money.

Before embarking on any project its purpose and potential usefulness need to be established through tabling elementary questions along the lines of:

- What is the problem that finding this piece of intelligence would help us solve?
- To what extent will we lose by not possessing it (or gain by obtaining it)?
- How will our actions be affected by getting it?

Once the objectives of the project are clearly understood and its prospective value justified the analyst can move to the second stage in the intelligence cycle and prepare to gather data.

---

3 Herring, J. (1999), 'Key intelligence topics: A process to identify and define intelligence needs', *Competitive Intelligence Review*, 10(2), 4–14.
4 Bernhardt, D. (2003), *Competitive Intelligence: Acquiring and using corporate intelligence and counter-intelligence*, FT Prentice Hall.

Data collection

If they are fortunate, analysts may enjoy the support of professional researchers who will hunt out the data they need. Many do not have this luxury so need a solid grasp of research technique in order to obtain their raw material. However, in either case they must have a good understanding of how research is conducted, even if they do not perform it themselves. Without this insight there is considerable scope for analysts holding unreasonable expectations as to the availability of data on acceptable terms and for relations with researchers that are less productive than they could be. So the second part of this chapter will explore the mechanics of research. Figure 7 shows its place in the intelligence production process.

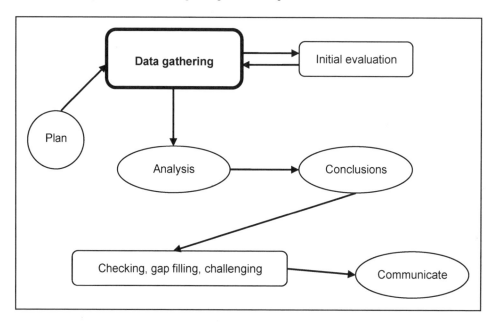

Figure 7   Data gathering stage of the intelligence cycle

Where to find the data sought – the golden rule of research

But where should we look for our data?

Information does not arise spontaneously. Its creation involves someone devoting the time, trouble and expense required for its collection, collation and distribution. Even if data are available on a topic, the compiler may have a reason for assembling them that bears no relation to our particular needs. Thus governmental bodies are key sources of information. Their focus on data collection, however, is primarily administrative, with provision of some of it to the wider world a secondary outcome. Furthermore, information held by the authorities relating to individual businesses or people is only made public in a minority of cases, with it being carefully screened out of published official statistics for example.

The erroneous belief that because they would like to possess it, information has to be available is shared by a vast array of people running from school students doing projects through to chief executives.

In the business world this problem is exacerbated by the dominance of the 'case study' method in teaching MBA courses. Although a powerful way of teaching analytical skills, the case study gives students the whole of the evidence they need to work with. Having all the data to hand (and being able to rely on their validity and accuracy) is a powerful boost to the perception that they will always be available in real life situations or are easy to find.

Being aware that information can only exist if someone assembles it leads to a very important conclusion. They must have a sufficiently strong motive for going to the bother of doing so. This principle is of such significance that I call it the *Golden Rule of Research* and can be stated as a simple question:

'Why might anyone collect information on this topic?'

It involves trying to identify those with enough motivation to do this. This is a key point of departure when we are about to commence research. It is also crucial later on if one has tried the obvious sources, drawn a blank and does not know where to try next. I shall show how it works in practice later (page 131).

The research framework

When starting a CI project a seductive temptation is to rush forward, buoyed by a wave of enthusiasm, and start collecting data on the topic, the second phase of the intelligence cycle. This should be resisted sternly. A more fruitful approach is to map out a research framework. This need not be an extended exercise, yet will considerably enhance the efficiency of research activities. Which sources to approach and in what order to tackle them are the first issues to be resolved (using the Golden Rule of Research as our lodestar). It usually makes sense to begin with those likely to provide the most enlightenment, although it can sometimes be wise to leave certain top grade sources until later in the research cycle. There may be only one opportunity to exploit a particular resource – a single interview with a person or one visit to an information resource such as library or a company's offices. So it might be better to garner what can be obtained from more accessible sources before approaching the most valuable source too early and thus failing to extract the maximum benefit from it.

It is particularly important not to be so enamoured of external sources of information that in-house ones are neglected. Researchers should be able to leverage both internal and outside sources when seeking data. Much of the information, many of the answers sought, may be sitting in a colleague's filing cabinet or in their heads. Liam Fahey estimates that 80 per cent of the data needed for effective study of competitors who have been active in the market for two or three years are available in-house. The techniques of knowledge management are directed at ensuring valuable facts and opinions are not lost within an organization, but can be retrieved when required. Obtaining data from in-house sources is naturally easier in firms where CI consciousness among the staff is already high and knowledge management systems well developed. Where they are not, the analyst will have to make the best of the situation through fostering contacts with colleagues to create a CI awareness and by devising their own facilities for capturing, storing and retrieving competitive information. On the other hand, external sources are often needed to validate in-house data and opinion as these can sometimes be incorrect or misleading.

Crafting a framework within which to conduct research ensures that it is less likely that you will overlook what later prove to be important factors in a headstrong rush to get to work. It also helps to reveal the interconnections between the various influences shaping a particular competitive situation. The absence of any framework may lead to these being neglected or at least not given their proper weight.

Tabling a hypothesis

When undertaking research, an initial hypothesis is needed to provide an analytical fulcrum. It is very inefficient to just keep gathering data and hope that somehow the story will 'jump out'. Nor does a hypothesis have to be correct for it to serve as the engine generating truth. Scientific advance is propelled by tabling theories, testing them against the observed evidence and validating, modifying or discarding them. Likewise a CI project should start with a proposition that can be confirmed or refuted. It would be gratifying if the hypothesis was right and subsequent research demonstrated this, but even an erroneous idea (provided the analyst is open to modifying or discarding it in the light of the evidence) acts as the launch pad for the project and provides its initial direction and dynamic. There is also the alternative and frequently powerful approach, discussed in the next chapter, of tabling several competing hypotheses.

Striving for excellence in research

Poor analysis will squander the finest previous research. However, fruitful conclusions can never be produced if the research supporting them is defective. Because of the crucial role of the information gathering process feeding CI analysis it is worth reflecting on some factors that lead to unsatisfactory research results.

In an ideal world, one would be able to obtain research:

- quickly
- cheaply
- which would cover all the key points of interest
- without the distraction of bundling in any irrelevance.

In reality researchers need to balance conflicting needs and are forced to make compromises. Getting data quickly will probably involve much greater expense because of the need to use premium rate services. On the other hand, keeping down costs usually means accepting slower delivery and/or poorer quality information. Highly focused data may miss out key elements in the story. A broader sweep will reduce the risk of omissions, conversely it will include more irrelevance in the haul landed. Before going fishing the researcher needs to have an idea of what they wish to catch, otherwise their efforts will merely yield 'inappropriate' information.

Inappropriate information covers a broad range of deficiencies:

FAILURE TO FIND ANY DATA – OR TO FIND IT IN TIME

A research exercise that produces no data must be generally counted a failure (while still accepting that, in some instances, a negative answer may be just what is hoped for. If an organization has developed a technology or process that they believe is unique, finding that someone else holds a patent for it is very bad news).

Likewise there is usually a deadline after which any information found – no matter how high its quality – is of no use.

PRODUCING IRRELEVANT MATERIAL

A common form of inappropriateness involves the researcher getting hold of the wrong end of the stick and delivering irrelevant results. This is more common, especially among less experienced researchers, than it ought to be. It arises from a lack of adequate understanding and usually there is fault on both sides. The person commissioning the research may fail to brief the researcher adequately (or does not really know what they are looking for). Or the researcher may fail to insist on a proper briefing because they cannot wait to 'get to work' on a project, wish to avoid looking ignorant, fear annoying a busy, pushy executive who gets impatient when being held up by questions or, in the worst cases, through sheer stupidity.

One can see that a researcher has missed the point if he or she clings to the words used in formulating the request, rather than digging out the meaning behind them. Lacking a proper understanding of what they have been asked to do they take refuge in key words that may well be insufficient to get good results or even completely misleading.

EXCESSIVE COST OF RESEARCH

Another danger comes from achieving the desired results at an excessive cost. This can be in terms of actual financial expense or time and effort. It can even involve an unacceptable risk to one's organization by exposing its interest in a particular company or topic. A rival who detects such inquisitiveness may actually *gain* a competitive advantage as a result of our activities – not at all the object of a CI project.

OVERLOOKING THE VALUABLE

Finally, the researcher may 'seize the jewel, yet miss the crown'. In other words, they achieve their original objective, but their vision may be so myopic that they fail to see something much more valuable. As has been wisely observed, imagine a CI analyst back in 1980 whose firm competes in computers against IBM. This person manages to come up with a detailed analysis of the 'Big Blue' cost structure – and, incidentally notes a strongly growing interest among customers in using personal computers. They neglect to alert their users about the shift in customer preference as it did not form part of the original research brief. But which information is more valuable – an insight into IBM's costs or an awareness that the economic weight of the computer market will soon shift radically from mainframes to personal computers? One is possibly 'nice to know', the other almost priceless.

Qualities of excellent researchers

To avoid retrieving inappropriate information an organization needs good researchers: ones who dredge up relevant data on time at an acceptable cost and add value to their findings. So I shall conclude this chapter by turning from failures in research to considering the personal traits that characterize the best researchers. An awareness of the need for these qualities and continuing to nurture them should help researchers striving to excel in their work. I believe it will also be of value to those executives and analysts who do not undertake research themselves, but who are responsible for recruiting and managing researchers.

PROPERLY BRIEFED

As has already been observed, successful information gathering depends upon the researcher having a clear idea of what they are looking for and why it is being sought. So they must insist on being adequately briefed before starting the search.

This understanding extends beyond clarifying an individual project. Good researchers are keen to develop a broader contextual awareness of their own organization, the sectors it operates in and the general business climate. This broader knowledge enables them to supply additional value when performing a specific task.

HARD WORKING

Researchers need to have great energy and determination. Business research is not for the lazy, the faint-hearted or the easily baulked. Sometimes the only way of finding the data sought is a relentless persistence that refuses to admit defeat despite serious obstacles and frustrations.

The cultivation of this quality is not helped by the 'black box' mentality that has developed among those who have never had to do their own research. According to this view a researcher merely has to table a question to an electronic database or the Internet and out pops the answer! For a very clear-cut query directed at a narrow, highly structured and standardized collection of data this can be true. Alas, for the bulk of serious research a lot of hard toil has to go into crafting and refining questions, coping with scattered sources of information that are not compiled on a mutually consistent basis and laboriously collating the raw data into something coherent and reasonably reliable. High levels of mental – and even physical – energy are needed to effect this transmutation.

INGENIOUS

However, the finest researchers work smart as well as hard. So another of their distinguishing characteristics is ingenuity. This is shown by an ability to quest beyond the obvious places to look for data, a talent that is related to their powers of imagination and capacity for original thought. It also demands the facility to isolate the crux of an issue from a tangle of distracting secondary considerations.

LUCKY

Candid researchers will admit that luck also plays a part in the ease or difficulty, success or failure, of a project. Sometimes they will find exactly what they want, in the form they want and at an acceptable cost, at an early stage in their search. I recall having an assignment on public procurement in western Europe where I was resigned to gathering my material from the national sources of 17 individual countries. I began by checking whether there was any international material on the subject. This was good practice and might yield something of modest help, yet my expectations were low. To my amazement and delight I found that a brand new report on this subject, giving me all the data I needed, was available.

Every researcher can relate similar instances of good fortune. They will also point to occasions when they found exactly what they sought – a day or two after the deadline for using it.

One key factor is the passionate intellectual curiosity of good researchers. They are like those (perhaps rather wearing!) children who want to know 'Why?' and demand, 'Show me', and 'How does that work?'. Other people want to know for instrumental reasons, in order to do something. The best researchers enquire out of sheer inquisitiveness, not motivated by practical considerations, but for the pleasure of relishing what the philosopher Bertrand Russell called 'the glory of new knowledge'.

WELL-ORGANIZED

A means of attracting good luck in research, noted earlier, is the systematic recording of past work for application in the future. When adopted across the whole of an organization this knowledge management helps preserve, at least to some extent, its corporate memory and experience. Even without the support of a formal corporate knowledge management system, individual units and individuals should devise ways of leveraging their experience to a greater extent. The obstacles to its deployment are:

- Time and resources must be diverted from working on present projects to recording old ones – something to which busy people have an understandable aversion.
- For this sacrifice to be worthwhile, a system is needed that will enable what has been preserved to be retrieved accurately and efficiently. The potential benefits of adopting this practice are very great. It is extremely frustrating to have a vague recollection of something done in the past, or a source consulted or technique used, and not be able to recall it promptly for current purposes.

NETWORKING SKILLS

Finally, for excellence in research it is not only what you know, but also *who* you know. To get the best results we need the help of human contacts as well as databases. These are the people (both inside one's organization and outside it) who not only provide the information being sought, but can explain its significance and implications. In other cases they may act as guides – while they do not have the information themselves they can point the seeker in the direction of someone who does. The most effective researchers place a strong emphasis on networking, mutual support and sharing knowledge. Those who undertake a substantial amount of interviewing as part of a project are also adept at getting the most from their interviewees, a skill that we shall be looking at in greater detail in the next chapter.

Researcher self-development

Some of these desirable qualities (such as intellectual curiosity) are clearly innate rather than acquired and it is undoubtedly true that they all apply to many other tasks besides research. Nonetheless they all can and should be developed. A creative, disorganized researcher who is good at finding data and weak at managing it can convert themselves into a well-organized researcher without harming their creativity. One who is brilliant at handling published sources and yet fails badly to get the most from human contacts can hone their interview techniques and cultivate a 'reach out' attitude. Good researchers become the best at their craft due to unremitting study, by attending formal training courses and learning informally from others and finally through practising what they have learned.

Management support for researchers is essential

My final point is addressed to those managing an information gathering function. This is about the vital importance of ensuring that their research staff members are given adequate resources if satisfactory results are to be achieved. Even the most brilliant researcher cannot make bricks without straw. All too often their talents are wasted and their organization loses out because those seeking data are not prepared to pay for it. It should be noted that this applies not only in an operational sense, but also in terms of encouraging and supporting the professional development of researchers.

Conclusions

- Adequate planning is the foundation of CI success both as a business function and in relation to specific projects.
- The Golden Rule of Research asks 'What would motivate someone to assemble information on this topic?'
- Collecting information is easier and yields much better results when conducted within a framework shaped by hypotheses.
- A stream of sound data provides the raw material for analysis and high quality researchers are vital in producing it.
- Good researchers can turn themselves into excellent, fully rounded ones by an unceasing commitment to self-development. It is also in the interests of their employers to invest in fostering this.

8 *Understanding Sectors*

This chapter considers the specific competitive space – call this industry, sector or market – that firms contend within. It has three sections:

- characteristics of demand for a product or service (customer aspects)
  - market size
  - the pattern of demand over time
  - market segmentation
- structure and organization of supply for meeting this demand (producer aspects)
- sources of information on sectors.

Constructing a research framework, the importance and value of which has already been emphasized, begins with sectoral understanding. Competing firms operate within the environment of their industry, *not* in some kind of splendid isolation from it. Their structure and activities are conditioned by, and must take place within, a sectoral context. So in order to understand the nature and behaviour of one's own company and its individual competitors, the first step is to have a good knowledge of the sector.

Even the most brilliant analyst is unable to make progress unless they have adequate direct experience or have studied an industry sufficiently so as to have reasonable grasp of its salient features, key influences and major current issues. This applies not only to the line of business the analyst's own organization is engaged in. They may also be called upon to develop a similar insight into sectors directly related to their industry or even those unrelated to it. Thus a good airline industry analyst should have a fair degree of awareness of what is happening in the tourism, business travel and freight spheres because these drive demand for space on flights. They should also be conversant with developments in competing transport industries such as rail, road and shipping. There will also be cases where the analyst has to explore hitherto unknown territory, supermarket chains looking to move into financial services being an obvious example.

Certain descriptive characteristics apply to all sectors, others will vary in importance or not apply at all depending upon the particular industry being studied.

Demand features

MARKET SIZE

A fundamental issue is the size of a sector. This is usually expressed in value terms (how much are its annual sales worth in pounds, euros, dollars or whichever currency used), but often also in volume terms. This can relate to the number of items (like cars or DVD players) or quantity (tonnes of stainless steel or litres of milk) produced or sold or the volume of transactions (mortgages completed or shares traded). Likewise its historic and prospective growth rates are clearly of vital importance. An analyst's understanding of their industry's size may be further enhanced by a feeling for how big and rapidly growing it is relative to other sectors.

An immediate difficulty arises because some industries are fairly well defined, whereas the boundaries of others are less clear. Market sizing becomes more difficult and uncertain once the dividing line between where the remit of one industry ends and another begins starts to blur. Such fuzziness reinforces the need to work out an operational definition of a sector before commencing the examination of individual competitors.

PATTERNS OF DEMAND OVER TIME

Demand in some sectors (utilities, healthcare or food supermarkets, for instance) is pretty immune from fluctuations in the national economic cycle. The buoyancy of other markets is much more dependent upon the general state of the economy. Thus spending on leisure services and among most branches of retailing will show greater sensitivity to the economic cycle. The analyst should, nonetheless, be cautious in applying a crude classification into cyclical and non-cyclical industries.

This is partly because there is a degree of uncertainty as to which category a number of them should be placed in. A lack of consensus on this issue was evident when the FTSE classification of London Stock Exchange sectors were revised in 1999 and 'consumer goods' and 'services' groups were subdivided between 'cyclical' and 'non-cyclical'. Another complication is that parts of the same sector may be at the mercy of the national cycle and others fairly independent of it. Finally, certain activities lie beyond the scope of such a simple model of demand patterns. Thus the construction industry is particularly subject to swings in overall activity, with sharper fluctuations in its level of demand than most areas of the economy. Primary sectors such as mineral extraction and agriculture have their own cycles of activity, often only tenuously related to the national one.

Seasonal influences on demand must also be taken into account. In some lines of business the level of orders is evenly spaced out across the year. However, most sectors experience a degree of seasonality in their order flows and for several important ones this can be very pronounced. Thus retailers experience a great surge in activity approaching Christmas, while business for tour operators is closely connected with peak holiday seasons. Again the analyst must take care against automatically pigeonholing a sector as seasonal or regarding its seasonality as a constant factor. Technological, sociological, climatic and other forms of change over a longer period may serve to moderate, accentuate or even change entirely the accustomed seasonal rhythms of an industry. Patterns of demand in some sectors may be unaffected by the season of the year, but still be noticeably 'lumpy', simply because orders are clustered at certain times and mainly absent during the intervals between them.

Less frequently the pattern of demand can be highly volatile due to exceptional circumstances. There can be sharp spikes in activity followed by a sudden falling-off, the massive impact of Y2K scare on the demand for IT sector products and services constituting a dramatic example. The effect of other one-offs may only partially dissipate afterwards, serving to propel the secular level of activity to new levels.

MARKET SEGMENTATION

Another crucial element in describing a sector is the nature of the market being addressed. This can range from a highly localized marketplace to one extending over the whole country through to a worldwide audience. Again it should be recognized that even a national, regional or global market may often be actually concentrated in certain hotspots.

It has already been seen (pages 22–23) that markets can be segmented into many other categories apart from that based on geography. The complexity of market segmentation is a major difficulty in sectoral analysis because companies in the 'same industry' may be offering very different goods and services or addressing completely dissimilar sets of customers.

A large swathe of the economy depends, to varying degrees, upon demand from the public sector. This factor should be given due weight when studying an industry whose fortunes are largely intertwined with decisions as to the level and direction of public expenditure. Conversely, in other cases a sector may derive none of its business from state customers.

SUPPLY STRUCTURE

After examining an industry's size and its particular demand profile, the analyst needs to consider its supply characteristics. There will be a huge diversity between those highly concentrated sectors where a few players, each with substantial market shares, dominate the market as against fragmented ones characterized by numerous competitors holding small individual shares. When concentration ratios are high, competition among firms will usually be fiercer than in the more muted competitive environment of a fragmented market. Again it can also be the case that different sub-sectors of the same industry furnish both concentrated and fragmented examples.

In some sectors a certain type of competitor predominates. For instance the players may be largely independent specialists. Alternatively, they might be subsidiaries of firms active in a diversified swathe of lines of business. Ownership characteristics are important – a sector populated by listed companies will be easier to research than one featuring mainly family-owned firms.

Another structural feature of an industry is the extent to which it is vertically integrated, that is, whether the same firm controls different stages of the production process or just one. As already noted (page 24), *backward integration* occurs when a firm owns its suppliers, *forward integration* when it owns those it would otherwise sell to. The oil industry is a good example of vertical integration with the same companies undertaking exploration, extracting the crude petroleum, refining it and transporting the refined products to its industrial customers and its own filling stations.

The ease with which new competitors can enter a market is also an imperative consideration. High barriers to entry offer protection to existing players. It is very difficult for a new entrant to break into the pharmaceutical industry owing to factors like the onerous regulatory requirements to be met, the hefty critical mass needed to compete effectively and the heavy demand for capital to sustain the business during the lengthy period between beginning research and the actual sale of drugs that have gained regulatory approval. In fields such as consulting and other forms of professional service barriers to entry may be very low. Relatively little capital is needed to create a new player whose competitive advantage lies in the skills, experience and reputation of its consultants. Indeed, many of the players in this sector are spin-offs from older firms.

There may also be formidable 'barriers to exit'; the huge costs of decommissioning nuclear power stations make it difficult for an energy producer to just pull out of the industry.

Organization of supply

Having examined the structure of a sector, its characteristics in terms of how it actually produces the goods and services it sells need to be reviewed. Production can be largely centralized, concentrated on just a single or a handful of sites – or spread over numerous ones. The output of a sector can be mass-produced or heavily customized. Again, both modes may be employed: in my role as a trainer I give both standardized, public access courses and in-house ones which are tailored to the client's specification in terms of content, structure and training method.

Some industries (such as transport undertakings) will be heavily labour intensive, employing many thousands of workers. Others will be capital intensive. So a private equity house or fund manager will generally have a relatively small staff, but need to deploy a great deal of capital in its investment funds. Technology levels will also vary between the low- and high-tech sectors. Certain industries, chemicals for instance, are markedly energy intensive and changes in energy prices will have a much greater effect on them than for, say, the website design sector. The degree and impact of regulation will also differ hugely between closely regulated industries such as utilities and pharmaceuticals and the unregulated areas of the economy.

All sectors have their special jargon and conventions regarding the types of goods and services produced, the technology used and the industry's structure and organization. Analysts must be able to decode these 'terms of art' in order to get to grips with understanding the sector they are studying.

Sources for studying sectors

Exploring all these factors provides a framework for learning about an industry. It is not a straitjacket, but can be adjusted to meet the idiosyncrasies of a sector. Analysts can muster a wide variety of types of source to fill that framework with the data required:

- trade associations
- official statistics
- individual companies
- market research
- brokers' research
- monographs
- journals
- regulatory authorities.

While the examples quoted are British, this categorization applies across most of the globe.

A splendid starting point for research is Karen Blakeman's business information portal which has numerous links to key sources (for other individual countries as well as British and transnational ones) arranged under various topics (www.rba.co.uk).

TRADE ASSOCIATIONS

These are an obvious starting point, being excellently placed to know their industry. A couple of points should be made about lists of trade associations on websites or in directories. First, a large number of organizations may be shown for a line of business. In some cases these may still exist only in name, being actually amalgamated with similar bodies. Be prepared for disappointment if you find them all being listed at the same address – instead of the multiple sources of information expected there may only be one.

Second, check that the organization really is a trade association – names can be misleading. The trade body for British farmers is called the National Farmers Union. It is not a trade union, but represents farm owners and employers.

CASE OF THE WRONG TYPE OF TICKET

While visiting a client, a global management consultancy, I was told that one of their other projects was concerned with the forthcoming privatization of British Rail. Through ticketing was a crucial issue, when the rail network was being split into over a score of franchises, to save passengers from having to buy several tickets from each operating company for a single journey. A new recruit had been given the task of gathering the information issued by rail industry organizations. She was delighted to find there was a 'Transport Ticket Society' and asked them to send her some material. When this arrived it included a specimen copy of the society's journal. This gave an entertaining insight into the hidden world of people who collected transport tickets as a hobby – including an article on an enthusiast who spent the whole of a holiday in Singapore riding on local transport merely to obtain the tickets – but did nothing to advance the project in hand!

Some trade associations are major publishers and information providers in their own right. Prominent examples include the Society of Motor Manufacturers and Traders for the automotive sector, Pira for printing and publishing and the British Venture Capital Association for private equity. They offer a rich array of products containing a great deal of detailed information.

One of a trade association's roles is to press the claims of the sector it represents with key decision-takers in government and other spheres. Another is to serve as an ambassador to the public for the industry as a whole. Consequently, many trade organizations collect information regarding the size of their sector, its rate of growth and major issues concerning it, and make this available to the public, often free of charge or modestly priced. Industry experts in trade associations are also often wonderfully authoritative and rewarding sources to contact.

Bodies representing a sector are thus essential ports of call and, being out of the competitive battleground themselves, a 'friendly' source. Even those associations who do not possess a large-scale external information function should be able to provide *some* help. While this may only be a list of their members, it does supply a platform for further research.

Nevertheless, some associations are frustrating for researchers to deal with. A number regard themselves as not having a public role, either for policy reasons or, more often, a lack of resources. A body that serves only its members is of little value as a source (although, as stated earlier, it is always worth asking for a list of these). In others the one person who actually has industry knowledge may be on holiday or otherwise unavailable, leaving the office to be staffed by administrative personnel who may know nothing about the sector. Another problem arises when a trade association's membership does not include all industry players. In this case statistical and other data obtained from the body will embrace only part of the sector. The larger the proportion of the total market these non-members account for, the less accurate the industry figures obtained from the trade organization.

A key resource for identifying and tracing industry bodies is the Trade Association Forum directory mounted on its website (www.taforum.org.uk).

OFFICIAL STATISTICS

Researchers will invariably make heavy use of these in terms of both macroeconomic indicators concerning national economic conditions and information relating to individual sectors and market segments.

The Office for National Statistics (ONS) publishes a superb *Official Yearbook of the United Kingdom* which can be downloaded free of charge from its website or bought in a hard-copy version. This compendium covering Britain's government, economy and society is a key reference work for broad overviews of sectors such as communications and the media or science, engineering and technology.

For more precisely focused research the ONS has a vast collection of data relating to individual industries and markets. The comprehensiveness and high quality of UK government statistics, plus the fact that many of the runs of figures on the ONS website can be retrieved free of charge, combine to make this a highly attractive source.

The sheer volume, breadth of coverage and complexity of the official statistics pouring out of government are daunting. Fortunately, the ONS provides a helpful handbook to guide users of their services through the maze. This can be downloaded or obtained in hard-copy form free of charge.

It is also important to remember that the series published by the national statistical office is only part of the vast array of data held by it. Individual researchers are often able to obtain much more detailed, disaggregated information at a reasonable cost when the publicly available datasets are not precise enough for their needs (www.statistics.gov.uk). Researchers can supplement the statistical services provided by governmental bodies with *non-official statistics*. These are produced by organizations such as trade associations, professional bodies, financial institutions, consultancies, economic research institutes and trade journals. Non-official sources may be more current and offer greater detail than official data and frequently supply the commentary and analysis that the latter tends to lack. The best sourcebook for them is *Sources of Non-Official UK Statistics*, compiled by David Mort and published by Gower (www.gowerpub. com).

INDIVIDUAL COMPANIES

An often-overlooked source for researching a sector is the information released by individual firms operating within it. Companies whose shares are quoted on stock exchanges will naturally refer in their annual reports to general market conditions and key industry issues that have already affected their business or are likely to have an impact on it in the near future. They may also produce freely available industry studies as part of their public relations operations. A classic example is BP plc's *Statistical Review of World Energy* which has appeared annually since 1951 (www.bp.com).

There has also been a growing tendency for technology firms to issue White Papers that can be an excellent source of enlightenment on major topics within an industry.

Another valuable source are the reports issued by the leading consultancies. Although most of these are restricted to those having a relationship with the firm (and hence a password), some of them are openly available. A good instance is Deloitte Touche's *TMT Trends Annual Report* covering the technology, media and telecommunications markets (www.deloitte.com).

If any companies operating in a sector have made public offers of their securities their prospectuses are also worth studying. When a company solicits the public to buy its shares or bonds it is legally obliged to produce one and this will include information, not only on the firm, but also the market environment which it operates within. Because they are used as a marketing tool in promoting the share issues, the financial advisers to the offer will give a copy of the prospectus to anyone requesting it free of charge. A copy also has, by law, to be filed at Companies House, so this is an alternative source of supply.

MARKET RESEARCH

Market research is the next broad category of sectoral information. Good quality market research should provide at least a partial answer to many of the questions tabled. A market research report will give an overview of an industry with information as to its size, structure, trends and other key aspects. It should also identify the main players and, in the better reports, profile them. Unlike trade association data, it will include *all* the significant competitors and not just those who are association members. This is very important if the membership accounts for a relatively low proportion of sectoral activity as a whole or some major market participants are not members. It will also include forecasts of future industry growth. These, like market share statistics, are hardly ever found in trade association data.

Despite its great usefulness there is often a reluctance to purchase market research. Mainly this is because it seems relatively expensive in comparison with other sources of information. High absolute cost can be a real barrier to acquiring a report. In many instances paying thousands for a report will simply not be feasible, regardless of how desirable it would be to possess it. There is also concern over value for money. I once spent $2000 on a 20-or-so-page report (as it was needed for a stock market flotation, we *had* to buy it to provide a legal defence, if something went wrong, that we had taken all reasonable steps to ensure the prospectus was based on the best available information). Certainly there was some good material within that slim document, but also a lot of very basic industry information that could be obtained elsewhere at moderate cost.

Besides these rational considerations inhibiting the purchase of market research, there is also an element of self-deception. I have often been amazed that people are not prepared to spend, say £100 or £200 on a report and instead opt for 'do it yourself' using their own researchers and analysts. This approach ignores the fact that the time of these staff costs money and (unless there is no other work for them to do) an opportunity cost is being incurred in diverting them to this task. It also will also certainly take longer – and probably produce an inferior set of findings – than simply buying the report. Failing to factor in the cost of staff time *in advance* is one of the worst – and most common – errors in research project management.

Given that market research is expensive, how can the most value be extracted from it? The first is to ask if it is really necessary to buy a report. In order to publicize their studies, market research firms issue press releases and similar publicity material outlining their key findings. In some instances these may suffice, at least in providing the springboard for in-house research. It may also be possible to consult (although not photocopy) reports held in business libraries. Apart from this the table of contents, assuming the report is of good quality, should offer useful clues as to how the market is structured, some of the terms of art used in relation to it and a list of the key players. In many cases it is possible to avoid buying the whole report and instead purchase those sections (and there may only be a few) that are essential for the project via the internet or online.

If the analyst's organization has an enduring interest in a particular market they should take advantage of any discount offered by publishers if next year's report is bought in advance as well as the current one. If they do not offer a discount it is worth trying to persuade them to grant one. A good report (from the 'Key Note' series (www.keynote.co.uk), for example) will contain lists of sources for the market such as trade associations, industry magazines and other relevant points of contact. These provide a ready-made set of new leads to follow up.

Apart from just studying the report, it can be very enlightening to contact its author. Some publishers are reluctant to allow this, while others use it as an additional selling point. The author can help in several ways. First, reports are only published annually or even less frequently. If the researcher wants to update figures quoted in a report, the author is likely to have them if they have subsequently become available. Second, only some of the information collected by the compiler will appear in the published document. If the analyst wants a section of it elaborated the author can probably supply useful additional material. Finally, it is always valuable to get an industry expert's view on the current situation and be able to have an interactive discussion with them. (Chapter 13 is devoted to getting the most out of such human sources.)

One caveat should be borne in mind with respect to market researchers' forecasts. I tend to be sceptical when confronted with a prediction of very rapid growth in sales. It occurs too often to be credible. We have to remember that market prospects must be attractive to persuade people to buy the report. Few firms want to enter a slow-growing market and hence have little interest in buying an expensive report focused on one, so there is an inherent bias toward a higher upside in these forecasts.

A number of services are available to help identify relevant reports, while market research content aggregators draw material from a large number of individual publishers and act as 'one-stop shops' for tracing and buying it. Karen Blakeman's portal, mentioned a little earlier, has very extensive set of links to these (www.rba.co.uk).

BROKERS' RESEARCH

The caution given above applies even more strongly when approaching brokers' reports, the fourth major resource for studying an industry.

Well before the scandals erupted involving brokers' analysts being used as a sales force rather than disinterested observers, shrewd investors treated their reports and comments with a healthy degree of scepticism. So the only surprise regarding the more recent technology stocks recommendations scandal was that so many people, especially among investment professionals, had not got wise to this kind of ramping far earlier. One good thing that has come out of the dot.com debacle is that the problem of objectivity is now recognized and moves have been made to offer more impartial research. As part of their settlement with US regulators of conflicts of interest cases, ten of the largest brokerage houses agreed to contribute over $400 million to finance independent research for five years from 2004.

Yet brokers' reports can be immensely valuable, especially when they are studies of sectors rather than individual companies. The best are treasure houses of useful facts and analysis provided one adjusts for their optimistic bias. Unfortunately, getting hold of them can be difficult if your company is not a client of the broking house, although several web-based services offer public access to a large number (but by no means all) brokers' reports including Reuters Research (www.reuters.com) and the First Call, Intelliscope and Investext databases of the Thomson Corporation (www.thomson.com). Investars.com rates the performance of analysts and research providers (www.investars.com).

MONOGRAPHS

The fifth major source of industry information is any books devoted to it. If the analyst is lucky and such a study has been published this can be the most comprehensive and cost-effective starting point. A major drawback is that industry monographs and conference proceedings date quickly, although they can help in understanding the historical background and secular progress of the sector. Analysis profits from being informed by a long-run perspective, encompassing a richer variety of experience than when only recent developments are taken into account. It is nonetheless frustrating to find an excellent tome that appeared seven or eight years ago and has never been updated. One way of trying to still extract some current value from it is to initiate a literature search to see if the author has written subsequent journal articles, delivered more recent conference papers or given interviews and to obtain their contact details. Someone taking the trouble to prepare a monograph on a subject will normally have an enduring interest in it and, even if they have not published anything concerning the topic since then, is an obvious source to approach.

The most comprehensive source for identifying monographs is the British Library's Catalogue (www.bl.uk).

It should never be forgotten that the term 'monographs' also embraces 'grey literature' – the sort of material not disseminated through conventional publishing channels – such as unpublished academic theses, scholarly papers, business school case studies and slides from presentations, technical reports and specifications or public sector documents. These works are usually available at a very reasonable price, indeed can often be obtained free of charge. Although tracing them presents special problems, some can be identified via Internet searches, while the British Library has made considerable efforts to make grey literature more accessible (www.bl.uk/services/document/greylit.html).

JOURNALS

Press reports and features are a crucial source of current (and possibly also retrospective) industry understanding. *Financial Times* sectoral surveys provide an excellent overview of different lines of business, outline the most pressing current issues affecting them and profile some individual players. Several trade journals offer annual surveys of major events and trends in their particular line of business, while a larger number run features on particular aspects of it.

The British Library Catalogue enables searches for individual titles, while two standard tools for tracing trade, professional and specialist journals with detailed subject indexing are:

- *Benn's Media*, published as a four volume hardcopy directory by CMP Information Services, details the business and consumer press worldwide. Volume 1 deals with UK periodicals (www.cmpdata.co.uk/ benns).
- *Willings Press Guide* appears in three volumes (Volume 1 deals with UK titles) and a web version. It updated quarterly (www.willingspress.com).

Details of reference works dealing with periodicals in other countries are given on page 105.

REGULATORY AUTHORITIES

If the analyst is fortunate enough to be dealing with a sector subject to public regulation a great deal of high quality information may be available at a modest cost. The reports and studies issued by the Competition Commission are full of useful data and analysis and provide a good model of how to undertake industry studies (www.competition-commission.org.uk).

Public watchdogs overseeing specific sectors are also excellent targets for research. The Office of Communications (which regulates radio, television and telecommunications), for example, publishes research on topics such as the digital TV market or telecoms providers on its website (www.ofcom.org.uk).

Other regulatory authorities can be identified using the *Official Yearbook of the United Kingdom* referred to above (page 70) and accessed through the UK government directory at (www.direct.gov.uk).

By drawing upon each of these different types of source, the researcher can leverage their individual good points and offset their deficiencies so as to produce a well-rounded and up-to-date picture of a sector. Such basic sectoral data, once assembled, should be organized, stored, updated and supplemented by the analyst. This knowledge base will be referred to frequently and should be available for immediate consultation, a solid foundation supporting many future CI projects.

Conclusions

- Where limited information is sought (perhaps to determine whether a sector is worth looking at in more depth) material from individual firms or trade associations may be a cheap and quick solution.
- However, when a more profound understanding is needed it is often a false economy to refuse to buy market research reports.
- A comprehensive trawl of the many sectoral sources will require a large commitment of research resources, yet will deliver the best results in terms of industry intelligence.

Armed with sound background knowledge of an industry, the analyst can now turn to the study of individual players within it.

9 *Refining the Search*

Research is an iterative process. Data found in the earlier stages guides the direction of subsequent research activity. This chapter:

- begins with some reflections on how iteration should be conducted in the light of criticism of the traditional intelligence cycle
- goes on to consider some of the options available to analysts once an initial search has yielded some results, including making comparisons between competing hypotheses and testing the validity of conclusions by dropping or reversing the assumptions underlying them
- ends by offering some guidelines (drawing upon analogies in the field of medical research) for deciding to abandon inconclusive research.

The traditional intelligence cycle begins by determining intelligence needs, then acquiring, organizing and analyzing the information needed to derive conclusions, with the dissemination of these to users as the final link in the chain. Some CI authorities have questioned its validity under contemporary conditions. Thus Robert Clark[1] argues that developments in information technology have made this model increasingly inappropriate. It follows a linear path from posing the problem through to finding the solution. This works well for simple problems, but is less satisfactory when applied to solving complex, non-linear ones. It also excludes the users of CI from involvement in the process apart from the first stage (defining intelligence needs) until the very end (presentation of analyst's conclusions).

He instead favours a new, 'target-centric' model, with more participation by users throughout the CI process. The goal is to create a body of intelligence that they both contribute to and draw from. Instead of all the analysis being carried out by CI staff, the users supply analytical insights (as well as raw data) based on their specialist knowledge and resources. This augments the range of expertise being brought to bear on intelligence problems and eases the information overload confronting analysts by doing some of the initial sifting to extract the significant elements from data and screen out the unimportant. In Clark's approach the role of the analyst becomes more of a facilitator and process manager for a network drawn from many different disciplines and functional areas. He rightly states their contribution is actually more one of *synthesizing* a diversity of information than *analyzing* it in the sense of breaking it down. Clark gives a number of examples of companies that have adopted a network-centred framework for solving problems (a development supported and accelerated by the availability of web technology for participants to communicate and manage information). Thus groups within Royal

---

1   Clark, R.M. (2003), *Intelligence Analysis: A target-centric approach*, CQ Press.

Dutch Shell, whose networks also include allies from outside the company, have been practising this approach for many years.[2]

A network-centric architecture for handling intelligence issues clearly offers many advantages over one in which analysts work in secluded isolation. I have already emphasized the value of networking. In reality I believe that CI analysts (certainly good ones) do not slavishly follow the traditional model in practice. Instead they treat it as an organizing concept and are aware that research is not only an iterative process, but also an *interactive* one, encompassing the insights and guidance of their colleagues and users and changing direction in response to their feedback. For this reason I have not used the usual neatly circular representation of the intelligence cycle in this book, believing a rather more jagged version captures better the interactive nature of the process.

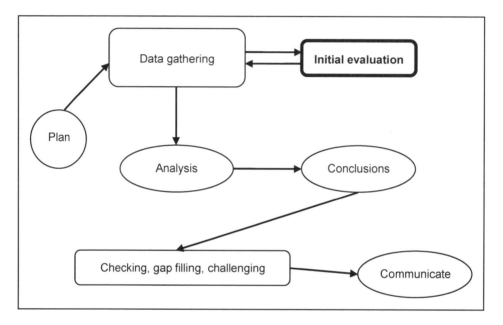

Figure 8   Interactive model of the intelligence production process

It is also worth noting that the CI practitioner has to exercise common sense when seeking this. Constantly badgering busy colleagues will erode their goodwill. I once observed an analyst at a client's who kept up what was virtually a running commentary on his work. Being interrupted by the colleague's excited announcements every time he found a new piece of information soon became highly annoying. In the end his manager, who described him as 'like a frisky puppy that's constantly snapping at your heels', had to tell him to cease his broadcasts to the rest of the office and that she wanted updates only once a day unless he found something of genuinely immediate import.

---

2   Schwartz, P. (1991), *The Art of the Long View*, Doubleday, 90.

Handling initial research results

A hypothesis, as noted earlier, may be convincingly refuted very quickly. For example, if our initial supposition that a particular technology was unique and a patent for it held by another party is found, the original belief was clearly incorrect.

More commonly a lengthy process of gathering and examining evidence must be followed before a premise is disproved (or proved). Information obtained in the first phase of research may support a theory, but still not prove it. Further testing is needed before the hypothesis can be accepted as validated, as illustrated by the following case study.

CASE OF AN ERRONEOUS HYPOTHESIS

A client's major potential customer was believed to be planning a significant shift in emphasis away from its traditional core business in favour of a hitherto relatively secondary line of business (one where our client's products and services were irrelevant). This suggested that the firm should become a lower priority target for the client's sales efforts.

The first indication of this potential shift came from the appearance as a speaker at an industry conference (attended by a representative of our client) by the fairly recently appointed head of the (until now) secondary division within the prospective customer. In his answers to questions from the floor, this divisional chief placed heavy emphasis on its far greater future importance to the firm. Subsequent research revealed that the division's premises had recently been redecorated (only two years after they were last painted), one of its customers stated that, having been somewhat lax in terms of chasing the payment of invoices, it had started pressing for prompt payment and there had been an unusual flurry of activity in filing patents relating to its products. None of these pieces of evidence refuted the hypothesis of a larger role for the division: indeed, they all supported it.

Then a new piece of information was uncovered. One of the division's competitors stated that there were rumours that it was up for sale. Sprucing up the premises, trying to speed cash flow and ensuring that its intellectual property was fully protected would also be sensible steps if that were true. However, what about the remarks of the divisional chief at the conference? Consulting the actual text of his address revealed no statements that a much greater role for the division was planned. Furthermore, he was an internal appointee who took over the post when the former head left at the normal retirement age. If the latter had quit before retiring or had been replaced by a high-flying outsider these might have been indications that the ex-chief had been ousted or that a 'new broom' had been brought in. Either of these would be much more likely to indicate a new strategic direction for the division than the routine replacement of its boss.

The address presumably represented the 'party line' agreed by senior management, while the much stronger remarks made in response to questions were merely the expression of the divisional chief's personal views. In the light of new data – and the re-examination of existing evidence – the original hypothesis now looked decidedly shaky. Further research activity was consequently directed at gathering material that would confirm or undermine the new theory that the parent company intended to dispose of it.

In fact the company's directors had decided to try and sell the division. Its new chief was opposed to this and his comments reflected his defensive feelings regarding its (and his own) future and a desire to quash rumours that it was to be sold. The division was eventually disposed of, thus providing the parent company with extra funds to invest in its mainstream businesses and making it a *more*, rather than less, attractive sales target for our client.

The original hypothesis, while not only wrong, but also downright misleading, nevertheless served as the ladder for climbing to the truth. This example is cautionary as well as encouraging. If the analysts conducting it had not been willing to explore alternative theories to account for the original evidence before them, their conclusion ('this potential client is going to be less attractive, give it lower priority as a sales target than before') would have been positively damaging if acted upon. An analyst can become so intellectually (and even emotionally) committed to a cherished hypothesis that they fail to consider alternative explanations of their evidence and simply ignore new data ('we'll forget about that silly "up for sale" thing – it's only a rumour after all').

Competing hypothesis analysis

Analysts normally consider hypotheses in sequence. In this example, the initial reasoning centred on 'they plan to give a hitherto secondary line of business a much larger role'. When this was undermined, it was replaced by the premise 'they plan to sell this division'. Another approach is to use *competing hypothesis analysis*.[3] This discipline involves the simultaneous evaluation of several theories rather than their sequential development. This has the merit of avoiding becoming over-committed to the 'correct' hypothesis and ignoring other possibilities. One way of doing this is to construct a matrix setting out the various hypotheses and seeing which pieces of evidence support or refute them. This provides a quick visual check on the degree of support each theory receives from the data (although it is a simplification in that it does not assign weights to the different kinds of evidence depending on their significance and reliability).

In this case the belief that the division would be offered for sale received growing support as additional evidence was uncovered, culminating in it being proved when the disposal was publicly announced. However, there might have been other explanations of the data, even allowing for the divisional head's comments being a personal view rather than company policy. Perhaps the new divisional chief and his colleagues hated the décor chosen by his predecessor so much that they decided to replace it, although it was only a couple of years since the last redecoration. The more robust approach to chasing invoices may be the company-wide initiative undertaking following a review of the accounting function by external consultants and not just confined to this particular division. Again the flurry of patent filings might extend across the *whole* group and might have been actually provoked by the loss of intellectual property through *another* division being slow to file.

An example of applying the technique concerns a division of a multinational company which caused serious damage to its parent when its new IT system crashed, leaving orders unfulfilled and leading to a loss of customers. This subsidiary had been bought from another global firm some four years before. Our initial working hypothesis was that the unit was a poor business, so its original owners wanted to be rid of it and were delighted when the acquirers took it off their hands. We viewed their later attribution of its troubles to the IT setback as just an excuse to mask more general weakness in the division. Given our lack of data at that stage this could well be a plausible explanation of what had happened.

However, we also tabled some alternative scenarios. Perhaps the subsidiary was a good business to start with, but went awry due to general mismanagement in the same year as the IT disaster. Another possibility was that the division was well managed on the whole and was

---

3 Sawka, K. (1999), 'Competing hypotheses analysis: Building support for analytical findings', *Competitive Intelligence Magazine*, 2(3), 37–38.

brought low simply because of the computer problems. The next stage was to match the evidence to each hypothesis and marshal these in a matrix.

Hypothesis	Evidence 1	Evidence 2	Evidence 3
1. Bad business from start	−	−	NA
2. Good business to start with – but later mismanaged	+	+	−
3. Good business in general – IT disaster specifically to blame	+	+	+

- − means 'refutes hypothesis'
- + 'supports hypothesis'
- NA 'not applicable, irrelevant to hypothesis'

EVIDENCE 1: PRE-ACQUISITION FINANCIAL PERFORMANCE

Division trading profitably, albeit unexcitingly so, and expanding in scale when sold:

- refutes theory that business was no good when sold
- supports hypotheses concerned with post-sale performance.

EVIDENCE 2: POST-ACQUISITION FINANCIAL PERFORMANCE

Division continued to expand sales, profits, profit margins and return on assets after being acquired:

- refutes theory that business may have looked good when sold, but had fundamental weaknesses
- supports hypotheses that it only went wrong later.

EVIDENCE 3: PERFORMANCE OF NON-IT ASPECTS OF BUSINESS DURING CRISIS YEAR

This is irrelevant to the pre-sale state of the subsidiary.
Nothing else went significantly wrong, apart from its IT, during the crisis year:

- refutes the idea that it was suddenly afflicted by more widespread problems
- supports the hypothesis that the IT failure was the crucial factor in its fall-off in performance.

This is obviously a greatly simplified version of our matrix, yet it shows the value of matching hypotheses against the different types of evidence. Although no weights are assigned to the categories of evidence it is pretty clear that the initial hypothesis was wrong and the IT debacle seriously damaged an otherwise well-run company. Once again a hypothesis, even though incorrect, has served as the engine of enquiry that leads to the truth being uncovered. In this case the process has been more rigorous because rival theories have been matched in competition. This makes it more difficult to remain wedded to an erroneous initial idea. One can well imagine an analyst considering just one hypothesis dismissing contrary evidence. Hence:

- 'The business looked good when sold, but that was due to creative accounting.'
- 'It flourished subsequently because new management actually turned it around.'
- 'They suddenly lost focus, lots of things went wrong and the IT debacle the best excuse on offer.'

Such warping of the evidence is more likely when there is only a single explanation on offer. So competing hypothesis analysis provides more compelling analytical judgements as it not only sets out the evidence and logic underpinning them, but also takes other possibilities into account and shows why they are less plausible. It has particular value in weighing up future outcomes (which is the main thrust of CI) where confirmation is only possible after the event.

Linchpin analysis

The conclusions reached by analysts rest upon a set of beliefs. As has been noted earlier, these can become so prevalent and long-held that they eventually become accepted as 'what is known' and thus unchallenged. Linchpin analysis is an attempt to counter such dangerous complacency by removing or reversing one of the key assumptions 'linchpins' underlying the existing analysis. Developed by Douglas MacEachin, a senior CIA officer in the 1990s,[4] applying this technique should help the user avoid 'intelligence myopia'. It was clearly not employed vigorously enough by those sections of the CIA involved in assessing Iraqi weapons capability, but this failure only goes to illustrate the great value of the linchpin approach to testing the reliability of intelligence, whether military or business.

In the case of Encyclopedia Britannica referred to in Chapter 1, the linchpins of the producer's market view were:

- our product, while expensive, is the finest in quality
- our customers are willing to pay for quality and are firmly loyal
- Microsoft's *Encarta*, although much cheaper, is inferior to our encyclopedia
- therefore their entry into this sector will increase the total size of the market, but have little impact on our part of it.

To reverse the assumption of customer loyalty – 'a significant proportion of our market is at risk because customers will be prepared to buy a product that is good enough for their needs, even if it is not the best on the market, if offered it at a much lower price' – would have radically changed the analytical logic. The company would have recognized that the new entrant threatened to seize a worryingly large tranche of its customer base and had more time to take the initiative with countermeasures, instead of having to react very late in the day under the pressure of having already lost half of its customers between 1990 and 1996.[5]

---

4   MacEachin, D. (1995), 'Tradecraft of analysis', in *US Intelligence at the Crossroads: Agendas for reform* (R. Godson, May, E.R. and Schmitt, G., editors), Washington, D.C., Brassey's.
5   Scapiro, C. and Varian, H.R. (1998), *Information Rules: A strategic guide to the network economy*, Harvard Business School Press.

Knowing when to stop

Medical research offers a number of useful lessons for CI.

- First, theories are crucially important in providing platforms to support the superstructure of research, with even erroneous hypotheses serving as tools for discovering the truth.
- Second, medical research efforts are concentrated on what are viewed as the most promising lines of enquiry and not dissipated in scattered 'let's see what happens' research initiatives.
- Third, a ruthless preparedness to drop research projects which are not making headway. This is an attitude researchers in other fields find hard to adopt. They become emotionally and intellectually committed to their pet project and hate having to write off the effort and expense that have been invested in it. This phenomenon occurs so often that the term *analysis paralysis* has been coined to describe it. Economic rationality, however, demands the objective approach of refusing to throw good money after bad.

Persistence, as I have stated earlier, is one of the qualities of a good researcher, so knowing when to stop goes against the grain for such dedicated people. However, resources for research are always rationed and should not be diverted to the pursuit of lost causes, while the research process is as subject to the law of diminishing returns as any other. Considerations to be taken into account before abandoning a line of research would include:

- How important is finding the information? We should obviously be less willing to give up on an issue that may be vital to our firm or client than one which would be merely 'nice to know'.
- Would getting the answer prove or disprove our hypotheses?
- How confident are we of obtaining the information *eventually*?
- In the case of market sizing and analysis, what percentage of the market do our results now cover? If it is, say over 80 per cent, they should be good enough to base management action on, with the extra costs in extending coverage probably not worth incurring.

CASE OF IT BEING SENSIBLE TO STOP SEARCHING

The dogged pursuit of an untenable project is stupidity rather than a virtue. Some years ago I was commissioned to write an article on tax havens for a leading accountancy journal. My thesis was that companies locate in these jurisdictions because they want to:

- reduce their tax liability
- preserve confidentiality.

The first reason was obvious, but the second had not been written up. I started interviewing executives of companies with parents based in havens such as the British Virgin Islands or Netherlands Antilles. After a few of these encounters not a single interviewee had been prepared to admit, even off the record, that the secrecy aspect might have influenced their decision to incorporate their parent company in a minimal disclosure jurisdiction.

It was, of course, possible that if I had conducted a lot more interviews I might have found someone who was willing to accept this suggestion. On the basis of my experience so far this looked extremely unlikely. So I outlined the results I had been getting and the prognosis to the editor, who kindly allowed me to rewrite the article from another angle. I was hardly overjoyed to have spent a fair amount of time on fruitless interviews, but would have been much more dismayed if I had not called a halt to a futile enquiry – even if the editor had refused to accept anything other than the original commission.

Conclusions

- CI research is both iterative and interactive. Its direction changes as new evidence is collected and responses elicited from intelligence users.
- Analysts should not become over-committed to hypotheses, but be prepared to revise or abandon them in the light of new information.
- The same set of facts can have different explanations. Rival hypotheses should be compared to see which is the most plausible.
- Lines of enquiry or CI projects that are not yielding useful results should be ruthlessly dropped.

10 *Systematic Sources – Regular Corporate Document Filings*

Equipped with the requisite industry knowledge, an analyst can begin to research individual enterprises. A key resource for this is the documents filed by them to fulfil legal obligations and which are available for public inspection.

This chapter examines the periodic filings businesses are legally obliged to submit to the public registry at Companies House, with ad hoc filings being considered in the next one. The documents filed by companies in other countries are discussed in Chapter 12. Because of their vital importance and complexity the contents of annual reports and accounts are considered separately in Chapter 16.

Business in Britain can be carried on under a variety of legal forms. The form chosen has important implications both for the business and for anyone trying to research it. CI analysts need to understand the legal background and be familiar with the public information disclosure regime set by it in order to know what data will (and will not) be available in these filings.

Unlimited and limited liability

Unless an enterprise assumes one of the particular legal forms discussed a little later, the law assumes that there is no distinction between it and its owner(s), business debts being treated as personal debts. Thus if its creditors are not paid as agreed they are entitled to confiscate not only any assets used in the firm, but also the personal assets of the owner(s) to discharge the debt or as much of it as possible. A business owner with such 'unlimited liability' stands to have their savings, home and other possessions seized if it cannot meet its obligations to creditors.

The perils of unlimited liability were dramatically highlighted in the massive losses sustained by 'Names' (personal investors) in the Lloyd's of London insurance market in the early 1990s. This led to considerable financial and emotional distress and a number of suicides among Names, exemplified by retired Admiral Sir Richard Fitch who took his own life in 1994.

One of the most powerful factors in the creation and development of industrial capitalism was the concept of limited liability, a privilege conferred by the state. The owners of a business with limited liability status stand to lose only the money they have invested (or promised to invest) in it if it fails. Their personal assets are insulated from its creditors, thus putting a cap on their potential losses. Hence the protection of limited liability is a huge comfort to those exposing their fortune to the hazards of business. However, Parliament recognized that the shield of limited liability also placed creditors at a disadvantage. Hence the privilege is only extended to certain legal forms (conferred by registration at Companies House) and, for the protection of creditors, a degree of public disclosure is expected from those possessing it.

Legal forms for carrying on business

There are three general types of business vehicle:

- sole trader
- partnership
- company.

SOLE TRADERS

These seldom need to be included in competitive analysis due to small scale of sole proprietorships. This is good news from an analyst's viewpoint as researching them is a difficult and often unrewarding task.

Operating as a sole trader (also known as a sole proprietor) is the simplest way to run a business. It is a popular form among those practising a trade (as a plumber, for example) or profession (single practitioner accountant) or running a shop or restaurant. The law discerns no difference between the enterprise and the individual carrying it on, hence the owner's liability is unlimited. A sole trader will have to report their earnings to the tax authorities and there may be some other filings (for planning permission, health and safety, regulatory supervision and so on) depending on the circumstances of the particular business.

However, no records relating to sole proprietorships are held at Companies House. Any public disclosure by the undertaking will be purely voluntary and made through brochures, advertising, the trader's website and entries in business directories such as the Yellow Pages or Thomson local directories. Some information as to the financial state of the business may also be obtained from a credit rating agency report.

PARTNERSHIPS

Sole traders can employ other people to work for them, but if these others have a stake in its ownership then the business is operating as a partnership. There are now three types of partnership available in Britain and some of these, such as the leading accounting practices, can be very large enterprises. The three forms are:

- general partnership
- limited partnership
- limited liability partnership.

General partnership

The limitations on research noted for sole traders also apply to general partnerships (also called *ordinary partnerships*), which are very much like a sole proprietorships in the eyes of the law. No distinction is made between the partnership and the individual partners who own it and consequently no limitation of their personal liability is granted. One potentially weighty legal factor is that the partners have 'joint and several liability' for the debts of their partnership. This means that a single partner may have to bear the whole partnership's liability if the other partners disappear or are found to have no assets. The form is very commonly used by groups of professionals like solicitors, accountants and surveyors.

Limited partnership

A business operating as a limited partnership has to file some information, but not financial data.

This legal form confers 'legal personality', in other words recognizes the business as a person separate from the 'natural persons' (the individuals involved) who own it. A legal person can take the same actions in law, such as suing or being sued in its own name, as a natural person.

As the name implies some of the partners in a limited partnership have the protection of limited liability. There are two key restrictions on this form. First, there must always be at least one general partner who cannot limit their liability and, second, the limited partners must not take any part in the work or management of the partnership – if they do, the screen of limited liability will be torn from them. So the limited partners are simply investors in the business, providing some of its capital and sharing in its profits or losses. A limited partnership is thus commonly used as an investment vehicle with the general partners deciding what to invest in and the limited partners contributing capital.

In order to enjoy the privilege of limited liability the partnership must register at Companies House. Limited partnerships are denoted by the letters 'LP' preceding their registration number and, in order to warn those having dealings with them that they have limited liability, they are obliged to include 'limited partnership' in their names on their headed notepaper and invoices. There are around 11 000 limited partnerships at present. The names and home addresses of the partners are recorded when the limited partnership is first registered and any changes in these must be notified to Companies House. However, no accounts have to be filed.

Limited liability partnership

Such partnerships are more attractive research propositions owing to their greater disclosure obligations.

Following the great corporate collapses of the late 1980s angry shareholders and creditors who had lost money sued the partnerships that had audited the accounts filed by the failed companies. Huge sums were awarded in damages against the accountants involved. However, the accountancy profession argued that this was unjust as many of the partners in these large firms had no personal involvement in the audits and yet had to meet their share of the damages under 'joint and several' liability. In response to their lobbying the government agreed to create a new form of partnership where non-negligent partners received the protection of limited liability, while those judged to have acted negligently would remain fully exposed.

The new form of limited liability partnership (often abbreviated to LLP, which is the prefix used before their Companies House identification number) has been available since 2000. Although taxed on a partnership basis, LLPs are treated the same as limited companies for filing purposes. Hence their accounts, as well as the names and addresses of the partners, are on the public record. The rules relating to the filing of accounts are described below on page 88. Originally conceived as a vehicle for professional services operations like accounting and law firms, the LLP form has proved more popular than expected with over 7000, drawn from a broad span of business activity, registered at the time of writing.

Companies

COMPANY LAW REFORM

In 2005, after a review of company law begun seven years earlier, the government issued a White Paper (policy document) on 'Company Law Reform'.[1] Some of its most important proposals relate to public disclosure by companies. At the time of writing no date has been set for a new Companies Bill to be submitted to Parliament and it seems likely that legislation will be quite a long time in coming. The present disclosure regime may thus continue for a number of years and the comments made below relate to it. However, I have also indicated the sort of changes being proposed concerning corporate disclosure in this and the next chapter.[2]

ANNUAL RETURNS

All companies, regardless of their size or status, are obliged to file an *annual return* (Companies House Form 363). This provides a snapshot of a company at a given date. It records the names of the directors and company secretary and any changes in those during the year. The directors' dates of birth, nationalities, occupations and residential addresses are shown in this document. The information as to occupation is useless in quite a few cases as the tautological entry 'company director' is supplied.

More recently, harassment (including physical attack) of some directors at their homes by protestors led to demands for residential addresses ceasing to be made public. There is a ministerial power to have home addresses removed from the Companies House record where a reasonable fear of assault can be shown, and some 4000 of these Confidentiality Orders have been issued to date.

The changes proposed in the review of company law would end the present openness. Under them Companies House would maintain two registers. One would be open to public inspection as at present. However, a director could choose to have their residential addresses entered on a confidential database with only an address for the service of legal documents on individual directors appearing on the public record. This would represent a considerable reduction in the personal data available to analysts.

The annual return also gives details of the issued share capital (shares actually sold or given to investors), showing the number and nominal value of each class of share in issue. Most importantly it also provides a list of the shareholders, giving their name, address, number of shares held and any transfers in ownership that have occurred in the course of the year.

More information regarding tracing shareholders is given on page 98.

TYPES OF COMPANY

Companies can be divided into:

- dormant companies
- unlimited companies
- private limited companies
- unquoted public limited companies
- listed public limited companies

---

1 Department of Trade and Industry (2005), *Company Law Reform*, Cm. 6456, Stationery Office.
2 Department of Trade and Industry documentation on the Review can be found at www.dti.gov.uk/cld/review.htm.

- quoted public limited companies
- foreign enterprises.

The rules for filing accounts vary according to the legal status and size of a particular company.

Dormant companies

A large number of companies are 'dormant', that is, they are still in existence but are not trading. Over a quarter of a million companies on the live register (20 per cent of the total filing accounts) are classed as dormant because they did not trade in their last accounting year. There can be a number of reasons for dormancy such as a desire to protect a trading name (the only way to do this in Britain is to establish a company with that name), because the legal and accounting costs of winding it up exceed the modest annual filing fee (£15 at the time of writing) or perhaps bad housekeeping by companies keeping now useless subsidiaries alive. Because dormant companies have not traded there will be no profit and loss account or cash flow statement and only a balance sheet has to be filed each year.

Unlimited companies

Limited liability and incorporation (that is, the act of creating a company) are actually separate concepts. Thus partners in two of the three partnership forms enjoy limited liability, even though these are not companies. It is also possible to have a company whose owners have no limitation as to their liability and some 5000 of these are currently registered. Solicitors are not allowed to limit their liability and thus must choose to operate as sole practitioners, general partnerships or unlimited companies. Certain firms may find incorporation (bringing with it a separate legal personality for their practice) attractive despite the absence of limited liability.

An unlimited company will have the same unprefixed registration number as a limited one and will be called 'XYZ Company' or abbreviated as 'XYZ Co'. Because the owners have unlimited liability they are allowed to maintain a large measure of privacy. While they have to disclose their names and home addresses through Companies House, they generally do not have to file accounts for their company. Public domain research opportunities are consequently limited.

Private limited companies

This is the most commonly used vehicle for operating a business, with over 1.8 million registered at Companies House. To warn those dealing with them that their owners have limited liability they must include 'Limited', 'Company Limited' or the abbreviations, 'Ltd' or 'Co. Ltd' in their names and on their company documents. The owners' liability can be limited either:

- by guarantee
- by shares.

The technical term for the owners of private limited companies, whether guarantors or shareholders, is *members*. This is also used to denote the shareholders of public limited companies. A company limited by guarantee does not have a share capital, each of the guarantors merely pledges a certain sum towards its debts. It is a popular legal form among charities and other not-for-profit bodies such as educational establishments. Bodies like the NSPCC, the

London Business School, the College of Law and the London School of Economics all operate as companies limited by guarantee.

Trading companies, on the other hand, will fix an amount for their total share capital on incorporation and divide it into a certain number of shares. These will then be allocated among the members and the more shares held by a member, the greater their stake in the ownership of the company. A fixed value, the 'par value', will be assigned to the shares at incorporation and this sum represents the total loss to the shareholder should the company fail.

Filing exemptions for private limited companies based on their size

Private limited companies that are trading are classed, according to their size, as small, medium and large and the extent of obligatory disclosure varies in relation to this. In recent years full accounts were filed by less than half of all active companies and the number exempted was greatly increased by the Government in 2004. As a result, although the larger and economically far more important companies will still have to file full financial statements, there are often cases where a smaller company is of analytical interest, but only limited accounting data will be available.

A *small company* is defined, from 2004, as one that, in its last accounting year, met two out of the following three criteria:

- turnover not exceeding £5.6 million
- balance sheet total (that is, either total assets or total liabilities) not exceeding £2.8 million
- average number of employees during the period not exceeding 50.

The reason for the lack of round numbers for the two financial criteria is that these are taken from an European Union Directive with the original amounts stated in European currency units (ECU) and then translated into sterling equivalents.

A *medium-sized company* is classed as one that, in its last accounting year, met two out of the following three criteria:

- turnover not exceeding £22.8 million
- balance sheet total not exceeding £11.4 million
- average number of employees during the period not exceeding 250.

If a company slots into either of these categories it can claim certain exemptions from the full rigour of public disclosure.

A small company only has to file a balance sheet and can avoid filing a profit and loss account, a cash flow statement or a directors' report.

A medium-sized company has to file all these items, but can conceal its turnover and suppress any details relating to turnover in the notes to its accounts.

The exercise of these exemptions often bemuses those obtaining such abbreviated accounts from Companies House or retrieving information from a company financials database. They assume that the profit and loss account has been omitted in error or that the database has lost some figures. In fact what is supplied is the information available, the gaps result from the legally permitted departures from full disclosure.

Large private limited companies or those filing accounts for *groups of companies* receive no exemptions.

This means that a minority of active companies actually trading file full accounts – very frustrating for someone researching a company claiming an exemption!

Standards of filing enforcement

Another practical difficulty from a research perspective is that a law is only as effective as its enforcement. In the mid-1980s many British companies failed to comply with the formal filing requirements set down in legislation. Compliance standards have greatly improved since then following an administrative crackdown on errant companies, with automatic fines on them for not submitting documents on time, personal prosecution of directors in seriously delinquent companies and other measures. The overwhelming majority of companies on the active register now file their accounts (the residue are presumably headed for liquidation although not yet formally in that state).

Nevertheless, many still file (especially annual returns) after the last due date. This is ten months after the end of the company accounting year for private companies, so if it has a year ending in March it should file before the end of the following January. One tip here is to complain to Companies House about a company's failure to meet its legal obligations. Common sense suggests that the minority of delinquent companies in which someone takes the trouble to express an interest should be chased more vigorously by a regulator, given the severe resource constraints Companies House has to operate within, than the many other non-compliant companies about whom no one apparently cares too much.

Under the changes to disclosure proposed by the Government, small-sized private limited companies, while retaining the right to file abbreviated accounts, would have to reveal their annual turnover. Medium-sized private companies would also lose the option of concealing their turnover figure. In addition the Government intends to reduce the time limit for private companies filing their accounts from ten to seven months after their year ends. When implemented these two reforms will give analysts a much better idea of the scale upon which smaller firms operate and place a company's latest financial data in their hands three months earlier than at present.

PUBLIC LIMITED COMPANIES

The law does not prevent a company or its shareholders from selling or otherwise transferring the ownership of some or all of their shares to another party by means of a private transaction.[3] It is illegal, however, to make a *public offer* of shares in a private company. This is a privilege reserved to those enterprises holding the status of *public limited company*, who are free to promote their share offerings using advertising and all the other marketing techniques employed to persuade the public at large to subscribe to the offer. Such firms will include 'Public Limited Company' or the abbreviations 'PLC' or 'plc' in their full names and company documents. To protect potential investors no exemptions from disclosure are granted to PLCs regardless of their size (and some private companies are considerably bigger businesses than many PLCs).

---

3   Although private limited companies often include a clause in their Articles of Association restricting the transfer of shares by members.

Unquoted public limited companies

It should be noted that, while a PLC's shares *may* be publicly traded this does not imply that they *are* traded on public markets, especially the London Stock Exchange (LSE). Out of about 12 800 PLCs on the register, only some 1800 are listed on the LSE, with a couple of hundred more quoted on other markets. Many PLCs assume this legal form because it has a certain degree of prestige or as a necessary preliminary step to floating on a public market. No share price information will be available for such nominally public companies because there is no formal marketplace for trading their shares. Unquoted PLCs have to file their accounts within seven months of their accounting year end (compared with ten months for private companies). Under the company law reform proposals this time limit would be trimmed to six months.

Listed public limited companies

Although there are under 2000 British companies listed on the London Stock Exchange their economic and business weight is vastly disproportionate compared to their numbers. In order to get and keep their listed status they have to meet sterner disclosure requirements than those set by ordinary company law. Originally these rules were set and enforced by the exchange, but now its role as the UK Listing Authority has been transferred to the Financial Services Authority (FSA), an official agency with statutory powers to regulate the whole UK financial services industry.

Significant additional information disclosure burdens are laid upon listed companies:

- They must file their annual report and accounts within six months of their accounting year end (unlisted PLCs have seven months to do this). Under the new disclosure regime they would have to mount their accounts on their websites within four months of their year ends.
- Apart from submitting their annual results they are obliged to produce an interim report covering the first six months of their accounting year. This requirement is stiffened for the 200 or so technology companies listed on the techMARK subdivision of listed companies: they have to file three quarterly reports as well as their annual one:
  - these have to be submitted to the FSA, but there is no remote electronic access to them and to inspect them a visit has to be made to the authority's offices in London's Docklands. Although several hundred companies voluntarily file interim reports at Companies House there is no legal obligation to do this and most do not bother;
  - company websites typically offer only a limited archive of their reports, so researchers must turn to commercial corporate document providers such as Perfect Information (www.perfectinfo.com) or Thomson Financial (www.thomson.com/financial) for longer runs of these;
- The requirement to publish prospectuses and the 'continuing obligations' listed companies accept as part of the price they must pay for their listing are dealt with in the next chapter.

Quoted public limited companies

'Quoted' and 'listed' are often treated as synonymous terms. However, a distinction now exists between the London listed companies and those British firms whose securities are traded on other exchanges. The shares of scores of entrepreneurial British PLCs, together with some well-established firms such as the Arsenal soccer club and brewers Shepherd Neame, are quoted on the independent Ofex market. Like the London exchange, Ofex is regulated by the FSA, but has its own rulebook. Companies quoted on it are obliged to issue six-monthly interim, as well as annual, reports.

Some UK companies have also chosen to be quoted on overseas bourses, particularly the American NASDAQ high technology market, in preference to being listed in London. They are then subject to the disclosure regime of these exchanges. This situation (together with 'dual listings' where a company is listed on an overseas market as well as the London exchange) can lead to greater disclosure of information – quarterly financial reporting for firms quoted in the US, for example.

Operating and Financial Reviews (OFRs)

From March 2005, instead of the present annual report and accounts, British companies with a full listing in London or quoted on some other major exchanges[4] have had to file a more extensive Operating and Financial Review (OFR). In the aftermath of Enron and other spectacular corporate scandals the Government decided that the requirement to prepare OFRs should be imposed without waiting for the enactment of a comprehensive new Companies Act.

While including topics that already have to be reported, the OFR ranges much wider than most current annual reports, with greater qualitative information on key issues such as a company's strategy and the factors influencing its performance having to be provided. The document's coverage is thus somewhat akin to a prospectus issued when a PLC offers its shares for sale to the public, particularly in the demand for risk factors to be identified and commented upon. However, a new reporting standard on the OFR has not yet been produced by the Accounting Standards Board and its practical impact remains uncertain. The Government contends that it will lead to greatly improved transparency and quality of disclosure, extending best practice from a minority of quoted companies to all them. Some observers are less sanguine, believing directors will eschew more informative disclosure for fear of exposing themselves to legal action or assisting competitors and confine themselves to bland, incontrovertible reporting.

Foreign enterprises

Most overseas enterprises establish incorporate local subsidiaries to carry on business in Britain. If a foreign firms merely operates through British agents (unless it is an insurance company) or takes the form of a partnership it is not obliged to register. However, if it has a long-term physical presence here it is classed as an *oversea company* and must register at Companies House. Filing requirements are similar for indigenous companies, but the accounts submitted will relate to the enterprise as a whole and not just its British activities.

Full details of disclosure requirements and Companies House forms are available on their website (www.companies-house.gov.uk).

Conclusions

- The extent of information that has to be disclosed varies according to the legal form assumed by an enterprise, its size (if a private limited company) and whether its shares are publicly traded.
- All companies have to file annual returns (which includes a list of shareholders).

---

[4] These are EU bourses (such as EuroNext), the New York Stock Exchange and NASDAQ. Firms whose shares are traded on junior markets like AIM and Ofex are not subject to this requirement.

- Although larger concerns must file full accounts, CI analysis can be frustrated if a smaller company takes advantage of exemptions from disclosure on grounds of size or neglects to file on time.
- More information has to be disclosed by quoted companies and hence these are easier to research.
- The new obligation for quoted companies to file OFRs should, if it works as intended, considerably extend the information (particularly of a qualitative kind) available in the public domain on them.

11 *Systematic Sources – 'One-off' Corporate Filings*

While the last chapter examined the regular, periodic filings made by firms there are also requirements to report certain ad hoc events to Companies House. This one reviews these disclosure obligations which CI analysts must be familiar with when using public registries to obtain company information and includes:

- an outline of the reporting demands laid upon all companies
- a sketch of the additional ones that must be met by *listed companies*
  - filing of prospectuses when securities are offered for sale to the public
  - immediate public announcement of certain developments through the Regulatory News Service
  - issue of circulars to shareholders and the special rules applying to the disclosure of shareholdings (including those held in the name of nominees) in Public Limited Companies (PLCs)
- details of other public registries which may hold useful corporate information on patents, trade marks, the ownership of land, ships and aircraft.

Every company is obliged to report the following events to Companies House:

- an alteration of its name
- a change in its registered office address
- appointment of a new director or company secretary
- resignation of a director or company secretary
- changes in the particulars of a director or company secretary. This provision relates to company officers who change their name, residential address or nationality
- the pledge of company assets as security for a loan or other credit, evidenced by the filing of a charge against those assets.

CHANGES IN COMPANY NAMES

Some of these events may be of considerable analytical interest – or none. Many reasons, for instance, can induce a company to change its name. It may reflect a change in ownership or perhaps a completely new departure in terms of its business strategy as the firm prepares to engage in new activities or address new markets. On the other hand it may simply indicate a decision to abandon a misleading or old-fashioned company name for a more accurate or contemporary-sounding one (although this can be associated with a change in strategic direction reflected in a new image). These filings merely record changes, they do not provide explanations as to why they have taken place. Other sources must be consulted in trying to establish the reasons for them.

CHANGES IN REGISTERED OFFICE ADDRESSES

A newly registered office address can mean that the company has shifted to another location – and this may be of significance. However, its address as recorded at Companies House is merely the one at which legal documents can be served and not that of a company's headquarters. There is no legal requirement for the actual trading address to be disclosed and in fact the address given for the registered office is often that of the company's accountants or lawyers. Thus in the latter case changes usually have no analytical import whatsoever.

CHANGES IN COMPANY OFFICERS

Changes in company officers should also be looked into further. The appointment of a new director(s) can again indicate a great many things – a change in ownership, an alliance with another firm, the injection of private equity funding, one of the consequences of buying another company or a reflection of the desire to bring on board specialist knowledge are some common examples. Likewise a resignation may result from a director moving to another firm, retiring, leaving following a takeover, quitting after a dispute or being ousted. Again other evidence must be obtained in order to elucidate the meaning behind the filing.

CHARGES AGAINST ASSETS

Charges against a firm's assets as security for a loan or other extension of credit are quite common and analysts need to understand the general principles governing their operation. The loan agreement pledging the borrowers' assets is called a *debenture*. If a company gets into financial difficulties these seemingly dull documents begin to cast a growing shadow.

They can take the form of either:

- fixed charges
- floating charges.

A fixed charge relates to a specific asset or asset class. The most common type is the mortgage debenture where the borrower pledges its freehold land and buildings as collateral for the loan. This is very similar to a residential mortgage where a lender will lend a sum secured against a house or flat. If the borrower fails to honour the terms of the mortgage agreement, the creditor can repossess the property, in other words, seize and sell it to repay the loan. In the same way the holder of a mortgage debenture can take possession of the shop, factory, office or other premises that has been pledged and offer it for sale if the conditions set out in the debenture are breached.

Companies also often offer debts owed to them, *book debt*, as security. Where a firm enjoys strong cash flow and has no serious problems with obtaining payment from its customers this form of collateral is often readily accepted (it should be noted that British case law has established that sums held in a company's bank account are *not* normally to be treated as book debt). Other types of asset pledged can include any intellectual property (patents, copyrights, trade marks or licences) owned by the borrower, ships or aircraft it owns and its goodwill. As was noted earlier, the latter is the extra it paid when buying another company over the balance sheet worth recorded for that business, minus an allowance for the decay in the value of goodwill over time.

The assets or classes of asset specified in a fixed charge cannot be sold without the permission of the chargeholder. However, an alternative approach is to accept a *floating charge* where no assets are designated as security. Some of a company's assets are constantly shifting in their composition: stocks of raw materials will fluctuate as they are acquired and used, work in progress will be commenced or completed and stocks of finished goods augmented or sold. Meanwhile equipment, furniture and vehicles will be scrapped, resold and replaced. The floating charge enables these more transitory assets to be used as collateral and does not prevent them being sold or otherwise disposed of provided this is in the 'normal course of business'. This stipulation is intended to prevent them from being got rid of in a manner intended to defraud creditors such as sales at bargain prices to associates of the debtor.

Floating charges do not take effect (a process which the law describes, for once rather poetically, by the term 'crystallization') until certain events occur. These will involve breaches of the terms of the debenture establishing the floating charge, the insolvency of the firm or its having to cease trading. When these take place the creditor is entitled to appoint an administrative receiver to assume managerial control of the company. The receiver can sell those assets not already subject to a fixed charge to meet the debts owed (this description somewhat simplifies a complex legal situation where many, often recondite, exceptions apply – neither must the right of certain 'preferential' creditors to be paid before those holding floating charges be forgotten – but it states the general principle).

Companies are required to file details of any charges, whether fixed or floating, made against their assets at Companies House. These records will show the name of the lender and identify the nature of the assets pledged in a fixed charge.

Time limits for filing and company's own public domain registers

The general rule is that any of these ad hoc events must be reported to Companies House within 14 days of their taking place (21 days are allowed for filing details of charges against corporate assets). They must also be recorded, as soon as they occur, in one of the company's registers. Contrary to widespread belief these registers are not confidential, but in the public domain and thus are often a little more current than the filings at Companies House. They are usually kept at the company's registered office address. The following registers must be maintained:

- Register of Directors and Secretary. This records appointments, resignations and changes in the particulars of company officers.
- Register of Directors' Interests. This contains details of shares and debentures in the company owned by its directors.
- Register of Members. This is a list of the company's shareholders (or guarantors if its liability is limited by guarantee rather than by shares) and records changes in these.
- Register of Charges. This reveals if any of the company's assets have been pledged through debentures as collateral and identifies the lender.

The Register of Members for private companies is generally quite brief, but can be huge for listed companies whose shares are frequently traded on the Stock Exchange. In the latter case the task of maintaining and amending the register, along with distributing company notices, annual reports, circulars and making dividend payments and so on to shareholders, will be outsourced to a firm of specialist company registrars. Where the register is held by an external registrar service, the place where they can be inspected must be publicly disclosed through a Companies House filing. The significance of the Register of Members for researchers lies in the fact that companies only have to notify Companies House of changes in their shareholders once a year in the annual return. While changes in directors have to be filed within a fortnight of their occurring, no similar legal duty is imposed where shareholders are concerned. However, special rules apply to public companies (PLCs) and these will be examined later.

Absurdly complex and incoherent rules relating to the inspection or copying of these registers are set out in the principal Companies Act (that of 1985). Essentially, anyone can insist on consulting them during normal business hours. There is no right to demand copies of the Register of Directors or Charges, but the company must supply a copy of its Register of Directors' Interests and Register of Members within ten days (counting from the day after the request was made) in return for a modest fee. I have already noted that many companies regard these registers as confidential, so anyone intending to exercise their right of inspection will be well advised to go furnished with a copy of the relevant sections of the Companies Act 1985 or, even better, a copy of the Act itself.[1]

Prospectuses for public offers of securities

These were mentioned in Chapter 8 as an often overlooked source of sectoral information, but their primary focus is, of course, on individual companies. In order to protect investors the law insists they have to be published every time a company offers its securities (whether shares or bonds) to the public and disclose a great deal of information about it. The content of prospectuses is laid down by the Financial Services Authority (FSA) in its Listing Rules, which sets out seven categories of information to be supplied:

1) Names and addresses of the issuer and those who have advised it in preparing the prospectus (its financial advisers, auditors, brokers and solicitors).
2) Details of the securities being offered such as their number, nominal value, issue price, voting rights, terms of conversion (if a convertible preference share or convertible bond can be exchanged for ordinary shares), rate of interest paid (if a bond) and all other conditions applying.
3) General information about the issuer such as its date of incorporation.
4) The company's activities.
5) Financial information for the last three years (this is not required for companies joining the London Stock Exchange's junior 'AIM' market or the independent 'Ofex' one, which will admit firms with a shorter trading record or even start-ups).
6) Data on the company officers such as their names, ages, education and professional qualifications, previous career history, other directorships and remuneration.
7) Recent developments in the company and an assessment of its future prospects.

Full details of what must be filed can be found on the UK Listing Authority section of the FSA website (www.fsa.gov.uk).

---

1   Companies Act 1985, HMSO.

Prospectuses represent a rich quarry of data for analysts, although it should be remembered that they are being used to persuade investors to buy the securities on offer and so the forecast outlook for the company will be on the optimistic side. Because of their use as a promotional tool for the issue, prospectuses are available free of charge from the financial advisers to the public offer. They also have to be filed at Companies House. A number of database services (such as Perfect Information and Thomson Financial, see page 90) carry archival texts which is helpful when a large number of prospectuses or rather old ones are needed.

Listed companies

Again to safeguard the interests of investors, a company listed on the London Stock Exchange has to meet sterner ad hoc disclosure requirements under the 'Continuing Obligations' laid upon it in the Listing Rules. Events such as the appointment or resignation of a director have to be reported to the market as soon as they take place through the Stock Exchange's Regulatory News Service (RNS). The key principle is that any development likely to move a company's share price either up or down has to be disclosed immediately. This is to ensure existing or potential investors do not make their investment decisions without having the opportunity to be in possession of the most current information. The RNS covers both fully listed companies and those listed on the second-tier AIM market, but Ofex has its own announcements service, Newstrack.

Where the fullest information is required the diligent analyst will not be content with the news items tabled by a company on its website. Many RNS announcements and Companies House filings are trivial. However, there are times when a certain disclosure has to be made to comply with the Listing Rules and the Companies Act, yet the enterprise carefully avoids any reference to it on its own website and in its communications to the media. Some of these filings then become of considerable interest to an inquisitive analyst.

Conversely, companies may choose to publish certain announcements or documents (the award of major new contracts or presentations by their management to investment analysts being common examples) that fall outside the scope of the continuing obligations.

One of the most valuable types of announcement is the *trading statement*. These are commonly issued by retailers to report on the vital Christmas period rather than leaving the market without guidance as to their performance until the next formal results appear, but can be released in many situations. They are prized by analysts because they provide more current data.

Another hugely important category of announcement is the *profit warning*, whereby a company informs the market that its own forecast for profits or those made by broking house analysts are not going to be achieved. An interesting debate in the City concerning profit forecasts has been settled by an excellent piece of research undertaken by the Bank of England.[2] Some fund managers used to argue that profit warnings (provided they were not too dire) were actually a 'buy' signal as the market would overreact to them, forcing down the share price so much that the shares were actually cheap in terms of the company's longer-term prospects. In fact the Bank's research shows that not only do profits typically take a long time to recover following a warning, but that the effect is also felt in weaker balance sheets, depriving the firm of resources needed to return quickly to growth in future years.

---

2   Kearns, A. and Whitney, J. (Autumn 2002),'The balance-sheet information content of UK profit warnings', *Bank of England Quarterly Bulletin*, 292–98.

Analysts will also be interested in announcements of disposals of subsidiaries, divisions or other parts of the business, acquisitions of new ones and major alliances or contracts. Mergers and acquisitions activity may also require a circular (which contains more information on the deal) to be sent to shareholders.

Circulars

Listed firms have to send circulars to their shareholders under certain circumstances. One example is 'material' acquisitions or disposals of other companies, businesses or assets. That every acquisition or disposal does not trigger a filing is often misunderstood. What is classed in the Listing Rules as material varies according to the size of the transaction in relation to the size of the company consummating it. Accordingly many deals by huge companies that are quite large in absolute terms do not need to be announced through the RNS or reported to shareholders in a circular.

Circulars are filed with the FSA and not at Companies House, so unless a personal visit to the authority's headquarters is possible they have to be obtained using a corporate documents archive service like Perfect Information and Thomson Financial (see page 90).

Shareholder data

Special rules apply to reporting changes in shareholdings among all PLCs (not just listed ones). The Companies Act provides that 'significant' shareholders in PLCs have to be recorded in the company's annual Directors' Report. Significant is defined as a holding of three per cent or more of the firm's total voting share capital. Each extra one per cent of the total capital acquired or disposed of must be notified by the shareholder to the company (as well as if a holding falls below the three per cent level). The company also has the right to demand notification in writing from a significant shareholder if they fail to submit this. A register of such notifications, which must be made within two days of the shares being bought or sold, is kept by the company. It is open to public inspection like those referred to earlier.

Listed companies receiving a notification must also disclose this through the RNS. Because of the risk of related parties building a substantial holding without breaching the three per cent ceiling (four holdings of 2.9 per cent each gives a total stake of 11.6 per cent) these must be aggregated. Thus holdings by their spouses or children under 18 years of age are also counted in when determining whether a shareholder has a significant stake. Holdings by 'concert parties', where several shareholders are acting together are also aggregated for this purpose.

From a researcher's viewpoint the value of this shareholding information is somewhat undermined by that fact that the shareholder named in the records may not be the real owner. This situation arises because a 'nominee' can hold shares on behalf of the actual 'beneficial' owners. In many cases the use of nominees is purely for the administrative convenience of fund management concerns handling a complex portfolio on behalf of numerous clients. However, it can also be used to conceal the identity of the beneficial owner. A predator preparing a hostile takeover bid for a listed company will often acquire a shareholding, sheltering behind the nominee, as a platform for its bid. Potential bid targets consequently take care to monitor their register of shareholders for signs that such strategic stakes are being built up.

PLCs have the right to demand that a nominee identifies the beneficial owner. Because this power is conferred under Section 212 of the Companies Act such approaches are commonly referred to as 'Section 212 notices'. Several database services can be used to research shareholdings (including the details of beneficial owners revealed in 212 notices) in listed companies: Argus Vickers (www.argus-vickers.co.uk), Computershare (www.computershare. co.uk), Thomson's 'Share World' (www.shareworld.tfsd.com).

Apart from Companies House and the registers held by individual firms, a number of other important public domain resources are available to researchers.

Patents

Searching through patents as a means of obtaining competitive advantage has a long history. Bayer started analyzing competitors' patents in 1886, just nine years after the creation of the German patent office. Patent analysis can yield useful descriptive clues regarding a company's technological trajectory and the markets it is concentrating on. It can also identify commercial opportunities presented by the expiration of patents held by rivals or those involving a potential to manufacture under licence (and other forms of joint venture) with other firms.

Thus firms whose patents cite their own early patents will tend to be technological pioneers, while those citing other companies' patents are usually imitators. It is also used to identify those individual scientists, engineers and other groups of inventors who are especially valuable as employees through either their prolific patenting or by devising a small number of particularly highly profitable innovations. Such research might reveal that a company's future prosperity rests upon a handful of talented people in the R&D department, rendering it highly vulnerable if they leave or become unable to carry on working.

The Patent Office website has many links to other national and international patent registries (www.patent.gov.uk/patent). The most extensive collections of patents and other documents recording intellectual property is held by the British Library (www.bl.uk/collections/patents).

There can be a number of difficulties in unearthing a company's patent portfolio. Those held by a small firm may have been filed in the personal name of the principal founder, a co-founder or a former partner. Likewise, in a joint venture the filing could be made under the name of either of the companies involved. Some firms operating under a group structure purposely try to baffle researchers by submitting patents under the names of numerous subsidiaries rather than that of the parent company. Thomson Derwent (www.thomsonderwent.com) assign codes to most companies in their Derwent World Patents Index, enabling patents held by both the parent and its subsidiaries to be identified in one search. This service is also helpful when there is uncertainty as to the way company names are treated (for example, are filings under 'Xerox' or 'Rank Xerox').

In the welter of patents issued by some companies it can be difficult to determine which ones are commercially important to them. Taking the trouble to renew a patent or filing it in other countries are probable indications that the owner places a greater commercial value on it. Robert Cantrell of ThomsonDerwent, the leading patent information provider, offers a number of extremely useful tips[3] for inferring which patents are merely routine ('this may be valuable some

---

3   Cantrell, R. (1997), 'Patents intelligence from legal and commercial perspectives', *World Patent Information*, 19(4), 251–64.

day, but not at present') and those they regard as promising products to bring to market. He recommends focusing upon the following indicators:

1) Patents that appear to represent the cumulation of earlier research activity.
2) Completely new patents.
3) Filing large blocks of patents together. This may indicate a new core technology being 'haloed' by intellectual protection for its associated applications. In other words, the patent holder is perhaps seeking to protect the spin-offs from the basic invention by simultaneously patenting many of them.
4) Where all research team members are named in a patent, if in other patents only some of them are recorded.
5) Patents being published worldwide within a short time of each other.
6) Foreign companies taking out a patent in Australia. This can be an interesting step as Australia is not a huge market like the USA, Europe or Japan and yet as a prosperous and technologically advanced country it is an attractive place to sell to. Cantrell warns against jumping to conclusions when this is observed. It is very easy to apply for a patent in Australia and he demonstrates that one major Japanese company files applications there as a matter of course. It is when an Australian filing is not part of a company's regular patenting practice that the analyst's interest should be aroused.
7) Widely cited patents. He also points out that this is a quick and easy way of assembling a list of competitors in a particular technology zone, while they are of additional interest if cited by a firm in a completely different industry.

As with the Australian example Cantrell counsels against hasty assumptions: 'Exceptions analysis [by which he means looking for aberrations in a firm's patenting behaviour] for commercial intent is an art form … For every example that works there is a counter example that does not.' When several of these exceptions to a firm's normal patenting activity are found, however, this does suggest the company regards a patent as commercially promising.

The PatentCafe information network provides many useful services for researching intellectual property issues throughout the world (www.cafeforums.com).

Trade marks

Trade marks filings, like patents, can provide insights that enrich descriptions of the company, tracing its development over time and in predicting its future strategic direction. They include not only symbols, but also words and shapes or a combination of all three. Coca-Cola's trade marks thus contain its name, a logo and a distinctive shape of bottle. It should be noted that, in the UK, trade names, as opposed to trade marks cannot be registered. The former is treated as merely the name of the company, while the latter distinguishes the goods and services it offers from those provided by other firms. The only way to safeguard possession of a trade name is to incorporate a company with that name (see the Trade Marks Registry www.patent.gov.uk/tm).

Land

A company or individual's ownership of land is a potentially interesting research topic. Details of the current owner of a specific property are normally available from HM Land Registry (www.landreg.gov.uk).

Unfortunately, as noted earlier, it is not possible to conduct a search to identify an individual person or company's holdings of land nor is information available as who the previous owners were.

Local authority planning permission records can also be useful to uncover a change in what a site is being used for or extensions to existing facilities.

Ships and aircraft

There may also be occasions where the analyst wishes to confirm the ownership of a vessel or an aircraft or to establish whether they have been offered as security in a mortgage. Two public registries provide this information: the Maritime and Coastguard Agency (Registry of Shipping and Seamen) (www.mcga.gov.uk) and the Civil Aviation Authority (UK Register of Aircraft Mortgages) (www.caa.co.uk).

On some occasions a search of other sources in this field, such as the Lloyds Register of Yachts may yield interesting results. This quote is taken from an official enquiry focused on the Fayed family, owners of Harrods:

> The Fayeds claimed that a very expensive yacht named 'Dodi' which was first registered in 1913 had been in the ownership of their family since before they were born ... A search of the Lloyds Yacht Register in the Guldhall Library, London, and the Reading Room at the National Maritime Museum, Greenwich, revealed that this story is completely untrue.[4]

Further information on Lloyds services and how to access them can be obtained from their website (www.lr.org).

Other regulatory filings

Regulatory bodies like the Competition Commission or the Office of Gas and Electricity Markets, as well as producing valuable material to help in understanding an industry, are also a good place to seek knowledge on individual companies. Although they are sensitive to the need for commercial confidentiality and thus do not publish all the information given to them by firms, their reports and filings are still an excellent starting point for obtaining reliable corporate information quickly. Links to these are available on the UK Government website (www.ukonline.gov.uk).

---

4   Brooke, H. and Aldous, H.G.C. (1990), *Report of the Department of Trade and Industry Inspectors Regarding House of Fraser Holdings plc*, HMSO, 618–89.

Conclusions

- Ad hoc corporate filings both extend and update the body of evidence available to analysts.
- Individual public filings should be interpreted within the broader context of the analyst's total knowledge regarding an enterprise garnered from other sources.
- Comparing several types of source is often instructive. For example, what is said in a regulatory filing compared with that stated in a company's press release, quotes from its management and media reports concerning the same event? Another instance would be where considerable patenting or trade mark filing was taking place in a certain field without this receiving much emphasis in a firm's public statements.
- Consulting less obvious public record sources sometimes produces surprising and valuable results.
- In many cases a detailed search of a large company's numerous filings will not be feasible or worth undertaking, but where an important issue is involved this should be carried out as far as is practicable.

CHAPTER **12** *Foreign Sources*

As this country is so economically dependent on international trading and financial activities, the overseas dimension has always been a significant part of business research in Britain. Now accelerating cross-border integration is making knowledge of the foreign information scene an ever-increasingly important part of researchers' work.

This chapter is split into three parts:

- the first, after some remarks on the problem of foreign language material, examines the key types of source for researching overseas industries
- the next is concerned with issues surrounding researching individual companies incorporated outside the UK
- because of its massive economic weight, the framework for company research in the US is considered separately.

The language barrier is often perceived as the principal difficulty in international research. For those who speak English it has been steadily lowered. There has been a massive growth in the past 20 years in the availability of material in English from official bodies, companies and other organizations in non-Anglophone countries.

A few points should be made:

- A huge amount of considerable analytical interest is still not published in English.
- On bilingual sites the English pages may be only a part of the content available in the vernacular. For example, many national statistical offices offer two sets of data: the full version in their national tongue and a more limited subset in English.
- Even someone fluent in a particular language may be baffled by the specialist jargon of business or not understand the local institutional background well enough to conduct effective research.
- American English differs from that used in Britain both in spelling and meaning: 'when I was at school' said by an American often means 'when I was at university'.

They illustrate the merits of involving someone with appropriate local knowledge of business terminology and the context within which research is conducted – in addition to linguistic expertise – in cross-border research projects whenever this is possible. This will clearly apply both in handling documents and when speaking to people in other countries.

Overseas sectoral research

For this type of research same kind of sources listed in Chapter 8 can be used:

- trade associations
- official statistics
- individual companies
- market research
- brokers' research
- monographs
- journals
- regulatory authorities.

A good starting point for international, as well as domestic, research is Karen Blakeman's business information portal (www.rba.co.uk).

Another excellent set of well-organized links, assembled specifically for CI research, is Fuld and Co's *I3* (Internet Intelligence Index) (www.fuld.com).

TRADE ASSOCIATIONS

Many trade associations are organized on a global or regional basis as well as at national level:

- A *World Guide to Trade Associations* is published annually by Thomson Gale (www.galegroup.com).
- American, Mexican and Canadian bodies can be traced through the online directory of the Federation of International Trade Associations (www.internationaltradeorg).

GOVERNMENTAL STATISTICAL SERVICES

One of the main functions of international governmental bodies like the United Nations and its agencies (such as the Food and Agriculture Organization, Industrial Development Organization and World Bank), Organization for Economic Cooperation and Development, International Monetary Fund and European Union is the collection and publication of macroeconomic, industry and social statistics. A major advantage of material taken from these sources is that considerable efforts have been made to ensure the comparability of the data between countries.

When researching an individual country more current and detailed figures should be available from its national statistical office. In countries with a federal system of government further information may be provided by provincial/state authorities, while public bodies responsible for inward investment can often be a useful source of extra material on their regions.

INDIVIDUAL COMPANIES

Multinationals and global financial and business services firms will be focused on both worldwide or regional sectors and, through their local offices, on national ones.

MARKET RESEARCH

Market research is available at the global, regional (Europe, South East Asia and so on) and national level.

BROKERS' REPORTS

Brokers' reports again provide global, regional or national coverage.

MONOGRAPHS

The British Library site has links to the national libraries of a number of other countries, such as the Library of Congress in the United States (www.bl.uk/catalogues/otherlibcats/htm).

JOURNALS

Three widely used international sources for tracing relevant periodical material are:

- *Benn's Media* published as a hard-copy directory by CMP Information Services details the business and consumer press worldwide. Volume 1 deals with UK periodicals, Volume 2 with those from the rest of Europe, Volume 3 with the USA and Canada and Volume 4 with the rest of the world (www.cmpdata.co.uk/benns).
- *Ulrich's Periodicals Directory* published by R.R. Bowker has global coverage. It is produced in the form of a CD-ROM updated quarterly or as a database with weekly updates (www.ulrichsweb.com).
- *Willings Press Guide* is published in three volumes (Volume 1 covers the UK, Volume 2 Western Europe and Volume 3 other parts of the world) and a web version. It is updated quarterly (www.willingspress.com).

REGULATORY BODIES

The most extensive set of links to these is through Governments on the WWW (www.gksoft.com/govt). The International Federation of Stock Exchanges site also has links to its member bourses throughout the world (www.fibv.com).

Researching foreign companies

WHICH JURISDICTION IS THE BUSINESS INCORPORATED IN?

The legal framework for carrying on business is determined by which jurisdiction it falls under. Jurisdictions are more plentiful than sovereign states because they include dependencies as well as the country exercising sovereignty over them. Most British law (such as the Companies Acts) covers the whole of the UK, but some legal provisions apply only to England and Wales and others only in Scotland. Thus there are slight differences between the law of England and Wales and the law of Scotland on business topics like insolvency and partnerships. Despite being ultimately governed from Westminster, Northern Ireland is a separate jurisdiction, while Guernsey, Jersey and the Isle of Man are tax havens with radically different legal rules from those set in the UK.

Most tax havens are dependencies like the three island jurisdictions listed above. So offshore centres such as the Bahamas, Bermuda, British Virgin Islands, Cayman Islands, Gibraltar and the Turks and Caicos Islands are British dependencies and the Netherlands Antilles a Dutch one. There also some sovereign tax havens like Cyprus, Liechtenstein and Malta. The US has over 50 jurisdictions as, apart from the national federal one, each state in the Union has this status, as does the federal capital area of Washington, D.C. and other US territories such as

Puerto Rico and Guam. Each of the Canadian provinces is also a separate jurisdiction and there are noticeable differences between the legal codes of Ontario and Quebec.

From the viewpoints of the legal constraints laid upon corporate action or researching businesses, the jurisdiction they are incorporated under makes a considerable difference. Some actions that are perfectly legal in one place are banned in others and radically different philosophies of the balance between corporate privacy and openness are adhered to. Certain jurisdictions treat company filings as confidential with only the authorities having access to them. There has been a move towards greater international cooperation in exchanging corporate information to combat money laundering and other kinds of criminal activity, but this is shared between the authorities and does not enter the public domain unless there is a court case. Other jurisdictions extend the right to access the filed records to groups such as shareholders or creditors. However, these have to demonstrate a financial interest in the company as part-owners or providers of credit – mere curiosity is not enough. More open jurisdictions allow anyone to inspect the records held in corporate registries, at least for certain types of company. Finally the most open (such as Great Britain) place filings made by *all* companies in the public domain.

The availability of information on unquoted foreign companies thus varies greatly between jurisdictions. Some insist on considerable public disclosure, while if the firm is incorporated in a tax haven or the Middle East for instance, virtually no information will be available from the official registry.

A company's choice of jurisdiction can be of analytical interest. Most companies naturally incorporate in their country of origin, yet a significant number register abroad. If there are good reasons for doubting the propriety of a business, its decision to incorporate in a jurisdiction with minimal disclosure requirements is another ground for suspicion. Robert Maxwell's empire was ultimately owned and controlled by a Stiftung (foundation) located in Liechtenstein, so no information regarding it was publicly available. However, analysts should beware of leaping to conclusions, this option may simply be driven by a desire to minimize tax.

HOW EFFECTIVELY ARE THE DISCLOSURE RULES ENFORCED?

In the European Union there has been an attempt to reduce some of the disparities between member states through a series of company law harmonization directives. The First Directive established broad rules for the registration of companies, the Fourth dealt with the form and filing of financial information, while the Seventh was concerned with the preparation of accounts by several companies operating together as a group.

Unfortunately the existence of a law is irrelevant unless it is enforced and variable standards of compliance can frustrate researchers even when there is a legal obligation to file accounts and other documents at a registry. Great Britain has enjoyed a relatively high level of compliance for many years in terms of companies filing their accounts (see page 89 for a more detailed picture).

However, this was not the case in the early 1980s and even now, as we have seen, overdue filing still vexes analysts eager to inspect documents that should have been submitted earlier. This also obtains in other jurisdictions with some authorities insisting on compliance and others taking a much more relaxed approach.

Hence, although Germany enacted the Fourth Directive into its domestic legislation, these obligations were largely ignored by private companies. There are giant German multinationals like Bayer, Deutsche Bank or Volkswagen but the backbone of the economy is the Mittelstand, the largely family-held small- and medium-sized private firms. These regard scrutiny by outsiders as highly unwelcome and as an offensive intrusion into family privacy as well as an attempt to deprive them of a source of competitive advantage. Consequently they prefer to pay the modest fines levied (if these are even imposed) as the price for not filing their accounts. Not surprisingly Germany's EU partners resent this financial secrecy when their accounts are in the public domain and agitated for the German government to enforce the Fourth Directive effectively. In 1998, after a campaign lasting 15 years, the European Court of Justice ruled that the authorities in Germany must impose 'appropriate penalties' on defaulters to ensure adequate compliance. However, at the time of writing the compliance rate for filing private company accounts was a mere five per cent, if anything worse than it had been some years earlier.

ACCESSING FILINGS

When a document has been filed the researcher is still faced with the problem of accessing it. Some European countries (Denmark, Great Britain, Ireland, Norway, Sweden) have centralized registries, while filings in others were traditionally made at local courts. Germany has some 500 of these local registries and France over 100. Difficulties in accessing official records has led to substitute services developing such as the Creditreform credit rating agency in Germany or the Cerved company information service run by the Italian Chambers of Commerce. I make some points regarding credit ratings data a little later in this chapter when discussing the United States.

COMPARABILITY OF ACCOUNTS

A major barrier to comparing companies operating in different places is the impact of national accounting traditions, with each country having its own set of rules for preparing accounts. In Britain the financial statements are required to show a 'true and fair view' of a company's affairs. This philosophy is dominated by commercial considerations and the accounts should reflect the economic reality of a firm's trading operations and resources. So strongly is this principle adhered to that if there is a conflict between the provisions of company law or UK accounting rules and giving a true and fair view, then the latter prevails (although disclosure of such a departure from the former is required, if material). Individual firms are the focal point of this system of financial reporting and a greater degree of subjective judgement has to be applied in compiling accounts.

The contrasting tradition is one in which accounts are prepared to satisfy legal and tax requirements. This framework is set at national level, rather than being focused on individual companies. Less discretion is available in preparing accounts, so there is narrower scope for applying subjective opinions and, provided the rules have been adhered to, the financial statements are legally and professionally acceptable – even if they do not provide a commercially true and fair view of a company's affairs.

Corporate taxation gives rise to a number of divergences between the 'true and fair' and 'legal/tax' systems. For example, in the UK the cost of replacing a computer would typically be spread over three years and reflected in a depreciation charge for each of these years. However, the government wishes to encourage IT and other forms of investment and therefore often grants accelerated tax breaks against company spending on fixed assets. The firm may thus receive 100 per cent tax relief for the cost of buying an asset in Year One, while the depreciation charge will generally stretch over Years One to Three. Because all the tax relief has already been received there will be none to set against depreciation charges in Years Two and Three, creating 'deferred tax' for these later periods. The financial statements produced as a company's accounts thus differ from those submitted to the Inland Revenue for the purpose of calculating its tax liability. In countries like Germany, where accounting rules are determined by the requirements of the taxation authorities, this does not apply and the same set of financial statements meets both situations.

Differences between national accounting rules leads to a wide divergence in the financial results reported. Daimler-Benz had prepared its accounts solely according to German standards, but in 1993 obtained a listing on the New York Stock Exchange. To comply with American rules the company had to file financial statements prepared according to US Generally Accepted Accounting Principles (GAAP). The profit and loss account in the German version reported a profit of DM614 million, while the American one showed a *loss* of DM1859 million. Another facet of German company financial practice revealed when US rules were followed was the creation of 'hidden reserves', not shown in the published balance sheet, which could be used to smooth out fluctuations in profits. Christopher Nobes, in his excellent *International Guide to Interpreting Company Accounts*,[1] cites other striking divergences between company accounts compiled according to different national codes.

The European Union member states have recognized that diverse national accounting standards create difficulties for investors wishing to make cross-border comparisons of companies and this inhibits the fullest development of a pan-European capital market. A major step forward in this respect was the decision to compel all EU listed companies to publish accounts prepared in accordance with International Financial Reporting Standards (IFRS) from 2005 (although unquoted companies will still be free to use national standards). It has also been recognized that there would be considerable benefits if a common set of rules applied across the world and New Zealand, for example, will adopt IFRS for quoted companies and some others from 2007. Reaching agreement on these has been difficult, however, as the Americans are unwilling to abandon their GAAP and replace it with IFRS, contending that their regime is superior. Since the US accounting scandals of recent years dented this self-confidence there has been a renewed impetus towards negotiating global standards, but this goal is yet to be achieved.

Analysts should thus be very cautious in making cross-border comparisons using accounts data unless they know they are all compiled according to a common set of accounting rules like IFRS or GAAP. This is especially important when their quantitative information is taken from international databases where the raw numbers of the original financial statements are standardized by the data providers. These databases are an admirable source for making rapid assessments of many companies in various countries. However, when deeper analysis has to be undertaken the original financial information should always be obtained.

ACCOUNTING JARGON

Differences in accounting terminology are another obstacle to understanding foreign company financial statements, even though many listed companies in the non-English speaking world now produce an English version of their reports. As well as US firms themselves, many overseas firms use American rather than British terms in their accounts (a concordance of these can be found as Appendix 4). Analysts will also need to get used to variations in the layout of financial statements. Thus French balance sheets typically begin by stating the shareholders' equity, an item that comes at the end of British ones. Again profit and loss accounts in France reverse the order used in Britain by reporting costs before revenues.

---

1   Nobes, C. (1999), *International Guide to Interpreting Company Accounts*, 3rd edition, FT Finance. Professor Nobes has also written a valuable textbook on the subject *Comparative International Accounting* (2003), 7th edition, Pearson Higher Education.

OTHER DISCLOSURE

Apart from the financial statements there will be other differences in disclosure between jurisdictions. Individual directors' remuneration has to be published for listed companies in Britain, while only aggregate figures for the board as a whole must be reported in Germany. As was noted earlier, the ownership of shares in Britain is recorded in a company's Register of Members, yet in France and Germany nearly all shares are held in *bearer* form. This means that whoever possesses them (until proven to hold stolen securities) is regarded as their lawful owner, even though there is no registration of their title. Consequently there is no publicly available record of a company's shareholders unless it is listed.

Major shareholders in quoted companies in the EU are obliged to declare their stakes when these exceed certain percentages of total voting share capital. Under the 1988 Major Shareholdings Directive these trigger points are set at 5, 10, 20, 33.3, 50 and 66.6 per cent. Individual countries can choose to demand greater disclosure, hence in Britain the level at which a holding is classed as 'significant' (as seen earlier) and has to be reported to the company and through it to the stock market is just three per cent, while every time a further one per cent of the total share capital is acquired or sold a public declaration is required.

A helpful shortcut to the websites of registries in many overseas jurisdictions is provided by Companies House at www.companies-house.gov.uk.

Jordan Publishing's encyclopedia *International Corporate Procedures*[2] is a very detailed description (updated every six months) of the formation, tax, accounting and public disclosure rules for companies, partnerships, branches of foreign businesses and joint ventures in some sixty jurisdictions (www.jordanpublishing.co.uk).

US company research

The company information scene in the US can be described as one of both feast and famine. The banquet is represented by the wealth of data available on US quoted companies, while there is a contrasting dearth of official filings on privately held companies. Quoted firms fall within the ambit of federal law and the Securities Exchange Commission (SEC), which enforces the rules relating to them, is an arm of the Federal Government. Companies not quoted on a stock exchange, but with total assets exceeding $10 million and over 500 shareholders are also subject to SEC supervision.

To protect investors the SEC demands considerable disclosure from these firms. When a company first comes to the market through an initial public offering (IPO) or makes a subsequent issue of shares or bonds to the public, it is obliged to file a prospectus known as a *Registration Statement*. The most common Registration Statements are made on Form S-1, with foreign companies using Form F-1, although there are some other types for special cases such as property companies and less detailed ones for small offerings. A great deal of information has to be revealed in these documents, with the section on risk factors being of particular interest in analysing a firm's vulnerabilities. Quite a large amount of capital is raised through private placements rather than public offers. These '144 placements' (named after the number of the SEC Rule relating to them) involve the purchase of shares by 'qualified institutional investors'. Since the latter are deemed to have the expertise and resources to reach an informed view on

---

2   Sealy, L. (editor) (1992), *International Corporate Procedures*, Jordan Publishing.

buying the stock there is no need for a prospectus to be published and any disclosure regarding them will be purely voluntary.

Companies subject to federal rules have to file a very detailed and audited annual report (Form 10K) within two months of their year ends (compared with six months for enterprises listed in London). As well as submitting an annual report, SEC-supervised companies are obliged to produce a quarterly, unaudited report in Form 10-Q (as was noted earlier, only fully listed technology businesses included in the London Stock Exchange's techMARK index are compelled to report quarterly, the rest just have to issue interim reports covering a six-month period). This must be filed within 35 days of the quarter end.

Ad hoc disclosures are made on Form-8K. Changes in directors or auditors will have to be reported within two days. Other events such as changes in the company's ownership, it filing for bankruptcy or agreeing major acquisitions or disposals should be reported on within 15 days of these taking place.

The threshold for disclosing major individual shareholdings is set, as in most European countries, at five per cent of total voting share capital (compared with three per cent in Britain). Form 13-D has to be filed within ten days of the acquisition of the holding. These filings not only name the 'street names' (that is, the nominee holders), but also identify the beneficial owners behind these. Company 'insiders', that is directors, other company officers or shareholders with holdings exceeding ten per cent of voting capital are subject to sterner rules.

'EDGAR' the corporate documents arm of the SEC, which is free of charge, can be found at www.sec.gov/edgar.shtml.

However, tracing specific SEC filings can be a daunting task. Fortunately, international business consultants PriceWaterhouseCoopers provide a useful search and retrieval service called EdgarScan (www.edgarscan.pwcglobal.com).

While some 11 000 companies are supervised by the SEC under federal law, the vast majority of American enterprises are governed by state law. Sole traders and general partnerships do not have to register as the liability of their owners is unlimited. There is also the option of trading as a limited partnership (a mixture of working general partners without a limit on their liability and limited partners who merely contribute capital) or as a limited liability partnership (LLP), both of which involve registration. The later is a more recent form, recognized in most, although not all, states and is a popular vehicle for private equity and other investment firms.

Limited liability companies are also found in the US. These are somewhat different from their British counterparts as they are treated as companies for legal purposes and have to register, but taxed as though they were partnerships. However, by far the most common legal form for conducting business is the privately held Corporation. Filing takes place at the Secretary of State's office in each state. Unfortunately, from a researcher's perspective, only minimal information has to be reported. No accounts will be available, hence the reliance on credit rating agencies such as Dun & Bradstreet.

Although credit reports are obtained by researchers as a matter of routine these often have severe limitations from an analytical perspective. They are intended to guide decisions as to whether to extend credit to a firm and/or accept it as a supplier and thus focus on financial strength and speed of payment. Credit rating agencies are much less concerned about other financial aspects such as its control of overhead costs or the return it generates for shareholders. Agencies have to rely on the information supplied by the companies themselves, which are often in the form of responses to questionnaires rather than independently compiled accounts. Many firms will only supply figures between bands ('sales are between $20 and $25 million') and not precise numbers. There may also be relatively little qualitative background information provided.

Information available from the Secretary of State's office will vary. Some states demand that the names and addresses of a corporation's directors are filed, in others (including such important jurisdictions as California, Delaware and New York) this does not have to be disclosed. A few states provide some other details regarding share capital or the value of property owned by the company in the state. However, filings made under the Uniform Commercial Code (UCC) may prove of analytical interest. This legislation has been adopted by all 50 states, with the information required by it being filed with the Secretary of State's office in the relevant state. If a company obtains a commercial loan to purchase equipment the lender is entitled to seize it if the borrowing terms are not honoured. The UCC records are intended to prevent the equipment being pledged to several lenders without their knowledge. They provide details of the equipment and the lender (typically a bank or leasing firm) and may also record the purchase price. UCC filings can be used as a starting point in gaining a picture of the fixed assets at the disposal of a company and if changes in these represent shifts in its level of production or range of products.

There can be ways of obtaining information on privately held US companies. For example, if they are subsidiaries of a listed firm references in the parent's SEC filings can be of interest. There may also be filings made under the Freedom of Information Act or those that have to be submitted at state or local level regarding the environmental impact of an industrial plant or to obtain planning permission to expand a facility. The file relating to a licence held by a firm operating in a regulated industry might yield interesting material, as may the papers concerned with bids for government contracts. An excellent guide to these alternative public domain resources is *The Sourcebook of State Public Records*.[3]

For those having to do a lot of this type of research, Washington Researchers' *Researching Private Companies* is a key textbook. They also provide a free guide, 'Sources of Information on Privately Held Companies', on their website (www.washingtonresearchers.com).

Conclusions

- Foreign research presents a number of challenges apart from the language barrier. Despite globalization significant differences in the institutional setting for business remain and these have important consequences for the researcher.
- Analysts should always be on their guard against assuming that the business and market context abroad are the same as in their countries.
- Hence appropriate local knowledge is needed both to find information and interpret it correctly.

---

3   Sankey, M.L. and Weber, P.L. (2004), *The Sourcebook to Public Record Information: The comprehensive guide to county, state and federal public sources*, 6th edition, Business Resources Bureau.

13 *Human Source Intelligence*

Some CI analysts seem to believe that published sources will provide all the data they need. This may be true for a number of narrowly focused projects, but a vast reservoir of intelligence lies unpublished in people's heads. To tap this, the researcher has to make direct contact with them.

So this chapter is devoted to getting the maximum return in intelligence gathered from human sources rather than documentary ones. It deals with:

- planning interviews
- identifying subjects to approach
- the benefits of email in making contact with potential subjects
- persuading them to be interviewed
- coping with refusals
- length and timing of interviews
- a number of key techniques for successful interviewing
- taking a record of the interview
- sustaining a longer-term relationship with the interviewee.

Planning interviews

An ideal conversationalist is both a good talker and a good listener. CI analysts must be able to communicate well – and cultivate the art of listening. It is essential for them to be adequately prepared before they start a series of interviews, with a reasonably clear idea of what they want to know, why they seek it and how long it is going to take.

They also need to gather background information on:

- the individual they will be interviewing. In some instances the analyst may only possess their name and/or department and job title before the meeting or phone conversation, but where possible further personal details should be obtained (further remarks on biographical research appear on pages 206–7)
- their interviewee's company or organization
- salient features and major current issues of the industry if dealing with an unfamiliar sector.

Well-briefed interviewers should produce superior results. Their preparation shows the respect and professionalism that those they are meeting expect. It allows them to develop a cordial relationship by being able to allude to a recent success on the part of the interview's subject or their company and avoid unwelcome topics. Such contextual knowledge also helps in formulating the content of the interview and direction it will take and in factoring the interviewee's biases into account in evaluating what they have said.

Who is to be approached?

The first task is to identify who to approach and their contact details. In some cases this information will be already available, in others some prior digging is required. Senior people are nearly always easy to trace, but there may be the need to interview someone who is not at board level or who has a specialist role. Individual company websites tend to be a poor source for this, although a web trawl using a search engine, a database scan or a directory may turn up the right person. A name or contact details taken from such a secondary source (which are never entirely current: a new person may be in post, the company may have been acquired by another firm or its corporate website not updated very often) should be confirmed by phoning the organization.

A call also has to be made if a named individual cannot be quickly identified. A well-trained switchboard operator should either be able to help the interviewer or put them straight through to someone who can. Unfortunately, in several organizations a caller will be passed from one extension to another – including some they have already spoken to. An even worse waster of time and generator of frustration is the Kafkaesque world of recorded telephone options where the caller wanders through a bewildering hierarchy of options, none of which meets their requirement. If all this is taking too long it is probably best to ring off, call back and ask for the PR department (which might be called public relations, public affairs, corporate communications or similar variants). Alternatively the personnel section (or human resources or whatever they choose to call this unit) should be able to locate the elusive postholder. If both of these courses fail, another potentially fruitful course is to ask to speak to a librarian or information officer. These are nearly always knowledgeable and helpful. If the organization does not have such people, the chief executive's personal assistant or secretary is worth contacting. Someone in such a position should be familiar with the structure of the organization and who does what and possess the professional motivation to steer the researcher in the right direction.

Approach by email

Writing to the interviewee prior to phoning has many advantages. An interview is more likely to be granted if the person one wishes to speak with has been forewarned and the timing arranged to suit their convenience. No one is keen on being interviewed by a CI analyst when they are grappling with a sudden crisis or preoccupied in closing a deal. For the same reason someone calling 'out of the blue', even when allowed to proceed with an interview, is generally going to get a shorter and less cooperative response than when the ground has been already prepared. Thanks to email there is no longer a frustrating time lag between posting a letter and waiting for the interviewee to receive it. A written communication also gives the approach a greater degree of authenticity as the recipient can see the interviewer's company details immediately. A disembodied voice is treated with more suspicion. Are you really who you purport to be? After all, the disc jockey Steve Penk notoriously managed to bluff his way to speaking to the British Prime Minister on the phone by pretending to be the then Leader of the Opposition.

An email also enables the analyst to set out the background to the interview and its purpose in greater detail than is usually practicable in a phone call, especially as having to give a fuller account to every person rung is time consuming. Being able to write a single text (with perhaps some slight adjustments made to the individual emails sent) is an useful time-saver. It also allows the interviewer to encourage recipients to cooperate by perhaps appending some material (such as industry data, case study or book review) likely to interest them and thereby increases their goodwill towards the researcher. Finally, it tends to improve the quality of responses as interviewees will have had more time to think about the issue (and to mull it over in their subconscious), assemble data that might not have been immediately at hand and perhaps talk to colleagues about it.

One drawback with emails is that they are easier to ignore or put off replying to than a phone call. It is therefore advisable to suggest a time for the interview and ask if this is convenient. They can then either accept or propose an alternative. If they do neither the interviewer should ring at the time they suggested. Many of those who did not respond will be willing to do the interview (and the caller starts with a moral advantage in that the person contacted should have replied even if only to decline the request). Some who would have turned away the researcher if cold-called may be more willing to participate when they have the chance to reflect on the appealing arguments for doing so advanced in the email. If these have failed to convince them, it is unlikely one would have succeeded by cold calling.

Persuading people to be interviewed

In approaching potential interviewees researchers must, in order to comply with professional ethics, truthfully disclose their identity, the name of the organization they represent and the purpose of the interview. Some people approached by a CI consultant may ask which client they are acting for. As was noted earlier, the consultant will have to refuse to divulge this, unless the client has given explicit consent for such a disclosure. If the interviewee is merely 'trying it on' such a refusal is unlikely to have any bearing on whether they agree to be interviewed or not. A more awkward situation is where the question is broached because of ignorance of the ground rules for consulting and CI activities. Someone who has never given such an interview before may be disconcerted when approached. They need to be reassured that this is a well-accepted practice and will be conducted in a completely ethical manner (that is, what is said will be treated in strict confidence and there is no intention of trying to winkle out trade secrets and suchlike). If they are still uneasy, it may help to suggest they have a look at the SCIP website to discover what genuine, legitimate CI involves or be prepared to offer contact details for past interviewees to testify to your good faith (having obviously previously obtained their consent for this). But you 'can't win 'em all'...

Handling rejection

One executive I phoned reacted with alarm and bemusement: 'I've never heard of anyone having the nerve to ask these sorts of questions before!' he thundered – it was as though I had asked him about his sex life. This was especially unexpected as I was working on a project for a US state government wishing to encourage inward investment by foreigners which had nothing to do with his industry or competitors as such. It was simply that his British firm had an operation in that state and the reasons why it had decided to locate there would be interesting. My reassurances made no impression on him and I could only apologize for having bothered him and ring off.

While it is always disappointing for a prospective interviewee to turn one down, there is no point in being too pushy in trying to make them change their minds. Would-be CI analysts who do this are likely to find themselves in an exciting new career trying to sell double-glazing over the phone. Rather than create lasting hostility, the best approach is to accept their refusal graciously. It might be worth asking them to nominate an alternative person to interview, either a colleague or someone in another organization. At a latter stage in the project they can always be contacted again to see if they have changed their minds. Although a refusal is often not overturned, there *are* cases where it is, either because their circumstances have changed (the major issue that was absorbing *their* whole time and energy has now been resolved) or that *the interviewer* now has more to offer them as the research will have progressed. It should also be remembered that this person may have to be approached as part of another future project and it is thus not a sensible move to have previously antagonized them.

However, most of those contacted will be willing to talk and provide some help. As Leonard Fuld has pointed out: 'Where money is exchanged, so is information.' The mutual exchange of information is the lifeblood of business, professional and academic life and participants are usually ready to offer data and opinions. Researchers who can swap some of their information in return are much more likely to receive a positive reception. If they can quote the name of a person who suggested they should approach the interview prospect or a mutual acquaintance the chances of success are also increased.

LENGTH OF INTERVIEWS

The interviewer should have a reasonably good idea how long one will take before starting (which will have an even firmer basis once a few actual interviews have been conducted). No one likes to be told someone 'will only take a few minutes' and find themselves still answering questions half an hour later. An interviewer may have to negotiate. If they want twenty minutes and the interviewee is only willing to grant ten, it is better to get some information rather than none. This means tabling the more important questions and regretfully skipping lower priority ones. In quite a few cases, once consent has been secured, interviewees will actually give more time than they initially offered (perhaps their original stipulation was a defensive measure against 'ten' minutes really meaning 'thirty' or they find the interview stimulating and become more willing to extend it).

TIMING OF INTERVIEWS

Interviewing in the morning, especially at the start of the day, is preferable if it can be arranged. There is less risk of interruption or cancellation if the interviewee has to deal with a sudden crisis and both parties are fresher. Mondays tend to be less satisfactory than other days for trying to arrange, or for conducting, interviews. Unresolved issues from the past week and plans for the coming one usually preoccupy interview subjects. Trying to fix an appointment during the height of the summer holidays may be difficult (although paradoxically if the person is available they can often be willing to give more time than during other seasons). National customs also influence availability. Thus in Brazil appointments are less easily obtained during late January and February in the lead-up to Carnival, almost impossible in Japan in the first week of May during the Golden Week series of public holidays and are very hard to organize in France and Italy during July and August when so many people take vacations and a large swathe of businesses virtually close down.

Conducting the interview

A job interview has been defined as a 'conversation with a purpose'. CI interviewing shares this conversational quality. While it has a structure and seeks specific information, the interviewer needs to possess the mental dexterity to depart from the script where appropriate. Unlike the 'closed' questions (which impose a single choice of answer on the respondent) asked by polling organizations or in certain types of market research, questions posed in CI interviews tend to be open-ended, allowing the respondent to qualify, elaborate or explain an answer. The questioner must also be on the alert for potentially valuable information on a topic that was not included in the interview brief. This may have to be incorporated into future interviews or even prove so significant that previous respondents have to be re-interviewed.

The interviewer thus has the sometimes tricky task of guiding the course of the interview without appearing bossy, impatient, bored or mechanical. Prolix respondents or those straying too far from the issue have to be tactfully nudged on or led back to the point. Yet questioners must resist the urge to jump to the next query before they have extracted all useful data. Valuable information may not be unearthed because the interviewer failed to give their respondent enough time or encouragement to develop a more considered reply. In TV chat shows the person asking the questions is as much of a celebrity and as centre-stage as their guests: in CI interviewing the respondent is the unquestioned star, the interviewer merely their feed.

Listening, far from being a passive art, is intensely active. The analyst must concentrate on what they are being told and ruthlessly suppress any inclination to think about other matters. Their understanding of what they hear and later recall of it will be improved by 'content paraphrasing' where they summarize what they believe they have been told. This not only reduces the risk of confusion, it also shows the respondent that the interviewer is listening intently and strengthens their willingness to be helpful.

VOCAL TONE AND BODY LANGUAGE OF INTERVIEWEE

It is not only what the interviewee says, but *how* they say it that must be captured. Exactly the same sentence may have an utterly different meaning when spoken. 'What a very pleasant person' can mean what is literally said – or can be delivered in such a tone that conveys exactly the opposite assessment of character. This very significant aspect of human communication, completely lost in a transcript, is readily available in a phone conversation. Telephone interviews are, in their turn, less satisfactory than where circumstances allow the analyst to meet the interviewee face to face (or via videolink as a second best opinion to meeting them in the flesh). Just as vocal tone enriches meaning, so does body language. Observing demeanour, posture, gestures (and visual clues from their surroundings if the interview takes place at their workplace) amplifies the information gained and enriches understanding.[1] Larry Kahaner[2] quotes the case of Sir John Egan, the head of Jaguar cars being asked in 1990 if the company was to be sold. Egan replied, 'No, I think we intend to remain fully independent', but the CI expert Andrew Pollard noted the hesitant tone of the CEO and concluded that the commitment to continued independence was not wholehearted.

---

1   The interpretation of body language is a major topic in its own right. A couple of helpful guides are: Pease, A. and Pease, B. (2004), *The Definitive Language of Body Language: The secret meaning behind people's gestures*, Orion and Morris, D. (2002), *People Watching: The Desmond Morris guide to body language*, Vantage.

2   Kahaner, L. (1977), *Competitive Intelligence: How to gather, analyze, and use information to move your business to the top*, Simon and Schuster, 108–9.

REFLECTING INTERVIEWEES' FEELINGS

Business interviewers are generally told to project an image of objectivity, neutrality and open-mindedness. However, at certain points it may be fruitful to become more subjective.

A powerful way of demonstrating that one has been genuinely listening is to 'reflect the feelings' of the person being questioned. This will take the form of statements relating to the emotions they are expressing – 'you are clearly very proud of this new product line' or 'that must be extremely frustrating for you', for example. Reflecting feelings helps to build empathy by showing that the interviewer understands the other person's position in *emotional* as well as intellectual terms. This practice also stimulates further revelation. An interviewee may say: 'Yes, we're really pleased with the new line – we're sure that it will be a big winner. Unfortunately, our marketing people just aren't pushing it as much as they should.' If their interlocutor responds with: 'That must be so frustrating for you!', they are more likely to obtain further information than someone who merely remarks: 'I see'.

Beaming back feelings also allows for an exaggerated impression to be corrected: 'No, although a bit irritating, it's not that important. What's really annoying me is…'. Maintaining eye contact (a reason to avoid taking too many notes), nodding or uttering short responsive phrases (such 'I see your dilemma', 'That's interesting, can you tell me a bit more about X') shows that the interviewer is alert and interested in their counterpart both as a source of enlightenment and as a person.

BECOMING THE INTERVIEWEE'S PUPIL

People like to bask in their successes, thus alluding to one or more of these will tend to stimulate a flow of commentary on these. Contrawise, recalling a criticism made against them, their firm or their industry is a good opportunity for them to put the record straight with a rebuttal to a sympathetic audience. An interviewer should have clearly done some research prior to the meeting and have at least some knowledge of the topics being discussed. However, they should never appear *too* well informed. Interview subjects are invariably irked by 'know it alls' (apart from such egotism being repellent, if the questioner *does* know it all, why on earth are they wasting your time doing this interview?). Someone who knows a great deal about a topic is usually delighted to share their expertise with an interviewer who is prepared to assume the role of a pupil.

PROVOKING DISCLOSURE

One tactic for drawing out a subject is to make a provocative statement ('we've been told that this segment of the market is saturated and yet you're still targeting it'). The interviewee will probably react with a vigorous denial laced with useful data demonstrating that it still has significant unmet sales potential. More rarely they may surprise the interviewer by agreeing ('Like most people, we believed this would be a growth area, but very recently we've begun to doubt this and are reassessing our marketing efforts towards it'). Often further clarification will result ('It's true that the market as a whole is pretty exhausted. However, there are a couple of very attractive niches still to be tapped and we're making a big push into those').

USE OF 'BRACKETED' QUESTIONS

Interviewers have to make the best of their opportunities. A subject may be willing to commend them to people outside their organization, give them documents for reference or greater detail or ask colleagues to provide further help. Other situations may be less rewarding and the approach modified accordingly. Precise figures on a topic may not be readily available to the subject and obtaining them may involve excessive effort for the subject or take too long to obtain to meet the researcher's deadlines. The interviewee may also be reluctant to be pinned down by giving exact numbers. Here the submission of questions in a 'bracketed' form can still elicit useable data. The path can be smoothed by asking: 'So the market size is between £20 to £25 million – or is it more like £35 to £40 million?' or 'Direct sales as opposed to those through intermediaries accounts for around 60 to 70 per cent of total sales? Is that a reasonable approximation?' On good days the subject may narrow the range: 'Well, more like 60 to 65 per cent').

ELICITING INFORMATION

One of the most powerful techniques for encouraging disclosure by those being interviewed, when they are perhaps reluctant to do this, is *eliciting* information. This approach eschews asking direct questions as may these cause the subject to feel anxious and suspicious and encourage a defensive attitude. Instead the interviewer adopts a rather meandering conversational approach, offering more information themselves than they normally would in other interview contexts and creating a relaxed, unthreatening atmosphere. Elicitation is a more difficult form of interviewing to master because it generally relies on the subtle as against the straightforward and coaxing as opposed to direct questioning.

Although a simple concept, its practice involves the use of many different tactics. It is often employed outside formal interview situations where intelligence is being gathered without this being made obvious, as in seemingly casual conversations with strangers. To avoid arousing suspicion elicitation is used, wherever possible, in the middle of a conversation. Displaying a lot of curiosity early on generates misgivings, while the opening and close of an encounter tend to be more clearly remembered. Thus the interviewer may have got the information they wanted towards the end of a conversation, but the subject may recall that there was something odd about it and, by reporting it, alert their organization that intelligence gathering has been taking place.

Recording the interview

Some interviewers like to make a sound or video recording of their meetings. This has the advantage of preserving a verbatim record, but these are outweighed by the disadvantages. It often makes interviewees more inhibited and operating the machine is a distraction for both parties. Recording also interferes with personal interaction and tempts the interviewer to be lazy and not listen or understand properly. Notes can be taken as an aide-memoire, although common sense should be applied. I was once the victim of an interviewer who painfully took down every word in longhand. She went away with a complete record – and had made a poor use of her time. It is probably best not to take notes right at the start of a meeting, where both sides are getting to know each other and working their way into the subject being discussed. Once this introductory phase is over the interviewer can ask if it is all right to take notes. A refusal is almost unthinkable; most people like to see their views are being taken seriously. Only key words or short phrases need to be written down, while diagrams or pictures are sometimes also helpful. More detail can be added immediately after the meeting, when the discussion is still fresh in the memory, thus avoiding excessive note-taking during it.

Keeping in contact with interviewees

When the interview is complete, the wise analyst will be suitably grateful to the subject for giving their time and contributing their knowledge. Apart from a courteous follow-up, it may also be appropriate to sustain a longer-term relationship. Detectives and government intelligence officers often keep their best contacts happy through financial payments and other incentives (or ensure their continued cooperation through threats). The corporate CI analyst has to maintain such relationships by the less obviously compelling means of getting in contact every now and again and sending information (journal articles, details of new websites or industry statistics) that will be of interest to the interviewee. This avoids the negative response provoked by people who 'only get in touch when they want something' and encourages the contact to feed back useful material in return.

A warning regarding being accused of anti-competitive conduct

One area where interviewers have to tread carefully involves directly obtaining price information from competitors. Most countries have anti-trust legal regimes where conspiring to fix prices is an offence and the exchange of price data could be interpreted as collusion against the interests of customers. Information on prices is thus more safely gathered by indirect methods such as publicly available lists, intelligence collected by the sales force and information supplied by customers.

Conclusions

- Using human sources gives researchers access to a vast reservoir of unpublished, current data and viewpoints. Unlike documentary sources people can be questioned and asked to elaborate or explain further.
- Interviews need to be adequately planned and background research undertaken before them.
- Those conducting them must not allow making a record of the interview to unsettle the subject or distract the interviewer from the main task of active listening.
- Direct interviewing (unlike reading a transcript) enables non-verbal clues to be picked up from the subject's tone of voice and, in face to face encounters, body language.
- Analysts should not stick doggedly to their 'script', but be flexible enough to gain advantage from unexpected changes in the direction an interview takes.
- They need to employ techniques such as reflecting feelings and elicitation to maintain the momentum of the interview and tease out the information sought.
- Former interviewees are often a precious resource and maintaining contact with them may yield substantial benefits in the future.

14 *Observing a Company*

Disclosure by businesses to meet legal requirements was dealt with in Chapters 10 and 11. The information extracted from these obligatory filings, valuable though it is, leaves many important CI questions unanswered or only partially answered. So the analyst must also sieve through publicly available material issued by a company of its own free will and observe it physically at first hand if this is practicable.

Hence this chapter explores:

- corporate communications with the wider world
- trade show CI
- visits to company premises.

It also emphasizes the analytical value of garnering *soft data* – impressions, intuitions, feelings – as well as accumulating hard facts.

Corporate external communication

Companies, unless they are relatively small, highly specialist operators who get all their business through referrals, have to provide some voluntary public information about themselves if they want to flourish. The vast majority of companies have to impress potential customers and maintain the loyalty of existing ones through publicity distributed via their website, advertising and similar promotional avenues.

Corporate websites vary in the extent of the information they provide. Smaller privately held companies often restrict the material mounted to describing their activities and the products and services they offer, with no details of personnel, ownership or financial performance. Others may add some company history and key facts such as number of employees. This limited data then has to be supplemented from other sources. When a firm operates from a number of sites, as was noted earlier, there is usually a handy directory of these included in its web pages. Many businesses place copies of their press notices on them. If an analyst is conducting a full-scale study of a company it can be instructive to compare these with any regulatory filings. A number of cases will be found, as we have also already seen, where a firm has been obliged to report something in a filing, but did not want it to receive the public attention that a press notice might generate. Any description of specific job vacancies is of great interest because it frequently gives clues as to the direction the business is taking and perhaps its future plans.

Quoted company sites will supply much more copious data in their pages directed at investors, particularly those containing the firm's annual and other reports. Analysts keeping tabs on a company over an extended period would do well to download these because most firms limit coverage to the most recent reports and will replace the oldest one on the site when a new document is issued.

Analyzing a firm's advertising can provide clues as to the market segments it is concentrating on, what it perceives as its strongest selling points, the mode of competition (price, differentiation or market segmentation) employed and the public persona it wishes to project. Corporate brochures and newsletters are also important initial sources for getting to know a company and often supply extra information not shown on the website. Junk mail is usually discarded unread. However, it can actually be an easy way of keeping tabs on a firm's direct mail campaigns. A leading financial institution asks its employees to bring in any mailings received from competitors. Obtaining detailed trade catalogues and product literature for non-consumer products like specialist tools is more difficult. Companies are naturally loath to send them to rivals or other parties that do not seem like genuine potential customers. Here one's own sales force or purchasing department can often provide the solution. Sales reps will acquire many such catalogues in the normal course of their work, while a competitor may also sell some items to your own company and the product literature may be readily available in-house in the purchasing unit (although care should be taken not to breach any contractual obligations regarding the distribution or use of such material).

In interpreting this material there can be subtle clues contained within it that are more useful than the direct information provided.

Analysts need to view corporate literature as not merely a quarry of facts, but as a more complex source with other dimensions. What is not said or shown may be of greater significance than that overtly stated. The style of presentation, in addition to the factual content, offers clues as to the sort of public image the company is trying to project. So analysts, among their many roles, also have to play the part of an art critic, combining what they can see with their other knowledge. Direct observation, when this is practicable, is worth undertaking and visits to trade shows and company premises will be discussed a little later in this chapter.

Finally, some others of corporate communications should be noted. Publicly held firms have to communicate with the investment community through presentations given when results are announced and on other occasions when there is something major to report. These will usually be mounted on their website and there will often be the opportunity to monitor their conference calls with investment analysts on the Internet. Some observers, when unconcerned by revealing their interest, will buy a tiny stake in a company they are particularly interested in so as to gain the right to attend shareholders' meetings and lob questions at management. *The Wall Street Transcript* (www.twst.com), which now covers European as well as US-listed firms, provides a verbatim record of what companies are saying about themselves along with analysts' comments.

Obviously privately held enterprises do not provide this type of information. However, many of them are prepared to make some public disclosure in the form of giving press interviews and delivering presentations at industry and scientific conferences.

Trade show CI

Trade shows and exhibitions offer splendid opportunities for obtaining a great deal of information on other companies and observing them, the whole point of firms taking part in these events being to tell the world about themselves and what they are doing. There is also the considerable convenience for intelligence gathering of having many players in the same industry group gathered under the same roof at the same time.

Participants are intentionally disclosing information on many topics of interest:

1) their product range, particularly their lead products
2) new or recent products and services – these will receive special emphasis and the industry event will often be the platform for launching them
3) forthcoming offerings and when they are likely to be available may be explicitly referred to or hinted at
4) which elements of the firm's portfolio are receiving the most attention (these will usually be new or those directed at providing solutions for major customers. Sometimes the show may be chosen to relaunch or revive interest in a seemingly promising product or service whose sales have not met expectations)
5) the technological level attained by a company as reflected in its offerings
6) which segments of the market or type of customer the exhibitor is targeting
7) reactions of attendees (potential customers, industry rivals, consultants and other third parties) to what is on offer.

As is always the case with CI, much more can be learned if data from one event can be compared with those from previous ones. Why has the much-trumpeted new product from last year been relegated to obscurity? Being able to roll out several new related offerings means a rival has extended its technology platform – what are the competitive implications of its broadened technological range? A little-known first-time exhibitor has been attracting a lot of interest and favourable comments from attendees; might collaboration in the form of corporate venturing or other type of alliance be of mutual benefit?

Visits to shows have to be carefully planned for maximum reward. CI will be gathered much more efficiently when appropriate arrangements are in place rather than having people wander around in the hope of seeing 'something interesting'. A well-developed CI function should already have a good framework in place for understanding the sector and its principal current concerns, coupled with assessments of players, key customers and third parties and their likely future moves. The focus of the visit must be to try and fill gaps in this framework and these assessments. CI representatives will be seeking evidence to confirm or refute unsubstantiated opinions and find information on topics where this is lacking. Apart from this directed searching, they must also be on the alert for other items of potential interest (like the first-time exhibitor who is not picked up in the existing analytical framework).

If resources permit it is desirable to send a team rather than a single observer. This allows technical, marketing and other specialists to contribute their expertise to the appraisal. However, it is absurd to see teams of representatives staying together as though they cannot bear to be separated, sharing what they have found with each other in public or individually approaching a stand and asking the same question three of them have already put. This happens all too frequently and is easily avoided given adequate planning – with the need to conduct debriefings where others cannot overhear them being especially firmly inculcated. Legal and ethical guidelines must be clearly laid down. Those attending should not be not wearing badges attributing them to an imaginary company and, if challenged at the show, have to be told to identify themselves and their employer truthfully (consultants will obviously disclose only their direct employer and not the client they are acting for). On the other hand they ought to know their rights as an attendee, as one sometimes sees competitors being asked to leave a company presentation even though the terms of admittance to the show do not confer a power of exclusion on presenters.

Trade show CI calls for the same mixture of activity/passivity and planning/spontaneity that is needed in other aspects of the discipline such as interviewing. A good slogan for observers, coined by Constance S. Ward, head of CI at Hoffman-LaRoche, is 'Teomwork' (that is, 'two ears, one mouth'). They need to be able to listen (and look) as well as ask questions. The apparently casual visitor can often learn more by saying little and showing no great interest. Unnoticed by oblivious attendees they take careful note of indiscreet conversations in refreshment areas and bars or careless reporting back to the office on mobile phones within public hearing. They can sometimes learn all they want to know by wandering around a stand while other attendees ask their questions for them. When they do ask questions or strike up conversations they will apply the same techniques as for effective interviewing already discussed in the previous chapter. They will also naturally collect as much relevant documentation as is on offer such as:

- lists of exhibitors and attendees
- transcripts of speeches and handouts at seminars
- press releases
- magazine reprints
- brochures
- price lists
- data sheets
- product samples and photos of products.

Debriefings need to be carried out quickly during breaks and at the end of the day as short term memories decay so rapidly, especially if team members are unobtrusively storing up information in their heads and not ostentatiously scribbling in their notebooks. The data obtained then has to be matched with the previous knowledge base and actionable conclusions drawn and conveyed to decision-takers within the organization.

Company visits

While companies attend trade shows and gather intelligence there as a matter of course, visits to a firm's premises can also be enlightening. Some of these will be made for the specific purpose of obtaining intelligence, but the CI unit should also seek information from colleagues, particularly the sales force, who undertake company visits in the normal course of business.

CASE OF A COY BANK

Some years ago a client was studying a new and apparently very successful banking operation, the Bank of Credit and Commerce International (BCCI). I referred to them earlier (page 23) as a good example of a firm competing on the basis of targeting a particular group of customers. I decided to call in at their nearest branch over the lunch break, have a look round and collect some brochures. Once inside there I was surprised to find that there were not the usual stocks of corporate literature displayed in retail banking branches. When I asked a member of staff if I might have some details of their services to read through, he replied that they did not have these in brochure form, but perhaps I might like to go to an office and discuss my specific banking requirements? This struck me as very odd and I pressed the point. I soon had to be back at work and did not have time for an interview (perfectly true), so was there nothing he could give me to read at my leisure? I received a polite, but decidedly firm 'no'.

I reported all this to the client and we concurred that this was unusual behaviour for a retail bank. It was agreed that I should visit their headquarters in the City, where surely a general brochure for the bank would be on offer, even if they did not produce leaflets on specific services. Once again I drew a blank. Apart from the extraordinary lack of such promotional material I was struck by the absence of any kind of information displayed in their premises – no adverts, notices or suchlike. Both the branch and the headquarters had the name plaque of the bank at the entrance and that was all. Such extreme corporate modesty was strange.

These observations proved nothing, yet they were suggestive. We later assembled other material that reinforced our misgivings about BCCI, but all of it was nebulous and subjective. There was no concrete evidence of any wrongdoing on the bank's part that we could bring before the authorities. Massive fraud and other criminal activities were hidden behind a genuine banking operation. What we had found was nevertheless sufficiently unsettling for our client to harbour strong suspicions about BCCI and act accordingly. Actionable intelligence does not have to be solid enough to meet the high standards of persuading a court. If seemingly insubstantial and vague indicators point consistently in the same direction when grouped together, this will often provide adequate grounds for a management decision. Waiting for confirmation that the bank was to be avoided until the extent of its criminality was publicly exposed would have been far too late for our client to escape unhurt.

A good analyst will be on the alert for any clues about a company that a visit to its premises offers. Are these well maintained or dingy and dirty? Do they look orderly or chaotic? Is there an atmosphere of calm purposefulness or is it highly charged and stressed? What sort of IT equipment is being used – current devices or ones that are now quite dated? Where other forms of technology are important, as in an industrial plant, it would be very helpful to be accompanied by a colleague with the technical knowledge to understand its significance. Verbal clues such as mottos, plaques, notice boards, signs on doors, titles of files or books should be noted and any brochures, newsletters or other material offered to the public taken away. One professional services firm I visited was reticent about naming individual clients, yet a plaque on the wall of its reception provided a list of the major ones. Poor security awareness in leaving client names and other information on flip charts or whiteboards in meeting rooms can give the watchful analyst very valuable data.

Images and artefacts on display may add to the analyst's stock of knowledge. On a visit to someone whose present job had nothing to do with heavy industry I noticed a photograph of a factory with a huge engine being lowered on a chain hanging on the wall of his office. It was a striking exception to the photos of his family, awards and paintings decorating the rest of the room. When I asked his aide about this he told me that his boss was an engineer by training and the picture was a memento of his first engineering project many years before. His early career had been bypassed in the biographical profile given on the organization's website and learning about it enabled our client to make a more technically oriented proposal to him than if he had been the life-long general manager we had assumed him to be.

A good non-business example of making deductions from visual clues comes from Sir Winston Churchill's home at Chartwell in Kent. This has numerous pictures, busts and other items depicting Napoleon. The guidebook downplays their abundant presence by saying they were collected preparatory to Churchill working on a planned (but never actually written) biography of the emperor. Later independent confirmation of Sir Winston's admiration for

Napoleon was found in an account by one of his closest colleagues, who recalled that he intensely disliked to be reminded of his hero's misdeeds.

Data obtained from visits has to be combined with other evidence to avoid erroneous conclusions being drawn. Interpretation can be often two-edged. A company may have opulent and impressive premises leading the analyst to conclude that it is wealthy and successful. This may well be correct. However, this splendour may also conceal the fact that the firm is heavily indebted and poor at controlling costs, while investment in its operations is being skimped in favour of spending on a flashy headquarters. Some very prosperous enterprises take a deliberately frugal approach to the accommodation of their central team, emphasizing simplicity and functionality in order to keep overhead expenses low.

Although visual observations on their own are too tenuous and ambiguous to be relied upon they do have a role to play in building a picture of a company and its operations. This is especially true when we are unable to enter its premises and are restricted to peering through its fence. A few examples:

- *Nature and productive capacity of a plant*   having a reasonable idea of the type of plant being operated by a manufacturer or utility, its potential output and any additions being made to this capacity are highly prized pieces of intelligence. An observer with the requisite technical knowledge can unearth a great deal about these topics.

- *Number of employees at a particular site*   this information is often sought to give an idea of the scale of operations at a site. A common technique is to send people to count the number of cars in its car park (excluding those in lots reserved for visitors) and estimate the number of employees from this. Carl Drott quotes the case of a firm which asks its staff to note the number of cars in the parking spaces of rivals and how many are occupied by workers or visitors:[1] a good example of involving everyone in CI.

   This is obviously likely to be more accurate for an out-of-town site without good alternative transport facilities. Applying it in city centre locations where driving to work is less common would produce a serious underestimate. Another factor to be taken into account is the extent to which an enterprise engages in hot desking (as in professional services firms where the majority of staff may be working at clients' premises at any one time) or has many of them working at home.

- *Property values and costs*   this example combines observation with other forms of research. Commercial estate agents can be a good source for data on the value of property and typical rents. Knowing that a business owns the freehold on a site that would currently fetch around £15 million if sold gives an insight into its potential resources (either through borrowing against the security of the property or realizing its value in cash by selling it).

   A visit to another firm's (rented) address revealing that it occupies two floors in an office block where rentals are typically £X per square metre, enables its accommodation costs to be estimated. The length and breadth of the block should be recorded in municipal planning permission filings. If there is no time to get hold of these, simply pacing them out will give a tolerably accurate figure for its area.

---

1   Carl Drott (2001), Personal knowledge, corporate information: The challenge for competitive intelligence', *Business Horizons*, 44(2), 31–37.

Businesses where the public have to be admitted such as shops and leisure facilities are easier targets for the analyst than those they can only get in to by invitation. Indeed for sectors like retailing, hotel and restaurants, nightclubs and many others such personal visits are a vital factor in gaining a proper understanding of the market and the companies contending within it.

CASE OF THE EMPTY SHELVES

Thomas Yake[2] recalls visiting shops of the US drug store chain Phar-Mor in the late 1980s and being amazed at how poorly stocked they were. Yet according to their published accounts sales were booming. In fact several senior managers were involved in fraud to conceal trading losses and embezzle money, with artificially inflated figures for stock being used in Phar-Mor's financial statements. This experience taught Yake 'how important it was to physically visit store locations of any retail company I was analyzing'.

A word of warning regarding store visits is necessary. Most retailers are well aware that their premises are being visited for purposes of CI and take countermeasures such as not permitting interior photography. I was once challenged by a security guard when I took a photo of a supermarket. In fact I was not interested in the store as such (I just wanted a picture of one to go in a presentation) and I was standing in the public road when I took it, but it would have been a more delicate situation if I had been within the supermarket's boundary. Similarly the big store chains are conscious that competitors and consultants tour their branches recording prices and have instructed their security personnel to hamper this. One colleague had the humiliating experience of being escorted off the premises by a guard, leading other customers to assume she had been caught shop-lifting.

The lesson here is that snooping analysts have to act discreetly to avoid being detected and asked to leave a shop before their research is completed. Indeed CI observation in all contexts should be as unobtrusive as is feasible.

Conclusions

- Where practicable, company research should include visits to premises as well as the study of corporate documents and information obtained from human sources.
- The CI unit should collect information picked up from visits made by colleagues, particularly the sales force.
- Trade show CI needs to be properly planned and executed in a disciplined way.
- While engaged in conversation tone of voice and body language are taken into account as well as the words actually spoken. Likewise, in observing companies and interpreting the results, a wider range of less tangible aspects need to be considered in addition to the purely factual.

---

2   Yake, T. (2001), 'Why retailers fail: Discovering the telltale signs', *Competitive Intelligence Magazine*, 4(3), 17.

15 *Creative Sources and Methods and the Craft of Analysis*

Although much useful material can be gathered from systematically working through documentary and human sources of intelligence, there will always be some questions to which they fail to supply answers. The researcher then has to use their ingenuity to find what Leonard Fuld terms 'creative' sources.[1] While the same types of systematic sources are used for every industry, a creative source is something used in a particular situation. Consequently, creative sources are virtually limitless in their possibilities.

The theme of creativity applies not only to obtaining data, but also to its interpretation. Business analysis requires fluid imagination as well as rigorous logic.

This chapter links the earlier material on data gathering in Part II with the chapters devoted to analysis that follow in Part III. Its three sections deal with:

- creative approaches to finding information when a blank is drawn using systematic sources
- taking a wider view, ways of enlisting creative techniques to solve those difficult problems in research and analysis where a straightforward logical strategy has failed
- setting the scene for the examination of specific modes of analysis in Part III through some general reflections on the craft of analysis.

Creative data gathering

A word of caution is needed here. Quite a lot of the advice on CI given in books and journals lays too much stress on ingenuity and not enough on what is practicable.

A favourite technique is rummaging in a target company's dustbins for documents that the firm has failed to shred. This, 'dumpster diving' as the Americans call it, can prove extremely effective. Benjamin Pell, known as 'Benji the Binman', has notoriously made a good living out of searching celebrities' dustbins and selling their secrets to the tabloid press. It was explained earlier how this led to the unmasking of Roy Lazzyman's abuse of his former employer's trade secrets (page 46). Neither is it open to legal challenge in that a company must take reasonable steps to protect what it asserts is a trade secret. The courts refuse to regard a document as confidential if it has been thrown away or discarded in a dustbin. So the bin archaeologist avoids the legal hazards run by the investigator who rifles filing cabinets or intercepts documents (although they may face a civil action for trespass if the dustbins were on the firm's property and not left out in the public street). However, I regard this kind of activity as the province of certain

---

1   Fuld, L. (1985), Chapter 8 in *The New Competitor Intelligence: How to get it; how to use it*, John Wiley.

private investigators and investigative journalists rather then CI professionals as it can stray beyond ethical (and even legal) boundaries.

Other cherished 'war stories' within the profession are legally and ethically acceptable, but often impracticable for CI operations carried on with few personnel and severe budgetary constraints. These include such famous episodes as spreading a suitable material across the access road to a factory and measuring the depth of tyre track left by the trucks going over it (in order to ascertain how heavily they were laden so as to estimate plant output) or having people stand outside an office armed with a handheld counter all week (to determine staff numbers).

Hence ethical and resource constraints force those most of those engaged in CI to be even more imaginative than people with less demanding business ethics or the luxury of ample resources at their disposal.

USE OF ESTIMATES IN THE ABSENCE OF RELIABLE DATA

Creative sources are ways of indirectly finding the information that is not directly available from the systematic ones. In some cases they can be highly accurate, but the use of a creative avenue usually means that the answer will be an estimate and thus subject to a lesser or greater margin of error. This is very similar to the situation often faced by military intelligence personnel who need to assess the size, composition and location of enemy forces. Unless they have 'inside track', thanks to spies in the opposing camp, direct information may be very difficult to obtain. So they are compelled to make estimates based on what they do know. Some examples of this approach follow.

Estimating market size without market research data

What if no market research is available to provide a market size for a sector (or if that available is too expensive or dated)? The total size of the market is made up of the sales of the companies operating in that industry segment. Hence if the individual players' sales are known the aggregate market size can be found by adding these together. Unfortunately there may be complications. If a firm is involved in more than one line of business merely using its total turnover is going to include income from other activities and will produce an overestimate. This danger is increased if a crude use is made of figures taken from a database where the sales figure quoted represents a company's aggregated turnover and not its revenue from a particular line of business.

Exports are another factor that may lead to an exaggerated domestic market size when company accounts are the data source. These will boost individual company sales, but do not relate to demand in the home market. A striking example is Danish bacon. The producers sell large quantities of this commodity, but it rarely features in menus in Denmark itself as the great majority of bacon output is exported. Trying to adjust for these distortions involves using the segmental data for turnover from the first note to the accounts (see page 153) to strip out sales generated by other activities and revenues from exports.

Employing proxies in market sizing

Another line of attack when trying to overcome a paucity of market research data is to use proxies or analogues. Paul Hague[2] gives examples such as estimating the size of the market for spark plugs. There will be data on the number of vehicles operating and all that is then needed is a multiple to be used with this (probably obtained through interviewing an industry source) for the typical number of plugs consumed by a vehicle over a year.

---

2   Hague, P. (1992), *The Industrial Market Research Handbook*, 3rd edition, Kogan Page.

He also illustrates estimating the market size for mechanical seals used in pumps, compressors and the like in Australia. This rests on the assumption that these will be used by Australians in the same proportions as in Britain. Figures for the UK market are available and he then employs electricity production, because the devices using the seals are electrically powered, as the analogue. Dividing the (known) British market size for seals by UK electricity production and multiplying this by Australian electricity output produces a rough estimate of their seals market. The final refinements are to adjust the figures to take account differences in the prices of seals between the two countries and convert Australian dollars into sterling. Other analogues include the number of registered vehicles or steel consumption (this is preferable to using steel production because of the distorting effect of exports).

A similar technique was employed by Ian Maclean[3] to calculate the market for dissolved acetylene (DA) in the absence of official figures. It was known that there was a close relationship between the demand for DA and employment levels in the various industries using it. Client records enabled typical consumption per employee in each of these to be estimated and then multiplied by the total numbers employed in the individual sectors to produce aggregate sales figures.

Using financial ratios where accounting data are not available

Where only limited financial data are available on an individual company (perhaps just annual sales and net assets) Leonard Fuld[4] advises using typical industry ratios to estimate the unknown figures. He recognizes there are potential pitfalls as the ratios may be distorted through the presence of an exceptional company in the population of firms used in compiling them or the enterprise being studied may have unusual financial characteristics. Fuld also warns against making comparisons between companies in the same industry that are of very different size. Other information, particularly that obtained through interviews with industry observers, is used to refine the estimates. The results are not to be relied upon too seriously, but can help to develop a crude financial picture of a firm when more precise data are just not available.

Creative ways of solving problems

When systematic sources fail to provide the information needed, the analyst has to return to the Golden Rule of Research and ask 'who would be interested enough in this subject to collect data on it?' For example, let us suppose we are looking for information on the level of children's pocket money. An obvious starting point would be in a standard official statistical source such as Social Trends. When this yields no data it is possible that the Department for Education and Skills has studied the topic. Child protection and welfare charities such as the NSPCC or educational bodies are also potential sources. If a blank is still being drawn then less obvious targets must be approached. Sectors that employ a large number of schoolchildren (such as weekend assistants in retailing) will presumably like to know how much pocket money is received to help as a guide to the wages they offer. Perhaps teaching unions have paid for research to support their case for higher salaries through showing that the pocket money given to the children they teach has been increasing far faster than teachers' pay? (The last suggestion is

---

3   Hurd, S. and Mangan, J., editors (2001), *Essential Data Skills for Business and Management*, Office for National Statistics and Statistics for Education, 13–14.
4   Fuld, L. (1985), Chapter 9 in *The New Competitor Intelligence: How to get it; how to use it*, John Wiley.

rather far-fetched, but illustrates the need to apply unconventional approaches when the more obvious methods are not yielding results).

What about businesses whose key customers are children making discretionary purchases (as opposed to those made on their behalf by adults)? This is where the answer was found. Birds Eye Walls Limited has been willing to pay for annual surveys to be made of pocket money for many years because this was such an important factor in determining the demand for their products such as ice cream. In fact data from the survey subsequently became available in a secondary source, NCT's *Lifestyle Pocket Book*.[5]

IMAGINATION – THE FOUNT OF CREATIVITY

Unlike systematic sources, which can be exploited using a straightforward 'checklist' technique, the creative ones are not obvious. Researchers have to draw upon the power of their imaginations to identity them. Creativity, according to Arthur Koestler,[6] is the fusing of two as yet unconnected ideas or pieces of data. Thus a pun brings together two unrelated meanings through a common word. Henry Ford saw that making cars in several colours was expensive, while producing only black automobiles would allow a significant reduction in factory costs and hence selling prices. Every other motor manufacturer knew that having to produce different coloured vehicles was costly, but accepted it as unavoidable. Only Ford dared to make the mental leap to ask the crucial question: 'what would most buyers prefer, a choice of colour or a cheaper car?' A glue that does not stick fast hardly looks like a very promising business idea: yet by applying it in 'Post It Notes' 3M had found a money-spinner. Koestler called this fusion *bisociation* and the stimulation of bisociative thinking promises enhanced creativity.

BRAINSTORMING WITH COLLEAGUES TO DEFEAT ORGANIZATIONAL INTELLECTUAL INERTIA

Fostering originality in solving problems has to begin by trying to generate as many ideas as possible and only making judgements on them at a later stage. There are powerful obstacles to creative thought, among them unchallenged assumptions (a particular danger when these have served well in the past even though the environment may now have changed), immediate dismissal of the unfamiliar (summed up in defeatist or isolationist philosophies such as 'it's impossible' or 'not invented here') and the herd instinct. Certain institutional measures can be taken to overcome these such as insisting that no options are ruled out until properly evaluated and compared and being prepared to at least consider 'unlearning' what has hitherto worked well.

Brainstorming is a favourite technique for trying to overcome intellectual and cultural inertia within organizations. The critical difference between brainstorming and simply trawling for ideas is that judgement is deferred. Participants are encouraged to 'think the unthinkable', no matter how far-fetched with their contributions simply being noted in the first instance. Instead of a serious, logical and realistic methodology, these sessions favour jokes, apparently crazy and fantasist thinking as the route to a solution. Only after the supply of ideas has dried up does their assessment begin.

Although there has been some disillusion with brainstorming I believe this is due more to the difficulty of coming up with new ideas *that actually work* rather than its weakness as a technique. It incorporates some valuable principles such as not ignoring less obvious possibilities and trying to make use of the widest range of talent. Provided it is combined with rigorous testing

---

5   *Lifestyle Pocket Book* (2003), NCT.
6   Koestler, A. (1975), *The Act of Creation*, Pan Books.

of new ideas (the brilliant new concept may not only have sounded absurd when first tabled, but may actually be simply silly), brainstorming can play a useful role in the quest for original thinking.

BISOCIATION TO THE CREATIVE AID OF THE LONE ANALYST

Related techniques such as role play or games can also help in triggering creative inspiration. However, all of these require the participation of others, what happens where the analyst is working alone? Here the stimulation has to come from things rather than colleagues. Koestler's method for fostering bisociation was to choose two unrelated objects at random and then seek connections between them. So the analyst might take a word at random from the dictionary and find a word associated with it (for instance 'car' might trigger the word chain 'wheel', 'ship', 'sail', 'canvas', 'tent', 'pole' and so on). They should be able to dredge up about 50 words in five minutes (persisting for longer is generally too tiring). Another method is to choose two words at random and then try to connect them. The imagination can also be fired by choosing a physical object and thinking about it in terms of its size, shape, colour, weight, texture and other qualities. Some creative consultancies post lists around their offices with the names of animals, plants, literary works, films, types of buildings or historical characters and other topics to act as a catalyst for new ideas. Visual works of art can also be a powerful imaginative aid. Thus celebrated animator Terry Gilliam goes to look at pictures in London's National Gallery when he needs a creative boost[7] and a range of collections across the world can be accessed through the Virtual Library (http://vlmp.musephile.org/galleries.html).

Creativity Unleashed Limited also has a superb range of resources and links for creative self-development at www.cul.co.uk.

Analysis

THE CRAFT OF ANALYSIS – ITS ESSENCE

I call it a craft such because analysis combines both scientific and artistic elements. Out of the complexity, confusion and uncertainty of the business environment the analyst has to fashion meaning and offer a credible guide to decision making. Intellectual rigour, scrupulous validation and conscientious testing have to be some of the hallmarks of their work. However, these qualities are not sufficient to produce good business analysis. This is not an academic exercise that can be extended over time and revised in the light of subsequent discoveries. Answers often have to be found and acted upon pretty rapidly. If they are incorrect and result in the wrong decisions being taken there will usually be a substantial price to pay in missed opportunities or unanticipated dangers.

The analyst must therefore also draw upon their intuitive and imaginative resources to be capable of delivering accurate guidance. There are good reasons for believing that some of the biggest errors in political, economic and business planning in recent years resulted from an over-emphasis on applying the methods of some of the natural sciences to analyzing human society. Leaders in many fields have placed too much weight on 'facts', 'statistics' and 'financial statements' – ignoring seemingly more intangible factors – only to discover that these apparently

---

7   The choice of works of art obviously depends upon what works best for individual analysts. I personally find the works of a great contemporary artist like Julian Rowe an unfailing source of imaginative stimulation (www.julianrowe.net).

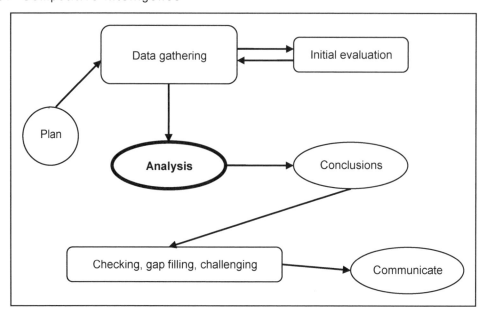

Figure 9   Analytical stage of the intelligence cycle

solid planks had serious limitations and flaws. Hence Friedman and colleagues jokingly call their wise and perceptive chapter (in *The Intelligence Edge*) on the art of analysis 'Lucky Guesses'.[8]

Socrates was the wisest man in Athens not because of what he knew, but because he understood the extent of his ignorance. Good analysts share this realism. It has rightly said that they must be 'comfortable with ambiguity' and not dismayed by it. On the more positive side this is true in many vocations – generals, politicians, business leaders and doctors have to cope despite imperfect understanding and the uncertainty of the future. A lawyer could win every case by only taking on clear-cut ones, but they have to take the risk of losing in court on the more doubtful ones if they want to rise high in their profession.

ACCURATE ANALYSIS IS POSSIBLE WITHOUT COMPLETE INFORMATION

Another source of comfort is that the analyst needs only some – and not all – of the information to make their lucky guesses.

Psychological research has shown that we can only absorb and process some of the information bombarding us every moment, yet this does not prevent us interpreting and acting upon it effectively. Thus:

> *It deosn't mttaer in waht oredr the ltteers in a wrod are, the olny iprmoetnt tihng is that the frist and lsat ltteer is at the rghit pclae.*
>
> *The rset can be a toatl mses and you can sitll raed it wouthit a porbelm. Tihs is bcuseae we do not raed ervey lteter by itslef but the wrod as a wlohe.*

This also applies to research conducted over the phone or radio conversations where only a minority of words can be heard and yet the message understood.

---

8   Friedman, G. and colleagues (1998), *The Intelligence Edge: How to profit in the information age*, Century.

In the same way accurate CI is possible even with a lack of complete information (a conclusion which fits well with the use of estimation to generate useable intelligence).

The process of undertaking it has often been compared to completing a jigsaw puzzle, although of course with that game one expects to have all the pieces – unlike many CI situations. Leonard Fuld uses the pleasing metaphor of comparing it to a Pointillist painting by an artist like Seurat. Observed close to only a series of tiny coloured dots are seen, but viewed from farther away these resolve into shapes and the artist's complete vision is revealed. Like this school of artists, CI analysts must attend carefully to fine detail while still retaining the big picture. They have the difficult task to achieve of being generalists who have a broad swathe of general knowledge, while capable at the same time of understanding a specialism in some depth.

GOOD ANALYSTS DO NOT 'FOLLOW THE HERD'

Finally, those who are going to enjoy long-term success in this craft have to be prepared to stand apart from the crowd as consensus judgements always eventually go awry. The world changes, but the viewpoint remains fixed. Recent intelligence disasters in the military and political spheres show the huge danger of this blinkered, 'comfort in numbers' thinking. Effective CI demands that analysts be willing to amend their opinions as circumstances alter and also be ready to plough a lonely furrow. As Friedman and colleagues rightly say: 'There are two kinds of analysts. The first type want to be right. The second want to have company.'[9]

Conclusions

- When the data being sought have not been captured through a trawl of systematic sources the analyst must adopt a less conventional, more imaginative tack.
- They should brainstorm with colleagues or use bisociation if alone to generate new avenues of enquiry.
- Creative CI usually produces estimates rather than exact data.
- This generally still suffices for the generation of actionable intelligence.
- Analysts should always rely upon their own judgement (provided this is adequately informed and well considered) – even if nobody else shares their view.

---

9   Friedman, G. and colleagues, 197.

PART III

Turning Raw Data into Finished Intelligence

Analysis and presentation

16 *Figuring Out the Numbers – Structure and Content of Company Accounts*

A company is judged on the financial results it achieves, hence analysts have to be able to use accounting information with ease and understanding. They do not need to possess accountancy qualifications to do this, but they must have a sound grasp of the concepts and principles of financial reporting, be familiar with the jargon of the discipline and be able to interpret accounting data. It is a vital tool in their repertoire of investigative techniques and sources of information.

The next two chapters are thus intended to provide a basic grounding in the discipline. To enhance their knowledge of accounts analysts should study some of the excellent books available,[1] attend courses and seek guidance from colleagues with accounting expertise. Some of the points discussed have been mentioned earlier in the text, but will now be considered from an accounting perspective.

This chapter explores the various documents that form a set of accounts and what they contain. It deals with the:

- balance sheet
- profit and loss account
- cash flow statement
- notes to the accounts.

Balance sheet

How much am I worth financially at present? To find the answer to this frequently asked question the first step to add up a person's *assets*, that is, anything they own that has a monetary value and any sums of money owed to them. The result is their *total assets*.

The second step is to ascertain the extent of their *liabilities*, that is sums of money they owe to others. Adding all these together gives their *total liabilities*.

Armed with these two numbers their *net worth* can now be calculated. Marketing people tend to avoid speaking of 'rich people', instead they refer to 'high net worth individuals'. The greater the surplus of total assets over total liabilities the higher the net worth. Another term for net worth is *equity*. This has nothing to do with the ordinary shares, the equity shares, which are sold to shareholders by companies. It is the sum a person would be left if they called in all the debts owed to them, sold their other assets and then settled their liabilities.

---

1   Walsh, C. (2002), *Key Management Ratios: Master the management metrics that drive and control your business*, Financial Times/Prentice Hall. Reid, W. and Myddleton, D.R. (2005), *The Meaning of Company Accounts*, Gower, 8th edition. Holmes, G. and Sugden, A. (2004), *Interpreting Company Reports and Accounts*, 9th edition.

A familiar instance of this usage relates to residential property. If a house or flat is worth £150 000 and the owner owes £50 000 on a mortgage, their equity in the property is £100 000. In other words if they sell it and repay the mortgage they are left with a surplus of £100 000 in cash. If their mortgage is £170 000 and the dwelling is valued at £150 000 they will still owe £20 000 to the lender even after selling it. During the recession of the early 1990s many households suffered such *negative equity*, when their outstanding mortgage was greater than the value of the property it was secured against.

The same concept of net worth applies to companies as well as individuals or households. Subtracting a company's liabilities from its assets reveals the firm's net worth. The more common term is *net asset value* (often abbreviated to NAV), which represents the value of the company's total assets minus its total liabilities. Details of the assets, liabilities and resultant net worth are set out in the balance sheet. Hence another term used to describe a firm's net worth is book value, the value of the company as recorded in the accounts. The great majority of companies will have positive net worth, in other words their assets will exceed their liabilities (as in the example shown in Table 1). However, companies, just like households, can be – and sometimes are – in a state of *negative net worth*.

So how do balance sheets actually balance – with aggregated assets and liabilities always equal? This is because the net worth of the business does not belong to the company, instead it is owned by the shareholders. It represents their stake in the firm and hence could be termed 'owners' equity' or 'shareholders' equity'. In British financial statements it is called *shareholders' funds*.

A typical balance sheet is illustrated in Table 1.

Table 1   Balance sheet as at 31 March

	2005	*2004*
Fixed assets (long-term assets)	27 278	23 801
Current assets (short-term assets)		
Stocks	40 041	31 997
Debtors	38 251	28 525
Cash at bank and in hand	6312	342
	84 604	60 864
Creditors falling due within one year (short-term liabilities)	(61 271)	(52 996)
Net current assets (working capital)	23 333	7868
Creditors falling due after one year (long-term creditors)	(19 893)	(8719)
Capital and reserves		
Called up share capital (issued share capital)	2408	1482
Profit and loss account (retained profit)	27 040	20 412
Share premium account (another reserve, arising from		
shareholders paying more than par value for new shares)	1270	1056
Shareholders' funds	30 718	22 950

It is important to realize that the book value shown in the financial statements is a figure based on past transactions and not a reliable indicator of the company's real worth. If the firm collapsed the sums that could actually be raised in *realizing* its assets (that is, turning them into cash) would usually be far less than those given in the balance sheet. Conversely, if a firm was sold as a going concern the buyer would normally have to pay more than the fair value of its assets. This premium paid to acquire a business is (as was seen in Chapter 4) known as *goodwill* and relates to those other attractive features of the company such as its reputation, its customer base, the skills of its employees or quality of its management.

Apart from stating the book value of a company, balance sheets provide more information regarding the structure of its assets and liabilities. These are analysed as:

- long-term assets
- short-term assets
- short-term liabilities
- long-term liabilities.

Short-term assets and liabilities are defined by accountants as those assets which will be used up during a company's forthcoming accounting year and those liabilities which must be paid within this year. *Long-term* assets will be used for longer than the next accounting year, likewise long-term liabilities do not have to be settled until beyond this period.

FIXED ASSETS

In British accounts long-term assets are termed *fixed assets*. These can be subdivided into three groups – tangible, intangible and investments:

Tangible fixed assets

Tangible fixed assets are those most commonly encountered and comprise all those longer-life items with a physical presence – hence 'tangible' – needed to support the company's operations. They include land and buildings, plant and machinery, fixtures and fittings, furniture and vehicles. Although there are now 'virtual' companies operating without dedicated accommodation, most enterprises need premises such as offices, shops, factories and warehouses to carry on their business. They also require IT equipment, lathes, refrigerated cabinets, desks, cars, vans and lorries and all those other items that will still be used by them beyond the next accounting year.

Intangible fixed assets

The copyright on this book also has a financial value, but lacks physical substance, hence it is classed as an *intangible fixed asset*.

- *Intellectual property rights* such as copyrights, patents and trade marks can be immensely important and may form the core of the value of a business. In sectors such as media, high technology and pharmaceuticals protecting and enhancing an enterprise's intellectual property is of particular significance.
- Another major category of intangible fixed asset is purchased *goodwill*, which arises (as noted earlier) where a company pays more than the fair value of another business's assets when

buying it. For a highly expansionary firm with a long tally of acquisitions this item can be one of the largest in the balance sheet.

- Other types of intangible fixed asset include *licences* and the *capitalization of research and development* (R&D) costs. The need to obtain licences or buy businesses already holding them is a salient characteristic of running a chain of bars, betting shops, casinos or pharmacies. A very prominent example were the costs incurred by telecommunications companies when granted licences by European governments to use part of the radio spectrum for their mobile phone services. Similarly, consumer goods manufacturers often make products, developed by overseas companies, under licence in their own countries.

Intangible fixed assets are usually only included in company accounts when they are the result of a previous transaction and will be recorded at cost rather at their current value.

Investments

The last category of fixed assets are *investments* in other companies. These will frequently be the shares held by a parent company of a corporate group in its subsidiaries, though such investments may take many other forms. These generally have strategic connotations, for example, investments in joint ventures and consortia or cross-holdings, where two companies take stakes in each other to cement a long-term alliance.

CURRENT ASSETS

Short-term assets will be used up in the current accounting year, hence accountants designate them *current assets*. They are divided into:

- stocks, also called 'inventories' in the US and some other countries
- debtors, or 'receivables' in American financial statements
- cash.

Stocks

The nature of *stocks* will depend upon the sector being looked at. In a manufacturing concern they will consist of:

- *raw materials* – companies will often hold supplies of these to avoid interruptions to production
- *work in progress (WIP)* – these are products which have been partly processed, but not reached completion. In some industries, aircraft and ship building for example, the value of WIP may be very considerable
- *finished goods or services* – these are now ready for sale, but have yet to be purchased by customers.

For a retailer stocks will be those finished goods they have bought with the sole intention of reselling them to consumers.

Debtors

These are sums of money owed to the company by other parties, its *receivables*. Most companies supply goods and services on credit and until they receive payment will classify the monies owed as debtors. There is naturally a degree of risk that the creditor will fail to pay. If they do not pay the company will have to treat the sum lost as an expense – *bad debts* – in its profit and loss account and subtract it from the total for debtors recorded in its balance sheet. Where there is uncertainty as to whether some debts will be paid it should make a provision for these in the profit and loss account under 'doubtful debts' and again deduct this from the sum shown for debtors in the balance sheet. However, bad and doubtful debts need only be disclosed in the accounts if the sums involved are *material*, that is, they would have a significant impact on the reported results.

Debts may also be due and not yet paid from:

- subsidiaries
- other businesses related to the company
- sums outstanding following the sale of subsidiaries or other fixed assets, or the disposal of investments
- prepayments – where payment has been made by the company in advance of receiving the goods or services to be provided under the contract and has to be returned if these are not supplied.

Current asset investments

It was noted earlier that enterprises will often buy shares in other companies as part of a long-term strategic plan. Some companies also make substantial short-run investments, buying securities with the intention of selling them on for profit or because they generate higher rates of return than they can obtain from leaving them in the bank in the form of cash deposits. These will be reported as *current asset investments*.

Cash

This is reported as *cash at bank and in hand*. The first element relates to the sums held in a company's bank accounts, the second to the bank notes and coins residing in the company's premises in its tills and safes.

LIABILITIES

As we have seen, liabilities can be divided into short-term *current liabilities* which must be paid within the coming accounting year and long-term *creditors: amounts due after more than one year*.

Assets in balance sheets follow the order:

- fixed assets
- current assets.

However, liabilities are presented in the reverse order:

- current liabilities
- creditors: amounts due after more than one year.

The reason for this treatment will be explained shortly.

CURRENT LIABILITIES

Trade creditors

One aspect of current liabilities mirrors that of current assets in that just as businesses often extend credit to customers, so they also typically obtain it on their own purchases. These *trade creditors* will be a major item in the current liabilities of many companies.

Short-term loans

It is also common for firms to agree overdraft facilities (theoretically repayable on demand) with their banks or obtain other forms of *short-term loan*. A company will also be liable to make payments to the authorities in respect of Corporation Tax, social security contributions in relating to employees and other taxes within the next accounting year.

Dividends

Another category of current liability is any *dividend* proposed by the directors. Although these cannot, by law, be paid until approved by the shareholders they are invariably anticipated as a liability.

Accruals

These are the reverse of prepayments and are future liabilities relating to goods and services that have already been partly supplied or for which invoices are still awaited.

NET CURRENT ASSETS

Comparing current assets against current liabilities (leaving long-term liabilities for later consideration) provides an indication of a company's short-term financial strength. Subtracting current liabilities from the current assets reveals *net current assets*. This is also the most widely used definition of *working capital*, which is the financial cushion that enables a company to pay its staff, suppliers and meet other current obligations. Having adequate working capital is vital for a company's health and perhaps its survival. Many businesses fail, not because they are inherently unprofitable in the longer run, but as a consequence of having insufficient short-term resources to survive.

LONG-TERM LIABILITIES

Finally, there are also *long-term liabilities*. These are items such as *term loans* from banks, mortgages, debentures or bond issues which do not have to be settled in the coming accounting year, but in the more distant future.

CAPITAL EMPLOYED

Adding fixed assets to working capital produces a value for the company's *total net assets*. This is also the most common definition of the 'capital employed' in the company. The proportion of capital tied up in fixed assets compared with that devoted to working capital will vary according to the line of business. Heavy industries such as bulk chemicals or transport will need to undertake massive investment in fixed assets. An employment agency, in contrast, may spend relatively little on these, but will require a lot of working capital to meet the gap between having to pay its temporary workers very soon and receiving payment from its clients some weeks later.

As was seen earlier net asset value equals shareholders' funds. Focusing on fixed assets and working capital shows where a company's capital is being employed.

An alternative approach is to look at where it is coming from. We have seen that companies can be financed either from internal or external sources. Internally sourced capital is that contributed by the shareholders – *issued share capital* – or the *reserves* owned by them. These added together make up shareholders' funds. External finance comprises lending to the company from banks, buyers of bonds and other suppliers of long term funding.

Reserves are in turn classified as either *revenue* reserves or *capital* ones.

REVENUE RESERVES

In most cases, revenue reserves are profits reinvested in the company under the reserve category of 'profit and loss account'. Revenue reserves can be used to pay dividends. Thus if a firm has experienced a bad year and lost money, profits retained in earlier periods can be drawn upon to maintain the level of dividend payments to shareholders.

CAPITAL RESERVES

Capital reserves can arise from a number of sources. The Companies Act 1985 divides them into three categories:

1) *Share premium account.* If shares are sold to investors for more than their nominal value, the surplus sum is allocated to this reserve. For example, if shares with a nominal value of one pence are issued for 200 pence, the premium paid of 199 pence is credited to the share premium account.
2) *Revaluation reserve.* This is typically created when the properties owned by the company are revalued. Fixed assets such as buildings are not revalued annually and will usually be found to have gained in value over the years since the last revaluation. This appreciation in the value of the company's assets is only a *paper profit* and would only become *realized profit* if the assets were sold. However, the increase in their value can be recognized in the accounts by it being assigned to a revaluation reserve.
3) *Other reserves.* These can be the result of several events, for example, the issue of share warrants (which give the holder the right to purchase a limited number of extra shares at a fixed price) or the acquisition of assets for less than the value recorded for them in the balance sheet. However, the most commonly encountered will be the capital redemption reserve. If a company wishes to buy back some of its shares using its profits, the law obliges it to assign a sum equal to that spent on purchasing the shares to a capital redemption reserve.

British companies are not allowed to use any of their capital reserves to pay dividends.

GROUP ACCOUNTS

Many companies have quite complicated structures, with the parent company involved with many subsidiaries (where it owns over 50 per cent of the shares) and associated companies (usually where it owns over 20 per cent, but less than 50 per cent of the shares). In preparing accounts for the group it would be misleading, should there be intra-group transactions, to simply add together the turnover and profit figures for each group member. This would include sales between members of the group and the profit resulting from them, yet these transactions merely reshuffle money within the group. To avoid this distortion the turnover and profits arising from intra-group trading are deducted from the totals reported for the group.

Another potentially misleading feature of group accounts involves debt. The great bulk of a group's debt may not be in the name of the parent, but scattered among the subsidiaries and associated companies. If only the parent company accounts are published or *special purpose vehicles* used to conceal borrowings it may appear to have relatively little debt. This 'off balance sheet' finance was a key element in both the Maxwell and Enron debacles.

The process of adjusting the accounts to remove these distortions is called *consolidation*. Since the 1989 Companies Act public limited companies and large private companies have been obliged to consolidate their accounts if they operate as a group. Medium-sized and small companies are exempt from this requirement (see page 88 for definitions of these). This provision applies to companies across the EU as the 1989 Act's requirements are derived from the 7th Company Law Directive.[2]

In group accounts there is a single profit and loss account and cash flow statement (both of them consolidated). Rather confusingly there are two balance sheets. The 'Company' balance sheet relates solely to the parent, while the 'Group' balance sheet is consolidated to take subsidiaries and associated companies into account. The group balance sheet gets by far the most attention because it gives a more accurate picture of the group's finances as a whole.

KEY POINTS

- The balance sheet tabulates a company's short- and long-term assets and liabilities and shows its net worth.

- It is *not* a valuation statement for the company.

- Reading the balance sheet is vital for understanding the financial strength of a company and the likelihood of its survival.

- For groups of companies, the consolidated Group balance sheet is much more useful than the Company one relating solely to the parent.

- Strong balance sheets feature low debt, adequate working capital and growing shareholders' funds.

- Weak balance sheets are characterized by heavy debt, show that finding sufficient working capital is a strain and reveal dwindling shareholders' funds.

- A strong balance sheet is not necessarily a good thing. It may be inappropriate in certain circumstances. Excessive amassing of cash piles and other current assets which only yield a low return hurts profitability. Likewise, taking on a lot of debt may be entirely appropriate if this permits a company with good prospects to grow more rapidly.

- A balance sheet is a snapshot of the financial position of a firm at a particular date – this may have looked very different during most of the company's accounting period or changed considerably since the date the balance sheet relates to.

---

2   It should be noted that while Enron filed consolidated accounts, these excluded borrowings made through special purpose vehicles. These entities were controlled by the parent company, but US consolidation requirements are based on ownership rather control. EU ones demand consolidation of businesses under the effective sway of a parent even if it does not hold the majority of their shares.

Profit and loss account

Company income minus expenses equals profit. Simple! Not quite. Profit and loss accounts are somewhat more complex than that. However, that equation still expresses their essence. The profit and loss account (P&L) details the company's income, expenses and the resulting outcome over a given period.

Four different formats for laying out the P&L are allowed under the Companies Act. Two of these involve the 'side by side' presentation of income on the left side of the page and expenses on the right. These will be used in the accounts prepared by companies on the Continent and other places, but are rarely encountered in British P&Ls. The other two options adopt a 'top to bottom' layout on a single page. One of them is theoretically more attractive to an analyst because key items of expense such as the cost of raw materials or staff may be displayed on the face of the P&L itself rather than buried in the notes to the accounts. In practice it is seldom used and even when it is a lot of the most interesting analytical detail is still relegated to the notes. So I shall concentrate on the format that is by far the most common, starting with the simpler version in Table 2.

Table 2   Profit and loss account for year ended 31 March

	2005	2004
1. Turnover	172 166	164 343
2. Operating expenses	(162 456)	(155 506)
3. Operating profit	**9710**	**8837**
4. Interest payable	(1724)	(1918)
5. Taxation	(2820)	(2624)
6. Earning attributable to ordinary shareholders	**5166**	**4295**
7. Dividends	3000	2800
8. Retained profit	2166	1495

A P&L will always start by showing the company's income from its trading operations (line 1 of Table 2) This could also be described as its 'revenue' or 'sales'. It Britain it is called *turnover* (although not for financial institutions).

The next item will be the *operational costs* of the business (line 2 of Table 2). These are all the expenses the company has incurred over the period (apart from interest on money it has borrowed or tax paid).

Subtracting costs from turnover gives the result (in profit or loss terms) for its operations during the period. This is called the *operating profit* (line 3 of Table 2) and is a key measure of the success of the company's activities. Another term for it is *profit before interest and tax* or *PBIT*. Financiers tend to give it another name: *earnings before interest and tax* or *EBIT*. 'Earnings' in this context has nothing to do with what the staff get paid, it is the profit earned by the company, its 'corporate earnings'.

As these expressions imply, a company has some other expenses to meet apart from its operational costs. Most companies borrow money and *interest* (line 4 of Table 2) must be paid on this. Furthermore all companies have to pay Corporation and other *taxes* (line 5 of Table 2), unless their trading record (featuring recurrent losses) has been too bad for them to be liable.

Subtracting the interest and tax charges yields the profit or loss the company's owners have enjoyed – or endured – over the period. This is described as the *earnings attributable to ordinary shareholders* (line 6 in Table 2) and is what is meant by 'the bottom line' in company results – for listed companies the actual bottom line is earnings per share (EPS) where the earnings are divided by the total number of shares in issue. When this result has been calculated the directors are faced with a choice. They can:

1) pay out all of it to the shareholders in the form of a dividend (line 7 in Table 2)
2) reinvest all of it in the business with the intention of growing it even faster (line 8 in Table 2)
3) a mixture of both.

Table 3   More complex profit and loss account for year ended 31 March

	2005	2004
1. Turnover	172 166	164 343
2. Cost of sales	(142 446)	(135 005)
3. Gross profit	**29 720**	**29 338**
4. Administrative and distribution costs (overheads)	(20 009)	(20 501)
5. Operating profit	**9711**	**8837**
6. Interest payable	(1724)	(1918)
7. Taxation	(2820)	(2624)
8. Minorities	(15)	(11)
9. Preference shareholders' dividend	(101)	(101)
10. Earning attributable to ordinary shareholders	**5051**	**4183**
11. Dividends	3000	2800
12. Retained profit	2051	1383

Their decision will depend on the company's nature and circumstances, particularly the evolutionary stage it has reached and its prospects. Young, rapidly growing companies will typically pay no dividend, but reinvest all the surplus generated by their trading activities back into the business (what the Americans call 'plough back'). Firms operating in relatively safe, mature, slow growth sectors such as water, tobacco and the like will tend to distribute a large proportion of their earnings as a dividend to shareholders. Most companies choose to retain part of their earnings to strengthen their financial base and distribute part to please the shareholders.

A rather more complex (and more typical) P&L is shown in Table 3. Here the operating expenses have been divided into two types. First, the *cost of sales* (line 2, Table 3). These are the direct expenses incurred by the company in achieving its turnover. The relationship between sales and the cost of sales is very close, although not directly proportionate. Subtracting the cost of sales from turnover gives the *gross profit* earned on goods or services sold by the company (line 3, Table 3).

Second, the *overheads* of the business. These are expenses the company must bear just to operate, even if it has made no sales. They include items such as:

- general administration costs including administrative staff salaries
- accounting charges
- legal fees
- human resources activities like recruitment and training

and where sales have been made:

- cost of getting the product to the customer

Overheads are both necessary and regrettable. They are an anxiety in that the relationship between sales and overheads is by no means as close as that between turnover and the direct cost of sales. A start-up will have to carry overhead costs before it earns anything in sales. Poor control of overheads can undermine a strong performance in terms of gross profits. In America they are sometimes referred to the as the 'burden' borne by a company, a term that well expresses the concern to contain them. Management consultants will often focus on overheads in the hope of identifying cost savings that will not have an impact on their client's capacity to serve its customers. On the other hand, a crass 'let's just slash overheads' approach may do significant damage to a company. A judicious balance must be struck, insufficient spending on these essential functions being as unwise as excessive expenditure on them is wasteful.

In British accounts overheads are described as *administrative and distribution costs* (line 4, Table 3). These are generally lumped together, although in some cases they are reported separately. Subtracting the administrative and distribution costs from gross profit gives operating profit (line 5, Table 3).

Additional complexities can occur further down the P&L. As has been noted many firms operate as groups, with a number of subsidiaries nestling beneath the parent company. If one of these is wholly owned, in other words all its shares are held by the parent, the entire profit earned by it is attributable to that parent. It is quite common, however, for a minority of shares in a subsidiary to in the possession of other parties. These will be entitled to their share in any profits it generates. Thus if a subsidiary with 20 per cent of its shares in the hands of minority shareholders makes a £1 million profit, £200 000 of this will be attributable to the minority shareholders. Stripping these out will be recorded as *minorities* (line 8, Table 3) in the P&L.

Most companies merely have ordinary shares. However, some may also issue preference shares that typically pay a fixed percentage of their nominal value as dividend each year, as opposed to the dividend on ordinary shares which will vary according to the annual decision as to how much should be distributed. No payment of dividend to ordinary shareholders is allowed until the holders of preference share receive theirs (hence 'preference'). Thus dividends paid to preference shareholders will be noted in the P&L (line 9, Table 3) before the bottom line total for the earnings attributable to ordinary shareholders (line 10, Table 3).

Another complication arises if a company receives income apart from that generated by its ordinary trading activities. This could be derived from numerous sources, such dividends or capital gains resulting from investment in other companies or the sale of subsidiaries, properties or other assets and will be stated separately in the P&L.

KEY POINTS

- The profit and loss account shows the financial performance of a firm over a period.

- It displays the company's revenues and expenses and the final result in terms of a gain or loss for the shareholders.

- Reading the profit and loss account shows how successful management have been in achieving returns on their behalf.

- The proportion of profit reinvested/paid out as dividend reveals what is being done with surplus generated.

- It is dangerous to focus simply on earnings per share – analysts must ask 'How have these earnings been achieved?' Is creative accounting being employed to flatter the results?

Cash flow statement

'Cash is king.' All businesses must generate cash or eventually go to the wall. The evil day can be postponed by borrowing, creative accounting or simply stealing someone else's money (as in the case of Robert Maxwell). There is still a moment of truth where liquid funds have to be available or the game is up.

The figures reported in other parts of the annual report are based upon the *accrual* principle. This means recording revenues and expenses when incurred rather than actually paid for, in other words, regardless of whether cash has changed hands. So firms can book a sale as revenue, even though the customer has been given credit and the sum owed included under 'debtors' in the balance sheet. Likewise they should treat an undisputed invoice as an expense even though they do not have to pay it until some time later. The accrual principle is intended to match the income earned and expenditure incurred to their correct time periods, ignoring the actual transfer of cash.

Companies are obliged to report their results for a specific time period (annually, six monthly or quarterly depending on their status). Unfortunately this is generally artificial and does not align with a firm's natural business cycle. Thus a grocery supermarket will have a short cycle with stock being bought and then resold within a few weeks. In contrast, the business cycle of a construction company or major utility will stretch over several years. It is this requirement to prepare accounts over set terms which forces a degree of latitude to be extended so that the varying reporting needs of companies in widely differing sectors can be accommodated. Alas, with this necessary accounting flexibility comes the opportunity to manipulate the accounts.

A growing realization of the fundamental importance of cash led to companies (only small private or dormant ones are exempted) being compelled to draw up cash flow statements. These show actual receipts and disbursements of cash as opposed to the nominal recognition of income or expense recorded in other parts of the accounts.

Creative accounting can flatter the balance sheet and enhance reported profits, but cash is difficult to fake. Subjective judgements may be made by a firm's management regarding the value of its assets or its profitability, conjuring cash out of the air is a much harder feat. While not impossible for a limited time in cases of extreme fraud, being able to maintain the deception becomes increasingly difficult.

Apparently favourable results stated in the profit account, but accompanied by weak or (worse) negative cash flow may indicate creative accounting is being practised. Yet there can be perfectly acceptable reasons for it such as a major acquisition or the repayment of debt. Whatever its cause such a situation merits further probing by the analyst. Directors should offer a plausible explanation for its occurrence in their public statements.

The inflows and outflows of cash are shown under eight headings, as displayed in Table 4.

Table 4 Cash flow statement for year ended 31 March

	2005	2004
Operating activities	9044	20 875
Returns on investments and servicing of finance		
Interest paid	(1053)	(1005)
Taxation	**(2093)**	**(2317)**
Capital expenditure and financial investment		
Payments to acquire tangible fixed assets	(2571)	(1916)
Sales of tangible fixed assets	1536	1503
Purchase of own shares for employee benefit trust	(315)	–
Acquisitions and disposals		
Purchase of subsidiary undertakings	(9659)	(2045)
Net cash/(overdraft) acquired with subsidiaries	1293	(578)
Equity dividends paid	(2600)	(2245)
Financing		
Repayment of bank loan	(94)	(73)
New bank loan	5000	–
Proceeds of shares issued for cash	137	320
Net increase/(decrease) in cash	**(1375)**	**12 519**

Operating activities

This covers the cash coming from the company's operations and from changes in current assets such as a decrease in stocks or debtors (an increase in these would be recorded as an outflow). The charge made for depreciation of fixed assets will be added back because the cash outflow actually took place when the asset was acquired and the deductions for depreciation from the profit and loss account are merely book entries not entailing any subsequent transfers of cash.

Returns on investment and servicing of finance

Records any interest received from loans made by the firm and interest paid on borrowing it has undertaken (in most companies the latter total will dwarf the former and there will be considerable net interest to be paid).

Taxation

An outflow of cash for the great majority of companies. It is important to be aware that the corporate tax regime is not directly aligned to the accounting system with, for instance, major differences between the rate and period over which tax allowances for fixed asset investment can be claimed and the depreciation schedules adopted in preparing accounts. These 'timing differences' result in tax payments and refunds having a limited relationship to the company's accounting period.

Capital expenditure and financial investment

Companies have to maintain and extend their fixed asset base. IT equipment soon heads towards obsolescence due to the speed of technological advance, machinery has to be replaced or shops refurbished. Adequate capital expenditure or *capex* is needed to ensure that the size and quality of a firm's assets is appropriate to its operational requirements. A company may also make investments in financial assets as well as physical ones through buying shares, bonds or other securities. Both capex and financial investment will represent outflows of cash.

Acquisitions and disposals

The balance between cash outflows and inflows here depends upon the company's strategy. Highly acquisitive firms will have heavy outflows to pay for other businesses (unless the payment is made in the form of giving the seller its shares rather than cash). Other companies may generate considerable cash inflows by a major programme of disposals. In some cases the proceeds of disposals from 'non-core' subsidiaries may largely match the cost of buying more core businesses and the net cash flow remain fairly modest even though large sums are both received and disbursed.

Equity dividends paid

Any distribution to shareholders will obviously result in an outflow of cash.

Management of liquid resources

Liquid resources are investments in current assets that can be easily sold off to raise cash. They are made not for long-term strategic reasons, but simply with the aim of making the best return while still being capable of conversion into cash at short notice. This section of the cash flow statement is often subsumed into 'Financing'.

Financing

As has been seen, companies can raise finance either by selling more shares to investors or borrowing. This section of the statement shows if cash has been raised by issuing equity or negotiating loans or disbursed in buying back shares or repaying debt.

KEY POINTS

- Without sufficient cash no business can survive for long.

- The cash flow statement shows the extent to which the firm is cash generative or cash absorbent.

- It acts as a reality check on other parts of the accounts – excellent reported profits accompanied by a cash haemorrhage *may* indicate creative accounting.

Notes to the accounts

A balance sheet, profit and loss account and cash flow statement are each single page documents. They are a précis of a firm's financial performance and condition. Much more detailed information is contained in the notes to the accounts. For example, the number of people a company employs will not be found in any of these three statements and neither will the proportion of current liabilities arising from borrowing as opposed to trade and other creditors. The notes are needed to reveal these details.

A major disadvantage of using original company accounts is that they only show the figures for the previous year and the one preceding that for comparison (listed companies publish longer runs of data for some key items in their annual reports). So three annual reports have to be obtained to span the five-year period needed to examine longer-term trends. Furthermore, anyone wishing to conduct competitive analysis on a sector has to obtain the reports for each individual company in order to extract the numbers required.

Hence those information providers offering longer runs of figures in standardized formats make both assembling the data and comparing the financial status and performance of a number of companies much easier for their subscribers. This is acceptable in either preliminary or 'broad brush' analysis, but insufficient if the analyst wishes understand a company in more depth. In the latter case the much richer level of detail provided in the notes can be of immense value.

One very obvious instance is where a company is an exporter and/or has more than one line of business. In order to discover whether it is heavily exposed to a particular geographic market the notes must be consulted. If a large proportion of its turnover was derived from, say, South East Asia in 1997 or the US in 2001, an analyst working at those times would have to allow for adverse economic conditions in those areas hurting the firm's exports. Likewise, if its main line of business is in a sector enjoying a boom, this would count for more in assessing the company as a whole than if a smaller part of its portfolio of activities was suffering from adverse market conditions. The value of such segmental data is plain. (It should be noted that the quality of disclosure will vary considerably, indeed companies are allowed to avoid providing a segmental analysis if their management consider this to be harmful competitively.)

Similarly, in trying to determine a company's indebtedness, the notes or data taken from them are required. 'Current liabilities' bundle together sums owed to suppliers, various tax and social security payments due, along with bank overdrafts and other forms of loan. The note relating to these there breaks them into individual categories enabling total short-term debt to be isolated.

A third example concerns *contingent liabilities*. These are liabilities that have not yet been incurred, but may be. They depend – 'are contingent' – upon a certain event such as the outcome of a lawsuit against the company. Mighty parent companies guaranteeing the debts of their subsidiaries have been felled when these get into serious trouble. There is no mention of them in the main accounts, only the notes can reveal this category of 'off-balance sheet' financial risk.

These illustrations demonstrate the potential value of the notes when a company has to be subject to a more probing scrutiny.

KEY POINTS

- The notes add a great deal of extra – sometimes crucial – information.
- They should not be neglected when conducting an in-depth study of a company.

17 *Running the Numbers – Understanding Financial Statements*

This chapter examines the techniques, such as ratio analysis, that are used to quantify a company's financial health and performance. It begins by considering the two fundamental (and conflicting) goals of a business enterprise.

The twin objectives of companies

Because of the inverse relationship between financial reward and risk, there is a tension between seeking profit on the one hand and ensuring the survival of the company on the other. Management's task is to reconcile these conflicting objectives. The actual point they choose on the continuum between high profit and low risk will depend upon a number of factors such as the appetite for risk among the shareholders, the personalities of the directors and the degree of individual power they hold within the organization or regulatory constraints.

A shareholder population composed of badly off pensioners will be (or at least should be!) considerably more risk-averse than one made up of wealthy, relatively young people. The former will show a greater concern about the security of their investment, preferring modest and predictable returns on it to larger, but more volatile returns or the danger of their capital being lost. They will also be far more interested in a steady flow of income from their financial assets rather than one-off capital gains. The latter group will tend to take a more speculative approach, not caring about immediate returns and having less anxiety about the possibility of the value of their investment being wiped out. They are comfortable with high risks as long as there is (at least apparently) a good prospect of big returns. Their focus will be primarily on achieving capital gains, with income as a very secondary goal.

Institutional investors, in constructing their portfolios, will likewise reflect the extent to which those contributing to their funds shun or embrace risk. A pension fund manager charged with preserving the capital of the fund members and providing a secure flow of income will weigh their portfolios towards safer, lower-return investments. In contrast, a private equity provider aiming to achieve relatively high returns for their sophisticated and well-heeled backers will concentrate their investments in the more speculative regions of the capital market.

What constitutes an acceptable degree of risk for a company to bear in the pursuit of making bigger profits also depends upon the personalities of those running it and the relative influence of each individual. The 'lifestyle' managers described in Chapter 1 (see page 3) will be unwilling to place their company in jeopardy by taking a certain course of action even if the potential gain could be very great. A willingness to 'go for gold' on the other hand is a defining characteristic of an entrepreneur. (It should be emphasized that a genuine entrepreneur is not someone who is unaware of risk or treats it largely with indifference, such people are better termed 'fools', 'gamblers' – or, in the worst cases, 'fraudsters'.)

Furthermore, there may be limits set by regulation on the risks management are permitted to take. For example, banks and insurance companies are obliged to maintain certain minimum levels of solvency which prevent them deploying all their assets in ways which they believe will capture the most profit.

There may also be a case for a company adopting a strategy of increasing sales and market share at the expense of profit *for a time*. A new firm, with its typically heavy start-up expenses, will usually have to accept several years of losses before its revenue outstrips its costs. Even established companies may choose this route at a particular stage in their evolution. However, ultimately a business must generate profits or it will cease to exist. The emphasis on building market share rather than profit worked well in helping South Korean firms expand rapidly for some years, but left them dangerously exposed when the Asian crisis struck in 1997. It is not a strategy that can be pursued indefinitely.

Then again, it may be possible to boost immediate profits by raising prices. However, if customers eventually switch to other suppliers or turn to substitute products the longer-term profitability of the firm will be undermined.

In the right circumstances, it may be appropriate for a company to borrow heavily to obtain the fixed assets, working capital or acquisitions it needs to fuel expansion. Yet growing indebtedness increases risk. If the sophisticated new equipment fails to work properly, the expensively developed product proves a flop or the trumpeted new acquisition turns out to have been unwise, the burden of this debt may become insupportable.

So the reckless pursuit of profitability, incurring excessive financial risk, may wreck a company.

KEY POINTS

- Firms seek to profit – without taking 'unacceptable' risks.

- High returns are very rarely achieved unless high risks are incurred.

- An aversion to risk taking diminishes returns.

- 'Acceptable risk' depends upon the company's particular circumstances.

Accounting policies

The policies a company adopts in preparing its financial statements determines the results they record. Hence it is essential to study that section of the accounts which sets them out. In a number of instances accounting standards allow management to choose between different ways of treating various items. For example, spending on R&D should normally recorded as an expense, but it can alternatively be deferred 'to the extent that its recovery can reasonably regarded as assured'. This capitalization of R&D expenditure increases apparent profitably, while management's opinion of what is 'assured' will tend to be on the sanguine side. Similarly a company is at liberty to change its financial year-end if it decides this is appropriate (most companies choose 31 March or 31 December, but they can select any date within the year).

Changes in accounting policies, year-ends or the length of periods over which fixed assets are depreciated should be noted. There may be good reasons for altering them such as aligning different year-ends when two companies merge or one is acquired. Yet they have been used as creative accounting devices, so analysts must be on the alert for them and ask if the case made for changes by management is convincing.

Ratio analysis

The numbers reported in financial statements are difficult to handle in their raw state. For example take:

$$5\ 917\ 486 \text{ divided by } 2\ 958\ 743$$

It is obvious that the first number is much larger and, if rounded up, is roughly 6 million divided by 3 million and thus approximately twice as big. It is only when the actual calculation is made that it is shown to be *exactly* twice as big. It can be expressed in *ratio* form as:

$$2{:}1$$

Ratios enable the unwieldy large numbers given in company accounts to be condensed into concise, easily understood ones and facilitate comparisons between firms.

There are four types of ratio:

1) *Financial ratios* – these measure the financial strength and health of a firm by assessing how well placed it is to meet its short-term liabilities, service its borrowing by meeting interest payments and maintain the current level of dividends paid to shareholders, and the extent of its indebtedness.
2) *Profitability ratios* – are used to quantify the returns being generated by a business in terms of resources such as the capital it employs, the investment made in it by the shareholders and the assets it owns. They also measure the amount of sales and profit achieved per employee, the speed at which stock is turned over and the efficiency with which a company handles collecting debts owed to it or the promptness with which it pays its bills.
3) *Investment ratios* – like the price earnings ratio or dividend yield relate to a company's stock market performance and thus only available for publicly traded firms.
4) *Management ratios* – provide data on the extent to which a firm's plant, vehicle fleet and other types of fixed asset are being utilized. Is a large portion of these fixed assets lying idle or under-employed or is the business operating near to capacity? While the other groups of ratios can be calculated using the published accounts and stock market data, management ratios are derived from a company's internal records for presentation at monthly board meetings. External analysts are thus unable to use them unless other companies agree to their disclosure.

In some industries it is common practice for certain management ratios to be disclosed in the annual report, for example, retailers commonly give figures for sales per square foot/metre in their stores, while transport concerns quote the number of passengers carried or passenger miles/kilometres travelled. Furthermore, consulting firms or academic bodies can sometimes persuade the players in a sector to provide them with these data. They may be willing to do this so long as it is merely aggregated for the sector, the information relating to individual companies kept confidential and, in return, some of this sectoral data is relayed back to them. It should be emphasized that there is *no legal obligation* on any of the industry participants to reveal those ratios to outsiders.

Two general points should be made with regard to using ratios:

- Some quoted companies helpfully calculate ratios and include them in their annual report. However, the prudent analyst will perform these calculations independently rather than rely on the company's own ratios. Definitions of ratios and methods of calculating them can vary and firms will naturally be more inclined to adopt those that flatter their results.
- The study of ratios over a period of five years provides more insight as to how a business is evolving than simply comparing last year with the previous one (one-off, exceptional factors may distort the results) or assessing it solely against its industry peers in a single year.

Financial and performance ratios

Financial analysts have developed a battery of numerous ratios that can be calculated from accounts. The DuPont chemical company did much to advance the understanding and use of ratios and developed a framework which traces the logical links between the different financial components of a business. In the DuPont Pyramid a family tree of ratios is used to explain the final return generated by a company. Because of the nature of this book and the constraints of space I shall not attempt to deal with more than a selection of the most crucial. Ciaran Walsh's *Key Management Ratios* (see page 139) offers a far more detailed treatment. Indeed, there can be occasions where the analyst is confused rather than enlightened by trying to handle a multitude of ratios. Calculating those shown below should provide considerable insight into the financial status and performance of a business and supply a sound platform to launch further probing.

LIQUIDITY RATIOS

As was observed earlier, many companies fail because they cannot meet their short-term financial commitments even though they are inherently profitable. Liquidity ratios provide a measure of how well placed a company is to meet its near-term obligations. Two principal yardsticks are employed: the *current ratio* and the stricter *quick ratio*. All ratios shown are rounded.

Current ratio

The current ratio for Company A is calculated using information taken from its balance sheet shown in Table 5.

Table 5   Balance sheet as at 31 March 2005

Fixed assets	2 587 724
Stocks	2 640 269
Debtors	4 930 187
Cash in hand at bank	4 532
Total current assets	7 574 988
Current liabilities	3 704 237
Net current assets	3 870 751
Long-term liabilities	872 435
Shareholders' funds	5 586 040

The formula for calculating the current ratio is:

$$\frac{\text{Current assets}}{\text{Current liabilities}}$$

For 2005 the balance sheet shows current assets total £7 574 988.

Current liabilities (described as 'Creditors: Amounts falling due within one year') incurred by Company A are £3 704 237

$$\frac{7\,574\,988}{3\,704\,237} = 2.0$$

Thus if Company A had to settle all its short-term liabilities immediately, current assets of around twice this amount are available to meet them. This is very satisfactory from the viewpoint of financial stability (although from the other angle there may be concern that profitability is suffering because excessive current assets, yielding very low returns, are being maintained).

The current ratio was once called the '2:1 ratio' because it was regarded as prudent to have current assets worth at least twice current liabilities. Nowadays it is recognized that profitability will be reduced if unnecessarily high levels of current assets are being maintained and that often a much lower ratio can be maintained safely. Indeed, in some sectors, the normal current ratio will be very low – grocery supermarkets typically have current ratios of only around 0.2 because their stock turns over so rapidly. Nevertheless, a current ratio below about 1.3 or 1.2 is likely to prompt questions from lenders and other parties, while one below 1.0 (with certain exceptions such as the food supermarkets) is almost certain to do so.

The quick ratio

As noted earlier, current assets include *stocks* (raw materials, work in progress and finished goods waiting to be sold). Unfortunately if the crunch really does come and a firm's short-term creditors demand payment very soon, it may have problems:

- if it resells its stocks of raw materials it will very likely receive much less than it paid
- work in progress may take a long time to finish and
- it may be unable to find ready customers for its stocks of finished goods.

The company might have to rely on its cash in hand or at the bank and any money it can raise by pressing its debtors to pay up or by factoring its debts (selling them to finance houses specializing in this form of corporate finance). The conservative, prudent accounting outlook therefore leads to another ratio being calculated to assess short-term liquidity – this time excluding stocks.

Stocks in Company A's consolidated balance sheet were valued at £2 640 269, so this is deducted from total current assets.

$$\begin{array}{r} £7\ 574\ 988 \\ (2\ 640\ 269) \\ =\quad £4\ 934\ 719 \end{array}$$

The quick ratio, the so-called acid test (a term derived from the use of acid in metallurgy to confirm the presence of gold), can now be calculated. The formula for this is:

$$\frac{\text{Current assets } - \text{ stocks}}{\text{Current liabilities}}$$

$$\frac{4\ 934\ 719}{3\ 704\ 237} = 1.3$$

The quick ratio was once called the '1:1 ratio' and a company with a ratio of less than 1 regarded as probably risky. As with the current ratio, there has been a growing willingness to accept lower quick ratios, although only very marginally below the traditional benchmark. Quick ratios under 0.8 in most sectors will prompt further questions.

Company A passes the second test with flying colours. If anything, it is perhaps being too prudent.

A very different situation is revealed by the balance sheet of Company B, a design consultancy, in Table 6. The current ratio position has improved fractionally, but is very weak, being below benchmark even for the quick ratio. The latter is barely half of the benchmark 1.0 in 2003 and worsened significantly in 2004. Shareholders, employees, creditors and customers should regard these figures with grave concern.

Table 6   Company B balance sheet as at 31 March

	2004	2003
Current assets	£388 872	£673 513
Stock	£130 815	£454 690
Current liabilities	£440 398	£722 881
Current ratio	0.9	0.9
Quick ratio	0.6	0.3

The working capital to sales ratio

Both the current and quick ratios are derived solely from the balance sheet. A less commonly used, but useful check on trends in short-term financial stability is explore the adequacy of working capital to support sales levels. The formula is:

$$\frac{\text{Net current assets}}{\text{Turnover}}$$

A decline in this ratio may indicate (even when the other two liquidity ratios remain stable) that a firm is 'overtrading', with insufficient working capital in relation to turnover. This arises either because it lacked adequate funding to start with or its sales have expanded far more rapidly than it increased working capital. Overtrading clearly endangers the survival of the business. Yet a fall in the ratio can also be a good sign and indicate that the firm is gaining in efficiency through improved management of inventories, more prompt payment by its debtors or reducing excessive levels of low-yielding cash holdings. Other evidence must be taken into account in arriving at a correct assessment as to which case it represents.

KEY POINTS

- Without adequate liquidity, insolvency looms.
- The current ratio compares short-term assets to the short-term liabilities they must meet.
- A sterner test is provided by the quick ratio – excluding stocks from current assets – and is the more important measure of liquidity, hence the 'acid test' of a company's short-term financial position.
- Examining the working capital to sales ratio can through further light on its financial health.

Interest cover and dividend cover

Another approach in assessing the financial strength of a company is to examine its longer-term ability to:

- meet the cost of servicing its debts
- maintain its current level of dividend payments out of its operating income.

If too large a slice of operating profit is swallowed by interest charges the business may be in a parlous financial state. Should trading conditions worsen in the coming year and operating income shrink this burden of debt may become far more onerous.

As always, the stress is on *may*. A high level of short-term debt will produce a substantial interest charge in the P&L. However, if the balance sheet reveals that the great bulk of this debt has been repaid and thus next year's interest charge will be far lower, a more relaxed view can be taken. Another, though less appealing, possibility is that the company has substantial assets and will be able to service and repay debt by selling off properties, intangible assets or subsidiaries.

Table 7 shows Company C's profit and loss account.

Table 7 Company C profit and loss account 2004–05

Turnover	**13 587 524**
Costs of sales	(11 317 511)
Gross profit	2 270 013
Administrative and distribution costs	(918 796)
Operating profit	**1 351 217**
Interest payable	(238 113)
Operating profit after interest	1 113 104
Profit on sale of subdiary	225 337
Pre-tax profit	**1 338 441**
Taxation charge	(405 742)
Earnings attributable to ordinary shareholders	**932 699**
Dividends	(241 211)
Retained profit	691 488

INTEREST COVER

The formula for interest cover is:

$$\frac{\text{Operating profit}}{\text{Interest paid}}$$

$$\frac{\text{Operating profit}}{\text{Interest paid}} = \frac{£1\,351\,217}{£238\,113} = 5.7$$

Interest cover of five times or more operating profit is usually regarded as indicating a prudent level of debt in relation to the revenue earned from operations. Cover of less than three times operating income would be considered insufficient.

DIVIDEND COVER

While a company borrowing money is obliged to pay the interest owed on its loans, the payment of dividends are, in effect, at the discretion of the board. Hence adequate dividend cover is less important in terms of a firm's short-term survival in business than having sufficient interest cover. Having said that, investors in listed companies are dismayed when firms they have invested in reduce the dividend. As was seen earlier, income-seeking investors value reliability in dividend payouts – they would prefer to receive an steady (though, ideally gradually rising) level of dividend declared over a period than to receive an extra large distribution one year followed by a reduction next year.

The formula for dividend cover is:

$$\frac{\text{Operating profit}}{\text{Dividends paid}}$$

$$\frac{\text{Operating profit}}{\text{Dividends paid}} = \frac{£1\,351\,217}{£241\,211} = 5.6$$

London listed companies presently have an average dividend cover of around 2, but the appropriate level of cover depends upon individual company circumstances. Companies in mature industries will pay high dividends. Fast-growing firms will pay out little or nothing, instead reinvesting the bulk of profit with the aim of gaining scale even more quickly. Company C has ample cover for its present level of dividend payments.

DEBT TO EQUITY RATIO: WHICH GEAR IS THE COMPANY DRIVING IN?

It has already been observed that companies are financed by a mixture of internal funding in the form of shareholders' funds (issued share capital contributed by shareholders and the reserves owned by them) and external funding in the form of loans. The balance between internal and outside financing is expressed by the *debt to equity ratio*.

The trade-off between financial security and profitability comes into play again here. If a company does not borrow at all or borrows very little in terms of its total capital – a low debt to equity ratio or *low gearing* – it is safer, but may be losing out on opportunities to be more profitable. If it borrows heavily – is *highly geared* – it can expand more rapidly, but it carries greater risk. The American term for gearing is *leverage*, hence a highly leveraged US company is like a highly geared British one in terms of the proportion of its funding derived from borrowing.

Taking the case of a newly incorporated company with £40 000 in the bank, where does its finance come from?

- Case A. £30 000 is provided by the shareholders, £10 000 from a bank loan. Seventy-five per cent of the company's funding comes from internal sources and gearing is obviously low.

- Case B. Only £10 000 is put up by the owner, £30 000 is contributed as loans from friends and relatives. Seventy-five per cent of the business's funding comes from external sources, those friends and relatives are taking on three times more of the risk of the business than the owner should it fail. Gearing here is clearly high.

Unfortunately, while the concept of gearing is straightforward enough, actually quantifying it is fraught with difficulties. These arise because:

- 'debt' is defined in various ways
- there are different formulae for performing the calculation.

Definition 1. Some people define a company's debts as its current and long-term liabilities (shareholders' funds are excluded because they belong to the firm's owners). As this includes all the liabilities of the business, apart from shareholders' funds, it is the broadest definition of debt.

Definition 2. Current liabilities bundle together a number of categories of sums owed (for example, overdrafts from banks, tax and national insurance payments due or goods and services obtained on credit from suppliers). A narrower definition of 'debt' is to ignore any groups of current liabilities where interest is not charged. So a bank overdraft is counted as debt, while an invoice from a supplier is not. In reality companies can be charged interest on the overdue payment of taxes or (under 'prompt payment' legislation) late settlement of supplier invoices. However, to simplify analysis, it is conventionally assumed that these types of liability will be settled by the due date, hence avoiding interest charges.

The bank overdrafts and loans, included under 'current liabilities', can be added to the 'long-term liabilities', which will include bank lending, the issue of bonds and the like, to arrive at a figure for total debt. A further complication arises in that there are some current liabilities – owed to parties other than banks – which are also classed as debts.

As noted previously, companies often lease some of their fixed assets rather than own them outright. Under an *operating lease* they merely hire the asset with no intention of keeping it. However, a *finance lease*, where they intend to retain the asset or least keep it for most of its useful life, is treated as the equivalent of borrowing money to buy the asset – even though the leasor retains formal legal ownership of it – and is thus regarded as a form of debt. Hire-purchase agreements are likewise classed as debt. The cash held by a company is deducted from the total of short- and long-term debt to arrive at *net debt*.

Net debt is the most commonly used definition and the one favoured by bankers. In terms of priority for repayment debts owed to a bank typically rank ahead of claims by suppliers. The 'banker's definition' thus ignores these subordinated claims against a borrower's assets when considering its level of debt.

Definition 3. An even more restrictive definition ignores current liabilities and includes only long-term debt.

As well as three definitions of debt, there are also three formulae for performing the calculating of gearing:

Formula 1: *Debt divided by shareholders' funds.* The most widely used method.
Formula 2: *Shareholders' funds divided by total liabilities.*
Formula 3: *Debt divided by total assets.*

I prefer to use the widest definition of debt (because a company is obliged to pay *all* its liabilities, not just its bank loans and quasi loans like finance leases. Furthermore, the balance sheet contains all the data needed, while the notes to the accounts are required if one uses the banker's definition). I also find that the third formula gives perhaps the clearest picture of how a company is financed. However, which one is used for calculating gearing is not really important, it is rather like having to travel the same distance whether it is measured in miles or kilometres. In this example I will use Formula 1 as it is the one generally used and also illustrates the calculation of net debt.

What is vitally important, though, is to be consistent in applying a definition and formula. Very misleading results will be obtained if data on gearing are assembled from several different sources and these vary in their definition of debt or use different formulae for performing the calculation. So we need to ascertain both the definition and formula which lie behind figures being quoted for leverage before using them.

Here is Company D's gearing (Table 8), using the banker's definition and Formula 1. Data on short-term debt are taken from the notes to the accounts, the rest of the figures come from the face of the balance sheet. The formula will be:

$$\frac{\text{Long term debt (balance sheet)} + \text{short term debt (notes)} - \text{cash}}{\text{Shareholders' funds}} \times 100$$

Table 8 Calculation of net debt

Short-term debt	
Loans	£1 000 000
Bank overdrafts (secured)	£12 093
Obligations under hire purchase contracts	£181 869
Total short-term debt	**£1 193 962**
We add long-term debt	£296 890
Total debt	**£1 490 852**
Then subtract cash in hand and at bank	(£4532)
Net debt	**£1 486 320**

Net debt = long-term debt £296 890 + short-term debt £1 193 962 – cash (£4532).

This is then divided by shareholders' funds

$$\frac{£1\,486\,120}{£6\,161\,585} \times 100 = 24.1\%$$

Company D is comfortably lowly geared.

Gearing (using the banker's definition) up to about 50 per cent of shareholders' funds is typically about as high as lenders will accept before they become concerned about the safety of the money they have lent. There are many exceptions to this (property companies, for instance) and the appropriate level of gearing depends upon a company's individual circumstances. Gearing in excess of 100 per cent will often be frowned on (the lender is taking on more risk than the owners of the business), although it can be justified if the company has exceptionally good prospects of rapid growth.

Where a high level of gearing is extremely dangerous is in a people-based business such as an advertising agency, public relations firm or consultancy. An advertising firm's key assets are its creatives (the people who think up and develop advertising campaigns) – and they can simply walk out the door. When the Saatchi brothers were ousted from the company bearing their name by shareholders in 1995, many of the former Saatchi and Saatchi creatives also resigned. The renamed Cordiant was badly hit by these defections and, if had been highly geared, its survival would have been in question.

In contrast, here are the gearing levels for Company B (*a design consultancy*):

	2004	2003
Gearing	177%	74%

This company was late in filing its accounts for 2004 and soon after submitting them to Companies House had to cease trading because it was insolvent (unable to pay its debts in full on time).

KEY POINTS

- Interest and dividend cover are useful measures of a company's longer-term financial strength.

- The level of gearing is crucial. The higher it goes the harder the potential fall if the going gets tough.

- Acceptable leverage varies according to sector and the individual company's prospects.

Profit margins

The analytical focus here switches away from estimating how financially sound a company is to discovering how efficient it has been in generating returns from its operations. To make a profit the business must receive more revenue than it pays out in expenses.

A first step is to consider its profit margins, starting with the gross margin achieved. The formula for this is:

GROSS PROFIT MARGIN

$$\frac{\text{Gross profit}}{\text{Turnover}} \times 100$$

$$\frac{\text{Gross profit}}{\text{Turnover}} = \frac{£2\ 270\ 013}{£13\ 587\ 524} \times 100 = 16.7\%$$

A firm obviously has to earn a positive gross margin to have any chance of yielding a final profit. More attention, however, is paid to its operating margin. This has to absorb the overheads as well as the direct cost of sales and shows the profit generated from its trading activities, hence it is sometimes called the *trading margin*.

Individual companies will have significant differences in their financial structures, with some carrying a lot of debt, others relatively little and even some being completely free of debt. A heavily indebted business may deliver lower profits, once interest payments are taken into account, than one with modest debts, even though the former is earning much better margins on its operations. Comparing operating profit margins is thus a purer benchmark of corporate performance as it focuses upon trading efficiency and ignores how a company finances itself.

OPERATING PROFIT MARGIN

$$\frac{\text{Operating profit}}{\text{Turnover}} \times 100$$

$$\frac{\text{Operating profit}}{\text{Turnover}} = \frac{£1\ 351\ 217}{£13\ 587\ 524} \times 100 = 9.9\%$$

Despite what was said above, the *actual* return to shareholders is nonetheless reduced when interest is paid, so another important measure of profit is that achieved after the interest charges are taken into account. The company may also receive income in addition to that gained from its trading activities from other sources such as dividends received on shares it owns or the disposal of subsidiaries or fixed assets. The pre-tax profit margin (which is also the post-interest profit margin) incorporates both interest paid and any income obtained other than from the firm's trading operations.

Why place the spotlight on the *pre-tax* profit margin when the potential profit available for distribution to shareholders as dividends will be *post-tax*? The answer lies in the limited scope available for companies to control their tax charge. Some companies, especially those with extensive operations overseas, may be able to mitigate their tax payments to an extent, but the corporate sector's tax burden is largely in the hands of the Chancellor of the Exchequer (who sets the rates of Corporation Tax and the rules applying to company taxation) and the Inland Revenue who administer the tax regime. Thus the tax charge (unless it is unusually high or low) is generally ignored when considering a company's performance.

PRE-TAX PROFIT MARGIN

$$\frac{\text{Profit before tax}}{\text{Turnover}} \times 100$$

Including the one-off profit on the sale of the subsidiary

$$\frac{1\,338\,441}{13\,587\,524} \times 100 = 9.9\%$$

Excluding it reduces it

$$\frac{1\,113\,104}{13\,587\,524} \times 100 = 8.2\%$$

KEY POINTS

- There are several types of 'profit' and hence several profit margins.
- Operating margin is the main focus of attention.
- Large absolute increases in profits may conceal margin erosion.

Returns on investment

Data on profit margins enable an observer to see how well a company has succeeded in generating revenue and controlling costs. Another approach is to examine its performance in terms of the returns it produces on the investment made in the firm. A standard measure of this is the return made on the capital employed in the business. Most analysts define *return* as the operating profit, though some favour including any profits accruing to the business such as income from investments. In the latter case before profit and tax, rather than operating profit, is taken to represent the return.

Capital employed is defined as the combined fixed assets and working capital used by a firm, that is, fixed assets plus current assets minus current liabilities. An alternative approach (already referred to), yielding the same result, is to ask where the capital employed comes from, rather than on which category of asset it is being deployed. This adds together the equity component of the company's capital (that is, shareholders' funds) and the long-term debt element (creditors amount due after one year).

RETURN ON CAPITAL EMPLOYED (ROCE)

Capital employed = fixed assets plus current assets minus current liabilities

or

= shareholders' funds plus long-term credit

$$\frac{\text{Operating profit}}{\text{Capital employed}} = \frac{£1\,351\,217}{£6\,458\,475} \times 100 = 20.9\%$$

Alternatively, if profit obtained other than from the company's operations is included, total profit before tax becomes the numerator.

$$\frac{\text{Profit before tax}}{\text{Capital employed}} = \frac{£1\,338\,441}{£6\,458\,475} \times 100 = 20.7\%$$

While typical ROCEs will vary between sectors, the fundamental criterion to obtain as much of a premium over the return on a risk-free investment as possible. Although no investment is absolutely risk free there are some places to place one's money that are extremely safe. In Britain it is very unlikely that any of the clearing banks or major building societies will fail, so there is no need for anxiety over funds entrusted to them. Neither is the British Government likely to default on its obligation to repay those who have lent it money by buying government bonds (called gilt-edged securities or *gilts*).

Hence a widely used proxy for a short-term risk-free investment would be gilts due to be repaid in between three and five years, currently yielding a return of about five per cent. (The risk-free rate of return used by corporate financiers is normally based on medium-term ten-year bonds, but a shorter time horizon is appropriate when looking at ROCEs). A ROCE that fails to beat this five per cent comfortably is clearly unsatisfactory as the risk of a company failing is much higher than HM Government defaulting on its bonds. No rational investor would invest in a company, thus bearing the higher risk involved, without a superior expected return to compensate for the greater risk.

ROCE shows the return yielded on assets financed by both shareholders and lenders. Shareholders are naturally more interested in the return generated by their investment rather than the broader ROCE. Hence the return achieved on the shareholders' financial interest in the business is of crucial importance to them. This return is encapsulated in the return on equity (ROE) ratio. Here, for once, most analysts use the bottom line figure, profit after interest and tax (that is, earnings attributable to ordinary shareholders) rather than operating profit. This is because the interest and tax charge will imposed before any reckoning of a potential profit attributable to them is made. I concur with this approach, but it should be noted that some analysts prefer to use operating profit as the numerator in the calculation of ROE.

RETURN ON EQUITY (ROE)

$$\frac{\text{Profit after interest and tax}}{\text{Shareholders' funds}} \times 100$$

$$\frac{\text{Profit after interest and tax}}{\text{Shareholders' funds}} = \frac{£932\,699}{£6\,161\,585} \times 100 = 15.1\%$$

However, this includes a one-off profit on sale of property of £225 337. Excluding this the figures are:

$$\frac{\text{Profit after interest and tax}}{\text{Shareholders' funds}} = \frac{£707\,362}{£6\,161\,585} \times 100 = 11.5\%$$

A third popular way of assessing return adopts the broadest canvas, taking the return on all the assets of the firm as its yardstick. Management's ability to obtain a good return on the totality of its assets underpins the gains to shareholders expressed in the return on equity. It is very difficult to achieve satisfactory returns on investment without the underlying support of a good return on total assets.

RETURN ON TOTAL ASSETS (ROTA)

$$\frac{\text{Operating profit}}{\text{Total assets}} = \frac{£1\,351\,217}{£10\,162\,712} \times 100 = 13.3\%$$

KEY POINTS

- Profitability ratios are a crucial test of management's ability to extract the maximum return from the assets being used.

- Returns from investing in a company should be well above those available from a risk-free investment.

Conclusions

- A reasonable understanding of the structure and contents of company accounts and how to interpret them is an essential skill for CI analysts.
- They should watch out for changes in the basis upon which accounts are prepared such as revised accounting policies.
- Too much weight should not be placed upon one or two ratios or numerical indicators, but the accounts should be viewed as a whole from several different angles.
- Despite their vital importance – hence two whole chapters being devoted to them – financial data can only be properly understood in a wider context. Qualitative information concerning the company and its business environment must also be given its due emphasis for this to be achieved.

18 *Interpreting the Non-financial Sections of Company Accounts*

Apart from the core financial statements, a set of accounts contains other documents of considerable analytical interest. So this chapter is devoted to examining what additional enlightenment these provide. It considers the:

- auditors' report
- directors' report
- chairman's statement
- chief executive's review
- divisional reviews
- finance director's review
- corporate governance reports
- list of subsidiaries and associated companies
- mission statement
- environmental report

and demonstrates how analysts can 'read between the lines' of corporate statements in forming their judgements.

Over a lengthy period dissatisfaction with existing standards of company reporting, combined with periodic rashes of corporate scandal, has forced greater disclosure in both the extent of coverage and the level of detail. The process typically begins with some companies doing this voluntarily. Pressure then mounts on others to follow their example and eventually it is made compulsory through legislation or accounting standards. Thus the Operating and Financial Review (discussed on page 91) was originally an innovative device for leading companies to communicate their performance and prospects in a more meaningful way. Yet its adoption beyond the top listed FTSE 100 firms remained patchy and this led the government, in the wake of the latest wave of financial collapses, to make OFRs compulsory for all quoted companies.

At the time of writing, much remains unclear as to the rules that will be framed for OFRs (and the requirement to file 'enhanced' directors' reports among non-quoted companies, for which no date has yet been set) never mind how they will work in practice. Analysts must also work with company reports from periods before they became mandatory. So this chapter deals with non-financial contents of reports currently being filed.

Auditors' report

A poll conducted among accountants some years ago awarded the auditors' report the wooden spoon for being the most useless item included in a company's annual report and accounts. In the vast majority of cases this 'report' is merely a boilerplate series of sentences stating that the auditors believe the financial statements show a 'true and fair view' of the state of affairs of the company and similar platitudes. If the auditors recite this standardized litany of approval, then the report is described as a 'clean' one.

Where an auditors' report gets very interesting is when there is a departure from the usual formula. This is always a bad sign.

The report can be 'qualified' for two reasons:

- The scope of audit is limited in some way. If, for example, part of the company's turnover consisted of cash sales and an adequate system for recording those transactions was not in place.
- Where the auditors and the company's directors cannot agree how a transaction should be treated, for instance the directors insist that a sum due from a company that has ceased trading is likely to be paid and therefore include it as an asset under 'debtors' in the balance sheet. The auditors, noting that there is no security pledged for this debt, disagree and believe that a provision should be made for it under the heading 'doubtful debts'. The latter course would result in a charge in respect of the doubtful debt being subtracted from reported profits and a reduction in the total figure for 'debtors' shown in the balance sheet.

A *qualification* relates to specific items in the financial statements – apart from these the rest of the accounts are given the auditors' stamp of approval. In more serious cases the auditors will have to either condemn the accounts *as a whole* or refuse to express an opinion on them.

An *adverse opinion* is recorded when the auditors believe that the financial statements do not give a true and fair view. This would arise, for example, if the directors insisted on ignoring accounting standards, the application of which the auditors consider would give the correct picture.

In other cases the auditors may have to issue a *disclaimer*. This would be recorded where the quality of the evidence available to them (the company's accounting records and other material) was so unsatisfactory that they were unable to form an opinion as to whether the accounts presented a true and fair view.

Finally, the auditors should flag up instances of *fundamental uncertainty* in even a clean set of accounts. These will have already been revealed in the financial statements, but the auditors' report should ensure they are brought to the attention of the reader. Here is an example:

Going Concern
In forming our opinion, we have considered the adequacy of the disclosures made in Note 1 of the Financial Statements concerning the uncertainty as to the continued financial support of the Company's creditors. In view of the significance of the uncertainty we consider that it should be drawn to your attention, but our opinion is not qualified in this respect.

Unless it is intended to wind a company up, accounts are prepared on the basis that it will continue to operate into the foreseeable future. The directors of this company are satisfied that it has adequate resources to carry on as a going concern. The auditors have approved the accounts. However, they feel that the degree of uncertainty as to its financial future is so great that it must be referred to in their report.

Translated into blunt English their message is: 'This company is on the edge financially and its continued existence depends upon the willingness of its bankers to extend it a line of credit.'

LIMITED VALUE OF AN AUDIT REPORT

It has already been seen how even a clean audit report can still be worrying. A more fundamental difficulty lies in the limited value of audit procedures in general. The huge corporate collapses in the US and Italy after the turn of the millennium (and in Britain during the late 1980s and early 1990s) when investors and creditors looked on with dismay as major companies – all of them having received their auditors' clean bill of health – collapsed, should convince anyone that an unqualified report is not some kind of guarantee that the financial statements can be relied upon.

KEY POINTS

- A clean audit report does not guarantee the accuracy of accounts.

- Any kind of deviation from the usual formula is interesting – even when it is not a qualification of the accounts in a technical sense.

- Always at least *glance* at the auditors' report to ensure there are no such deviations – surveys by Company Reporting show that four out of the top 400 listed companies in their sample had some form of auditor qualification attached to them in a typical year.

Directors' report

All limited liability companies, except those private ones able to claim the small company exemption from disclosure, are obliged to file a directors' report. It would reasonably be thought that this statement by the board of directors on the company's performance during its last accounting year would be the most interesting of the bundle of documents comprising the annual report and accounts. Unfortunately, the directors' report has decided limitations in terms of what it reveals.

First, its review of the results achieved merely replicates financial information given in richer detail in the accounts (or refers the reader to them) accompanied by an often banal comment that 'the directors consider the results for the year and the financial position of the company to be satisfactory'. Second, for quoted companies, management's assessment of performance is to be found instead in the chairman's statement (and chief executive and finance director's reviews if they have supplied these). Finally, the directors' report is not viewed by the board as an opportunity to explain the financial results, but as a rather tedious chore of complying with the filing requirements set down in company law and (if listed) the additional demands of the Listing Rules.

Despite all this, the directors' report should not be ignored as it does contain some useful information.

COMPANY ACTIVITIES

For a start the directors' report is the document which states what the company actually does. The Memorandum of Association traditionally outlined the 'objects' of the company, that is, what its purpose was and this objects clause set limits upon the activities that could be lawfully undertaken. Thus a retailer was debarred from providing financial services unless its Memorandum was amended to include this among its objects. Companies wishing to retain the maximum scope for operation responded by drafting lengthy objects clauses allowing them to engage in any business activity they could think of. An alternative later permitted was to pen an objects clause so vague and all-inclusive as to be meaningless, making it unnecessary to update the Articles before entering a new area of business. Although over time the restrictions of this 'ultra vires rule' withered away, its legacy has been to make the Articles an often unrewarding source for finding out what line of business a company is engaged in.

Consequently, the section on principal activities in the directors' report is where management defines what the company does. It is worth emphasizing that this is self-definition and that the quality of disclosure will vary between companies, with quoted companies describing their activities in other parts of their glossy annual reports. Consulting the directors' report may nevertheless reveal additional information as to activities that would be missed using just the description given at the start of the glossy version.

Those studying a company need to remember that players competing in the same area of business may describe themselves in very different ways. A cross-check on the principal activities as recorded in the directors' report is offered by the annual return (see page 86) where the company has to assign one or more SIC codes and this may assist in clarifying vague statements as to activities. Again, though, it has already been admitted that these codes are of modest precision and have to be treated as indicative rather than definite.

DIRECTORS

The names of the directors and their interests in the company (that is, how many of its shares they each own) have to be disclosed in their report. This should be cross-checked with the annual return and other Companies House filings (see page 93–94). It is unlikely that these will not tally (although possibly very interesting if they do not!), the reason for doing this is to pick up variations in the way they are named. It can be helpful to know that the 'H.T. Zog' recorded in the list of directors in their report is more fully named as 'Hieronymous Theophrastus Zog'.

Directors having bought or sold significant numbers of shares is something that merits further investigation.

Listed firms will provide additional personal details of their directors (such as directorships they hold in other companies) in a page devoted to them in the glossy annual report. Much more information as to what each receives from the company in terms of pay, bonuses, contributions to pensions and share options will be revealed in the Remuneration Committee report (see page 180).

SIGNIFICANT SHAREHOLDERS

Public limited companies have to list all shareholders owning more than three per cent of their total voting share capital and this conveniently available information is of self-evident analytical interest.

SHARE BUY-BACKS

If a company has bought back and cancelled any of its shares during the accounting year, details must be given in the directors' report. However, more copious information on this will have been given in the circulars to shareholders relating to the buy-back.

POST-BALANCE SHEET EVENTS

If an event considered important occurred between the end of the accounting year and the subsequent approval of the accounts by the board of directors this should be reported. The relevant accounting standard defines these as:

- *Adjusting events* – a later change in pre-existing features of the company which means the reader of the accounts should revise them in the light of the new occurrence (such as a downward revaluation of a building owned by the company which is now found to be suffering subsidence).
- *Non-adjusting events* – new occurrences such as major acquisitions or disposals of subsidiaries agreed after the accounting year ended.

CHARITABLE OR POLITICAL DONATIONS

These should be disclosed if they exceed £200 in the course of the accounting year (the Government intends to raise this to £2000). Some companies (for example, The Body Shop, Ben & Jerry's ice cream business) use charitable giving as a key element in their marketing strategies, so a high level of donation will be of interest. Contributions to political parties or organizations pursuing political ends must also be revealed.

CLOSE COMPANY STATUS

A close company is one controlled by its directors or by five or fewer shareholders. The concept was originally developed by the authorities to prevent the avoidance of personal taxation by families or small groups of business associates and special rules apply to close companies on topics such as loans made such firms to the individuals controlling them. Listed companies must state if they are close companies. Those with a free float (shares in the hands of the public) of over 35 per cent are exempt from making this statement.

The culture of a close company, dominated by a family or a tight-knit set of individuals, is likely to be considerably different to that of a firm where voting power is dispersed over a wider body of shareholders.

EMPLOYEE RECRUITMENT AND CONSULTATION

Once again this tends to be dealt with by serving up platitudes and banalities. No company is going to admit that they practise unfair discrimination in hiring or promoting or that its employees are there to do what they are told and are not canvassed for their views.

A general principle here would to be to regard a longer and more detailed statement as an indicator that the company does take its obligations to treat employees fairly in terms of recruitment, promotion, development and consultation more seriously.

CREDITOR PAYMENT POLICY

Many large, powerful companies used to abuse their suppliers, forcing them to wait unreasonably long times before being paid. Complaints about this led to public companies and their subsidiaries classed as 'large' private companies (see page 88) having to state their policy towards the payment of creditors. This statement again tends to be bland – companies are not going to admit that they are helping their own cash flow at the expense of long-suffering suppliers.

The average number of days the firm takes to pay its creditors will usually be given as at the balance sheet date. More useful from the analytical perspective is when the average waiting period over the accounting year is revealed.

KEY POINTS

- Directors' reports have a limited research value as they repeat a lot of information found elsewhere in the annual report and are written in stilted language to meet legal requirements.

- While a dull read they should still be studied.

- Descriptions of what the company does and its significant shareholders are certainly worth noting.

Chairman's statement

Given the deficiencies of the directors' report as a vehicle for communicating with shareholders, chairmen started to supplement the annual report with a letter unconstrained by the need to comply with the recitation of details required by the Companies Act. This chairman's statement or review, although not demanded by law, eventually became an expected part of the accounts sent each year by listed companies to their shareholders.

A firm's financial statements, auditors' and directors' reports are almost exclusively collections of facts (albeit, as we have seen, containing a subjective element in the decisions taken on how to treat its transactions when preparing the accounts). The chairman's report, in contrast, is largely *qualitative* in character. The other documents report what happened, this one offers an *explanation* of the company's results.

Another reason that the chairman's review is so important is that at least part of it is *forward-looking*. The accounts and other statutory reports present *historic* information on how the company fared in the previous accounting period, while the chairman will comment on its future prospects and plans.

A typical statement will discuss the general economic climate and specific trading conditions in the sector the company operates in before going on to outline how its management responded to these. It will also refer to significant corporate events in the period such as major new ventures, disposals of subsidiaries or changes in the membership of the board of directors. The chairman concludes by offering an assessment of the current and future trading environment and perhaps saying something about the strategic posture management are adopting to meet this.

One of the roles of a chairman is to maintain the morale of shareholders, so one cannot expect a statement shot through with doom and gloom. Adverse factors will be passed over lightly and positive ones highlighted. There will be an inevitable and understandable bias towards optimism and this is something the person reading the review must mentally compensate for when appraising a company. Having said that, a hard-headed, realistic analysis and purposeful future programme from the chairman of a firm which has gone through a bad patch is reassuring. An honest admission of problems or mistakes, coupled with a plausible course of action for putting things right, is impressive. This approach is the business version of Winston Churchill's 'I have nothing to offer you but blood, toil, tears and sweat' speech in the darkest days of the Second World War, combining frankness as to the gravity of the current situation with unwavering confidence in eventual victory. A chairman's statement that ignores or trivializes difficulties should arouse suspicion, as must one offering a limitless, untroubled, golden future. Shrewd investors know that 'if it's too good to be true, it probably isn't true' and analysts should apply similar caution when reading this document. Another warning sign is where the statement is lengthy, but actually provides little additional information. As Zweig and Chamberlain observed: 'the chairman's verbosity increases in direct proportion to the severity of the company's problems'.[1]

An analyst interpreting the chairman's review has to overcome the obstacles of its subjective and biased nature. Here the techniques of literary criticism can be of help. When something that is obviously important is never discussed in a novel or play this is taken by critics to denote its extraordinary significance. A 'great unmentionable' is something to examine more closely. So when the chairman's statement ignores or pass lightly over a major issue, the analyst's interest should be piqued.

Another useful borrowing from literary critics is to compare what a character says with what they actually do – there is often a considerable discrepancy between their statements and their actions. In the same way a chairman's words must be matched against what the company has done and achieved.

CASE OF THE UNCONVINCING TEXT

During the dot.com frenzy, one of the brightest stars of the overheated equities market was internet stockbroker Durlacher. The collapse in its share price was consequently particularly dramatic. Since then the company has tried to revive its fortunes by repositioning itself. The December 2000 interim statement by its chairman, Geoffrey Chamberlain, makes a good case study in this type of textual analysis.

In his first paragraph he states 'Re-focusing and transitioning our specialist investment banking business model'. 'Transitioning'? Not a word I had ever encountered and indeed one unknown to *Chamber's Dictionary*.[2] Now the English language does evolve and there are many instances in which a noun eventually spawns a verb form. However, a chairman's statement is not the proper forum for linguistic innovation. Turning to the review of online services, the first paragraph begins with 'During the period under review', the third paragraph has the same opening phrase, as does the first paragraph of the discussion of corporate finance, institutional sales and research, the third paragraph of which starts with 'During the period'. This lazy repetition jars on the reader.

It might be argued that company chairmen are not employed to be literary lions, so what does a poor written style matter? I would contend that good business leaders are highly conscious of the power and value of words in persuading people to accept what they are saying. The ability to influence and persuade others is a core skill for a chairman or chief executive. Poor expression is also often a symptom of feeble thinking. Here's another example from the Durlacher report. One paragraph lists

---

1   Zweig, J. and Chamberlain, J. (3 August 1997), 'Windbag theory', *Forbes*.
2   I have subsequently seen it used in an American newspaper article.

three conditions for the repositioning of the firm's corporate finance business. The third one is described as 'a mandatory pre-condition of the above [two]'. Surely the precondition should be the first item with the two conditions depending on it following, not preceding, it?!

In fact the rest of this document fails to convince a careful reader. The introduction enthuses that, 'Despite difficult market conditions, nothing-ventured and Sharecast [two of Durlacher's online services] have strengthened their UK and European rankings.' Here one is unsure what is meant by 'rankings' – ranking in terms of market share, perhaps? When we turn to the part dealing with online services we discover the improvement in ranking is in terms of the perceived quality of these. In fact the section devoted to online services is mainly an account of awards won by Durlacher's various internet offerings. As we noted at the beginning of this book, the principal goal for a business is to increase its profits through boosting sales or cutting costs. If general market conditions are adverse, then increasing sales depends on seizing market share from rivals. Winning awards is commendable and indeed may be a stepping stone on the way to growing sales, but in itself does not produce profits.

Neither does the description of the Principal Risk Department engender confidence: 'While the number of trades … was significantly lower than the corresponding period last year, our market share barely changed.' Holding on to relative market share in a shrinking market is better than losing it, but hardly a cause for rejoicing. There is also a reference to freeing 'the corporate finance team from its previously wide ranging responsibilities to our investee companies which had greatly restricted their ability to earn revenues elsewhere'. This puzzles rather than informs. Who is now looking after the investee companies? Later on we are told about a 're-organization of staff to reduce the opportunity cost of managing the portfolio', yet there is no indication that the headcount has been increased. An obvious question to management would be 'Are the investee firms being neglected while your people concentrate on seeking business elsewhere?'

Finally, it is interesting that the role of chief executive vacant, with the chairman holding both jobs until a new CEO is recruited! What happened to the former chief executive, why has this situation arisen? There is a screaming need for an explanation of this very important point. All that is offered is silence.

KEY POINTS

- The chairman's statement, liberated from the constraints applying to directors' reports, is of vital significance in trying to understand a company.

- It differs from the other documents in the report and accounts because it is qualitative, explanatory and forward-looking.

- A chairman's review will 'accentuate the positive'.

- However, read with care, much of value should be learned.

- It should stimulate the reader to ask the types of question that an alert brokers' analyst or shareholder would lob at management.

Other reports

THE CHIEF EXECUTIVE'S REPORT

Since it became the norm, in the wake of the Cadbury Report on corporate governance, to have a separate (non-executive) chairman and CEO, this document (although not obligatory) is also found in the annual report of many listed companies and offers additional material for analysis and consideration.

DIVISIONAL REVIEWS

These are again most welcome if included. Sometimes they will be included as part of the CEO's review, though it is more usual to print them separately.

Divisional reviews not only enable readers to understand better the company's different lines of business. They are also very useful if the primary focus of research is on an industry rather than individual companies. When the subsidiaries of a company are congruent with its divisional structure, such divisional data can be augmented by obtaining their accounts. However, if they are organized in a different way (perhaps by geographic area rather than activity) then this will not be possible.

THE FINANCE DIRECTOR'S REPORT

A most valuable document if included (again it is not compulsory), this review *explains* the company's finances as reported in the financial statements. An informative finance director will also outline the firm's *policies* in handling its finances. Below are some extracts from a financial review:

Is the company taking good care of the cash passing through its hands?

Surplus cash deposits are invested with a variety of financial institutions chosen after a close study of their relative credit ratings. Limits are placed on the sums that may be placed with each house. The list of approved institutions is periodically reviewed by the Board.

This is reassuring. The firm's cash is not all placed with the same bank and the list of authorized banks has to be approved at board level (not just by the financial director, treasurer or chief accountant).

'Where foreign exchange commitments are entered into, forward contracts to cover these are negotiated by our treasury department. No speculative positions are permitted.' Another comforting statement. Some firms have suffered serious damage from trying to boost profits through currency speculation.

What are the financial criteria for making acquisitions?

The board has set hurdle rates that require a return in excess of your company's cost of capital (currently nine per cent on equity funding) to be achieved by each of its operating units. Because the gains from acquisitions usually take time to be fully realized, these newly acquired businesses are generally allowed up to three years to deliver them.

Explicit details of the hurdle rates used by a firm in its internal investment appraisal are of considerable interest in assessing its strategy and performance. Estimates for an enterprise's cost of capital (that is the price it must pay to obtain either equity or loan finance) are found in a number of American and multinational company accounts, but more rarely in those of British listed companies.

CORPORATE GOVERNANCE REPORTS

Listed companies now have to state the extent of their compliance with the Combined Code on Corporate Governance. Departures from the code have to be disclosed, along with the reasons for them. The auditor is also obliged to check the accuracy of these statements.

Rather like the directors' report, the documents devoted to corporate governance have very limited informative value, consisting mainly of a series of pious formulae as to the soundness of the managerial regime. One element of potential interest is the Remuneration Committee Report detailing the salaries, bonuses, pension contributions, share options and other forms of compensation paid to individual directors. The distribution of rewards is often a good indication of the relative balance of power between board members.

LIST OF DIRECTORS

This can be included in the corporate governance section of a listed company's annual report, but is more usually given a place of its own. It will show whether a director is executive or a non-executive, which board committees they sit on, their ages, other directorships or offices held and, in many instances, their role (marketing director or research director for example) and perhaps contain a brief biography. The list enables a researcher to trace rapidly individual directors' relationships with other firms. It can also contribute to the appraisal of managerial capacity. A director holding a sheaf of non-executive, public or industry body appointments is unlikely to have the time or focus to contribute fully to the firm. On the other hand, such external relationships (if not too distracting) can be useful in raising the company's profile and (provided these are not merely sinecures for old friends) offer a wider perspective than a purely in-house team of directors.

LIST OF SUBSIDIARIES AND ASSOCIATED COMPANIES

This is either printed as a discrete item or is included as part of the notes. Only material-related enterprises have to be listed, that is those having a reasonably substantial effect on the group's results. The percentage of the parent's shareholding in the subsidiary and the jurisdiction in which the related firm is incorporated will be shown. Some will be *wholly owned subsidiaries* where the parent owns all the shares, others *subsidiaries* (parent owns the majority of shares, but not all of them) and the associated companies (where the parent has only a minority stake, yet exercises 'significant influence' over it – generally demonstrated by a holding in excess of 20 per cent).

MISSION STATEMENTS

Analysts typically read company mission statements with little enthusiasm. Faced with so many examples of the risibly absurd ('we're not in business to make money, but to make the world a better, happier place for all those little children'), the bland, vague and vacuous, this is understandable. It would be wrong, nonetheless, to ignore them. At their best they represent a firm's most profound attempt to explain and justify its purpose or purposes (and it should not be forgotten that a lot of people in business *are* genuinely idealistic). Sometimes the change of a few words in its self-definition can have major implications for its strategy.

Larry Kahaner[3] quotes the example of Trammell Crow who originally described themselves as a 'real estate services company', redefining their ambition 'to be the premier customer driven retail estate company in the United States' in their vision statement. This trivial change in wording was an alerting signal that a major realignment of the firm's strategy and operations towards becoming a far more customer-focused enterprise was planned.

ENVIRONMENTAL REPORT

Many companies now comment as the impact of their activities upon the environment. In some cases this will be limited to topics such as the consumption of natural resources and energy and recycling. For manufacturers this will also include the disposal of hazardous waste and emissions from plants into the atmosphere, water and soil. Where environmental issues loom large for a firm, such as a chemical or oil company, it often produces a specific report containing fuller discussion. Analysts study these to discover what decommissioning costs (for power stations, oil rigs and the like) will have to be met in future, the risks it bears in terms of accidents causing pollution or other damage and what internal mechanisms are in place to avert risk or minimize its consequences. They can also provide clues into a company's general business philosophy, although the statements made have to be compared to its actual record in terms of care for the environment.

---

3   Kahaner, L. (1997), *Competitive Intelligence: How to gather, analyze and use information to move your business to the top*, Simon and Schuster, 104–5.

19 *Assessing Information Quality*

Competitive analysis would be a lot easier and far more reliable if the information that served as its raw material were of a uniformly high quality. Unfortunately, the evidence analysts are compelled to use varies from highly trustworthy through to positively misleading. They thus need a data quality assessment model to apply to the material gathered before attempting to draw conclusions from it.

This chapter outlines a two-stage scheme for judging the reliability of a piece of information:

- What kind of data is an analyst dealing with? They can classify each part of their body of evidence according to a hierarchy of information trustworthiness. Such categorization helps sort solid data from the less well founded.
- Where do they come from? Source criticism is a powerful tool for exploring the background and motives of the person or organization from whom data emanate and then taking account of their bias when making use of it in CI.
- It also warns analysts to beware the pernicious analytical menaces of misinformation, disinformation and source contamination.

Data quality hierarchy

VERIFIED FACTS

The most dependable category of information can be termed *verified facts*. These usually result from some kind of legal requirement. For individual companies these will include annual reports and accounts, annual returns, prospectuses, offer documents and other regulatory filings. At the industry level these embrace, for instance, official statistics, competition authority reports and those resulting from parliamentary enquiries. From the national perspective population censuses, national income and production statistics or formal statements of government policy are obvious examples.

When I describe them as 'verified' I mean that there is a strong incentive for them to be accurate in terms of the facts they retail. This is because those submitting them face legal sanctions if they knowingly give false information or do so recklessly without taking reasonable steps to ensure it was factually correct. Hence there will be considerable political trouble when official publications contain factual inaccuracies. I am laying so much emphasis on the factual element because, of course, there will also often be a degree of judgement involved. We have seen that company accounts involve both aspects. Likewise a prospectus offering securities for sale or an offer document for the acquisition of another company is going to 'accentuate the positive'. Just as the British House of Commons asserts one of its privileges is 'for the most constructive interpretation to be placed upon its debates', company boards are going to place the most favourable interpretation upon their firms' results and prospects. An analyst may arrive at a very different conclusion, but should not have to worry too often that the *facts* are misstated.

Directors who deliberately or recklessly misstate facts in these documents expose themselves to a number of legal punishments. The Finance Reporting Review Panel can ask the courts to compel a company to restate its accounts at its own expense – an infrequent occurrence, but one which will have almost certainly have a devastating impact on a quoted company's share price. The courts also have the power to disqualify a director from holding this office for up to 15 years. In addition, the directors may be personally sued by investors for losses incurred as a consequence of them relying upon false information, while fines or imprisonment can be imposed on those convicted of acting with criminal intent. Board members of American publicly quoted companies now operate under stricter rules and sterner penalties in the aftermath of Enron and other corporate scandals.

A different kind of problem arises when using governmental material. Like corporate managements, governments will use facts to make their performance look good (or at least not so bad) and to support the line of argument they are advancing. Yet although the facts may be selective or emphasized and interpreted in a partisan way they are unlikely to be incorrect in themselves. Political opponents and the media are quick to pounce on what can be shown to be factually wrong. Ministers not only want to avoid such embarrassment, but have the resources of the Civil Service available to avoid it (while civil servants are keen to do this for reasons of professional pride and because it might damage their promotion prospects).

Part of the difficulty arises because a great deal of government data are estimated rather than exact. We know exactly how many new vehicles are registered or companies formed each year because this is recorded in a central registry and a direct count can be made. For many other topics we have to rely on raw figures that may not be wholly comprehensive or that are based on sample surveys. The National Income is measured in three different ways. In theory these should produce the same figure, but they actually yield slightly different results. Fortunately analysts do not need absolute precision to deliver effective CI, so long as the margin of error in the figures used is not too great.

A more insidious danger with official statistics lies in attempts to manipulate them. The Thatcher Government received much criticism for revising the definition of who was counted as 'unemployed' 30 times between 1979 and 1989. Although only seven of these were statistically significant their cumulative effect was to reduce unemployment by half a million through redefining it instead of actually placing the jobless in work. This manipulation of official statistics particularly affects projections of population growth, which tend to be on the high side in some European countries because this will provide grounds for demanding extra public money to provide homes, schools and hospitals to meet this supposed future need.

Furthermore, official statistics may simply become inaccurate because the traditional measure no longer works or something has gone wrong in collecting them. The Boskin Report of the US Senate Finance Committee issued in 1996 found that American consumer price inflation had been overstated in published official statistics. Its authors estimated that actual annual inflation had been 1.1 per cent lower than reported because the effects of the 'New Economy' were not given enough weight in the traditional statistical process. In the UK figures for vacancies were traditionally compiled using returns from the state-run employment offices called Job Centres. These became increasingly unreliable as private sector recruitment agencies played an ever-growing role in matching job-seekers and employers and were eventually abandoned in

1997. Despite the very high professional standards of British official statisticians, there have been problems with some series, most notably the Average Earnings Index which was suspended in 1998 after increasingly strident complaints about its inaccuracy.

From an analyst's perspective the consequences of verified facts turning out to be incorrect are clearly grave. The only defence is a sensible level of scepticism (as opposed to a totally self-defeating cynicism) coupled with as much background knowledge as possible. Hence the shrewd analyst will always question company results that are 'too good to be true' or that seriously conflict with other information. They will also be on the alert for expert complaints about the veracity of industry or governmental statistical data. Two respected sources for monitoring these are the Royal Statistical Society (whose website has links to other national statistical societies sites: www.rss.org.uk, and the Business Statistics Users Group: home.btclick.com/bsug).

REASONABLY SECURE FACTS

Next in the hierarchy of information quality comes what can be described as *reasonably secure facts*. Unlike the verified ones these usually come from secondary rather than primary sources and are not the result of a legal imperative. Market research reports are an important group within this category (albeit that information taken from interviews and surveys undertaken by the market researcher is primary material), as are investment bank reports. A sound rule in ensuring that such evidence is 'reasonably secure' is to double check it. It is always comforting when the original source is quoted and the analyst can obtain it (if the source is a document) or communicate with it (if it is a person or organization).

Less reassuring is where the source is given as *estimates* by the body that has compiled the document. This can sometimes just mean that multiple sources have been used and it would hinder the flow of the argument or take up excessive space to list them. It can also occur where the author has decided the raw data must be adjusted to provide a more accurate picture. However, a long list of sources or a complex set of adjustments can be relegated to an appendix so that they are still open to outside examination. In the worse case an estimate can be an euphemism for a wild guess.

PROBABILITIES

Further down the information quality ladder are *probabilities*. In many cases we have to rely on these as it may be impossible or impracticable to obtain proven facts. Probabilities become more reliable if we have several pieces of evidence supporting them. Accepting the likelihood of something on the basis of a single fact or observation increases the risk of our being wrong. For example, if we discover that a company is undertaking a major recruitment drive through advertising and placing jobs with recruitment agencies we may be correct to deduce that it is planning to expand its scale or range of operations. On the other hand this may just be the result of high staff turnover, with a pressing need to hire new employees to replace those leaving! So if we found that staff morale appeared good and its workers tended to remain with the firm for lengthy periods of service our deduction would be more likely to be valid.

RUMOURS

Next the most untrustworthy and dangerous category of information: *rumours*. These can be simply the result of something being half-understood or poorly communicated. In one firm, operating in cramped and inconvenient premises, management launched a search for better accommodation. In order to partially finance new premises, they also requested a valuation of their existing building. To avoid raising their employees' expectations before they had a better idea of what was available and affordable, the directors were discreet in carrying out these tasks. Unfortunately, one of the staff found out about the valuation and a rumour swept the firm that the company was going to be wound up, its premises sold and the workforce laid off. These kinds of Chinese Whispers can be a fertile source of false rumour and confuse analysts.

Apart from a simple mix-up, a rumour can also arise for a more sinister reason. The motive behind it can be malicious or it may be a canard used in an attempt to manipulate events. Identifying the original source of a rumour – and thus getting the chance to make a better evaluation of it – may be impossible once a story gets widely disseminated.

Dangerously beguiling though they are, rumours cannot be ignored. Analysts must undertake the difficult task of being on the alert for them, while avoiding falling for untrue ones. It is well known, for example, that 'talk on the grapevine' at scientific conferences regarding the failure of a particular drug to obtain regulatory approval is often the precursor of a public announcement of this.

Unsourced material can be reliable, however, if consistent with other evidence. The correct approach is to regard it as a starting point for further investigation, as the following case demonstrates.

CASE OF THE MYSTERY SOURCE

An associate told us that he had overheard someone at an industry event say that a company we were interested in was up for sale. Unfortunately our contact failed to find out the identity of this person, never mind the grounds for her statement. Once we started to investigate we discovered several reasons for believing it to be true such as the auditors working at its premises (even though the preparation of the annual accounts was still a long way off). The company had also been somewhat aggressively trying to extend its intellectual property at the expense of its collaborators, while the present owner of the business had bought a home abroad and was spending an increasing amount of time there whereas he had hitherto been a workaholic, coming into the office seven days a week. None of these facts on their own was conclusive, but their cumulative effect (in addition to some other indications) was to support the veracity of the unsourced statement. Final confirmation came quite soon with the public announcement that the business had been sold.

ERROR

There is also the possibility of plain error, even in what should be rock solid sources.

The following table is taken from Lloyds TSB's 1997 profit and loss account:

Table 9 Lloyds TSB – original data

	£ millions
Interest receivable from debt securities	572
Other interest receivable	9616
Interest payable	6016
Write-down of finance lease receivables	58
Net interest (interest received minus interest paid)	**4114**

A glance at these figures shows that they appear to add up to around £16 billion, so why only £4 billion? This is how they should have appeared:

Table 10   Lloyds TSB – data corrected

	£ millions
Interest receivable from debt securities	572
Other interest receivable	9616
Interest payable	(6016)
Write-down of finance lease receivables	(58)
Net interest	**4114**

Better practice would have been for the negative numbers to be bracketed in accordance with accounting convention (as was done further down the profit and loss account for 'Commission payable'). A simple mistake or perhaps deplorably slack inconsistency, but one committed by one of Europe's largest banks which was not picked up by the auditors before publication. An example of the dangers of such a seemingly trifling error was where a leading multinational corporation issued a summary of its results enclosing all negative numbers in brackets – apart from the figure showing the percentage change in net debt. This then appeared to show a substantial increase of 41 per cent in the company's indebtedness, when it had actually paid off a large slice of its loans. The figure was included by a researcher in a table, illustrating shifts in debt levels within a sector, which would form part of a major public presentation. Fortunately the apparent surge in debt was so striking as to provoke a query from colleagues and the mistake rectified before the presentation was made. It was noted that the multinational's next results summary had the figure showing a further three per cent repayment of debt correctly encased in brackets.

A less readily apparent mistake in ICI's 1999 annual report was that the trading profit for its Quest division was given on page 31 as £82 million, yet the other references to it all stated £92 million. The lower figure was an undetected input error, but again might have been used unwittingly by an analyst who did not compare it with other parts of the report.

Thus analysts must always be on the alert for inconsistencies or surprising data. If found these must not be ignored as tedious irritations that should just be accepted at face value, but rather investigated more closely.

THE UNKNOWN

Finally, contrary to the more optimistic view that good CI will uncover anything one wants to know, there is the unknown. We have to accept that there are some things it would be useful to know, but which we will be unable to find out. Indeed, sometimes a target company may not possess the information itself. One area that is particularly hard for an outsider to fathom are the inner dynamics of a firm in terms of the personalities of its people and their relationships with each other. We can gather some clues from interviews they give, unintended leaks of information and statements by their ex-employees, business associates, family and friends, but it would be wrong to downplay the difficulty of the task.

READ WITH CARE

At the risk of stating the blindingly obvious, a media report or other published material should not be treated as verified because it appears in print or on a database. Such is the reverence for the written word that clients have often protested 'but it says it here' when even a little reflection would have shown the statement to be very dubious or totally absurd.

The same principle applies to uncritical trust in material retrieved from the internet. A MORI survey commissioned by leading business information providers Hoover's Online Europe reported that net searchers were 'exchanging objectivity and accuracy for speed and convenience when it comes to online information on which to base business decisions'.

This depressing conclusion serves to introduce the second stage of the data quality assessment model which focuses on the sources generating the information.

Source criticism

Given that the quality of sources ranges from the solid and dependable through the generally reliable (but sometimes wrong on details) to the purely invented, we need a means of probing a source more deeply.

The standard method for burrowing deeper is source criticism. The essence of this technique is taking a text and asking 'where did the author find that information?' In other words – if they are not themselves the primary source – what sources did they use? Source criticism developed in German universities in the nineteenth century as a way of furthering a profounder study of the Bible and the classical texts surviving from ancient Greece and Rome. It is heavily employed in the academic sphere by historians and literary critics – and also used by intelligence agencies and the best journalists and business analysts.

They often have to use material without its source being named. In some cases the original source can be identified with a high degree of probability, even though not specifically recorded. In others this can only guessed at.

The status of sources must also be considered and analysts should table a number of questions to test their quality:

- Are the source's statements made first hand or are they relying on information given by others?
- Did these follow immediately an event occurred or are they made a long time after it?
- Was the source at the centre of affairs or on the periphery?
- Is the information soundly based, probably (though not definitely) correct or mere speculation?
- Does the source have the specialist knowledge to understand a situation fully and arrive at an informed evaluation or could they misinterpret (and thus mislead) through lacking this?
- What is their previous record? Are their statements generally accurate, fair and proportionate or are they prone to errors, misrepresentation or exaggeration?
- Are they disinterested or are they trying to promote certain views or interests?

In general statements regarding events made straight away by those well placed to know what is happening are preferable to those made later by an external observer. Yet knowledgeable insiders will often be biased and immediate pronouncements may be inferior in reliability to more considered subsequent ones. Analysts thus have to make judgements, weighing all the relevant factors, on each individual case.

Misinformation and disinformation

Watzlawick in *How Real is Real?*,[1] his study of how erroneous data are generated and spread, calls it *misinformation* where they arise from simple error (as in the Lloyds TSB example) or misunderstanding without any intent to deceive. There is also the situation – *disinformation* – where it is deliberately intended to mislead recipients. This term was a translation of the name of the KGB's 'dezinformatsiya' division which was responsible for creating and disseminating false stories. The most virulent form of disinformation, 'black propaganda', aimed at damaging opponents rather than persuading neutrals and reinforcing allies, has a long history of use in war and politics.

A notorious commercial example of this type of attack was the falsified announcement that Dial & Save, a small US telecommunications operation, was offering free calls to Cuba. Some subscribers misled by this seeming bonanza ran up very large bills and the company spent around $2 million in calming irate customers and other corrective measures. The perpetrators and their motives remain unknown.

A distinction can be drawn between active (as in the Dial & Save case) and passive disinformation. The passive version is the suppression or manipulation of information that may reflect badly on an organization or be of use to its rivals. This can involve the destruction or concealment of such data or their presentation in an unhelpful form. Firms preparing hostile takeover bids for quoted companies have often paved the way by buying shares under the cover of a nominee holder or holders. Equity purchases by obscure entities are less likely to trigger early awareness of the move than if a known potential predator buys them in its own name. An individual may use several variants of their name (perfectly legally) to confuse others as to which companies they hold shares in or on whose board they sit.

Exceptionally complex company structures (often involving the use of minimal disclosure tax havens) can be devised so as to hamper research into the true situation, especially if ultimate ownership is impossible to ascertain. (However, we should note that they may simply result from a historical legacy or legitimate operational reasons.) The Maxwell Group of companies was a cobweb of interlinked businesses with a top level of ownership (taking the form of a foundation in Liechtenstein, as was related in Chapter 12, so no public disclosure required) that was impenetrable to outsiders. Enron's tangle of obscurely related associate firms also defied external analysis.

Companies may also draw a veil over their activities by creating subsidiaries to carry on sensitive work such as R&D. These will then file patents under their own name rather than that of the parent. An even more opaque version of this is to have friends and allies appear in the public record as the formal directors and shareholders. The 'directors' will have a purely nominal role, all the actual decisions being taken by the 'shadow directors' behind them and the shareholdings will be in nominee names (unless a court orders this, there is no legal requirement for nominees in private companies to disclose their status or reveal the identity of the beneficial owner they represent). An enterprise may also try to screen promising research from the attentions of observers by moving its most sensitive R&D activities off-site.

---

1   Watzlawick, P. (1983), *How Real is Real?: Communication, disinformation, confusion*, Souvenir.

NEWS MANAGEMENT

There is also the option of *news management*. This involves tactics such as releasing bad news at the same time that some major story is distracting public attention or just before weekends or holidays. An alternative is to blanket the key data, if publishing they cannot be avoided, by placing them deep in a lengthy, highly technical and seemingly boring document or accompanying it with a blizzard of mundane announcements that are quickly dismissed once a couple or so have been read. That provides a convenient future defence against a charge of concealment, while reducing the chances of it actually being picked up by external observers.

NOT AVAILABLE FOR COMMENT

Another approach is complete passivity, simply to make no comment, refuse to discuss something or utterly ignore it. This approach is used in those difficult situations where saying anything could be dangerous, hence we commonly find 'X declined to comment' or 'Y was not available for comment' or 'Z did not return our calls'. This is an effective way of deterring questions in the short term.

It should also be conceded that in some instances it can be justifiable: there may be legal constraints (such as when a case is before the courts or an official investigation in progress) or practical ones (where, for example, not enough is known about a situation to make an informed statement or matters are so pressing that there is no time for distractions). These difficulties should nevertheless be explained if they are to be accepted as anything other than feeble evasions.

EXAMPLES OF DISINFORMATION

One form of corporate *disinformation* is the announcement that non-existent products are coming to the market. This is so common in the IT field that it has received its own name, *vapourware*. It has the twin advantages of persuading some buyers to postpone purchase of competing products in expectation of a better one being soon available and also tricking rivals into poor counter-moves based upon this erroneous assumption. A publisher of reference books also uses it as a form of market testing, announcing a forthcoming title and either quietly forgetting it if there is little interest or hurrying to actually commission the book if there is a lot!

Paul Dishman[2] gives a number of examples of corporate disinformation. One of these involved interfering with a rival firm's test marketing of a new product in a limited area before attempting a nationwide roll-out. The company sent out its staff to buy large quantities of the item being tested, at the same time as cutting shipments of its own version of the product. Acting on the favourable results of this distorted test the competitor proceeded with an ambitious national launch, which its cunning rivals wrecked by a substantial price cut that prevented the new product establishing itself in the market. A hi-tech firm maintained customer loyalty by spreading a rumour they were developing a new product. When asked about it by clients, the sales force was told to say they couldn't talk about such matters, while at the same time smiling and winking. As Dishman notes: 'one year's annual sales meeting actually had a training session devoted to perfecting the sincerity of smiling and winking'.

Active disinformation can be outright lying or shuffling true facts so as to mislead. In British courts witnesses have to swear or affirm that the evidence they give is 'the truth, the

---

2   Dishman, P. (1999), 'Red herrings and disinformation: A strategic component of counterintelligence', *Competitive Intelligence Magazine*, 2(4), 11–14. See also Dishman, P. and Nitse, P. (1999), 'Disinformation usage in corporate communications: CI'ers beware', *Competitive Intelligence Review*, 10(4), 20–29.

whole truth and nothing but the truth'. It is providing the whole truth that separates honest statements from disinformation.

Disinformation can act as a fog or as an illusion, confusing rivals and provoking them into making false inferences as to how the disseminator is placed, what it is doing and what its plans are. Fortunately you can 'fool all of the people some of the time, but you can't fool all of the people all of the time'. A study of a company's past indulgence in disinformation (and the practice tends to become habitual) should warn analysts that they should be suspicious of any statement it makes. Even if a firm has got not a previous record of engaging in it, the wisest course is to try and cross-check the information.

SOURCE CONTAMINATION

In many ways misinformation is more dangerous in CI analysis than denial and deception. A shrewd person will probe deeper when confronted with evasion and can uncover previous example of ruses used to confuse external observers. The worst situation is *source contamination* where the same erroneous statement is repeated by others and becomes generally accepted. Here are some examples of 'facts' that 'everyone knows':

- 'Ostriches hide their heads in the sand when in danger.' (They don't.)
- 'Red Square in Moscow is named after the Bolshevik Revolution.' (It was called that in Czarist days.)
- 'The flight recorder in a plane is a black box.' (It is actually coloured orange to aid its identification.)
- 'Lightning never strikes twice.' (Not only can this happen, it is actually more likely to occur as an electrical current takes the route of least resistance and uses anything that will conveniently bridge the gap between cloud and ground.)

None of these popular fallacies (with the possible exception of the last one) is likely to cause much harm, but the unquestioning acceptance of similar falsehoods in business can led to serious financial loss. Many instances have been pointed out earlier in this book where the managements of individual companies or even whole industries misjudged their competitive environment because of shared false beliefs. Classic statements of business self-deception include:

- 'There's no demand for that sort of product/service.'
- 'It's an interesting invention, but will have no practical impact.'
- 'This upstart rival's products are clearly inferior to ours – they pose no threat.'
- 'We've prospered for years, why change a winning formula?'
- 'Bigger is better.'
- 'If we seize first-mover advantage our competitors will never be able to catch up with us.'

In many contexts these assertions may indeed be true. The danger arises when they pass unchallenged as what 'everybody knows' and are complacently assented to. Should they prove to be erroneous the business consequences will usually be painful.

The danger of source contamination is greatest when the untrue statement is something which accords well with the existing general outlook of commentators and executives or is what they would like to believe.

CASE OF SOURCE CONTAMINATION

A relatively new company was gaining a great deal of attention. Its flamboyant chief executive stood out markedly compared with his dull, uninspiring rivals. This sector had only been growing at a slow rate for many years, but a major shift in technology seemed to promise a much faster paced expansion of the market. His company, which had achieved high visibility through aggressive marketing, looked well placed to reap this new harvest and was seen as an exciting investment prospect.

We carried out a review of the literature and found certain 'facts' consistently repeated. More searching investigation showed that the first press reports had incorporated grossly misleading statements made by the entrepreneur without their authors trying to check them. Later reportage simply incorporated these 'known facts' and many of those working in the industry that we spoke to also repeated them.

That this chief executive was addicted to misrepresentation was one of the principal reasons for us recommending our clients to avoid investing in the company, advice amply vindicated by its subsequent pedestrian performance.

In principle information supplied from several sources is more trustworthy than that derived from a single one. However, this may be due to source contamination. Once again the only defence is to refuse to accept data at face value whenever it is possible to trace them back to their original source or to assay them in other ways.

Conclusions

- Information provides the planks upon which analysis stands. The poorer the quality of the data the less analytical weight should be placed on them.
- Analysts must always ask: 'What is the status and reputation of an information source and from which sources did it obtain data?'
- The overt or detectable biases of a source should be taken into account.
- Corporate misinformation and disinformation, together with the disturbing possibility of source contamination, hold special dangers and the analyst has to be on the alert for them.
- Wherever possible data should be validated from different sources or through applying other tests.

20 *Describing Companies*

The next three chapters consider different modes of analyzing the information that has been gathered. These embrace:

- descriptions of individual organizations
- positioning each one in relation to its peers on a variety of criteria
- seeking to anticipate future competitive landscapes.

Describing companies is one of the key intelligence topics mentioned in Chapter 7. Furthermore other types of CI analysis rest upon – and must be preceded by – accurate and adequate description. In this chapter we shall consider:

- a checklist of items in describing an organization is set out
- some ways of describing the culture of an organization are then considered
- the role of individuals within the firm is explored.

The checklist is a general descriptive framework. Some items will apply to all companies, others may be irrelevant (such as litigation if a firm has never been involved in a court case), while a particular item may assume special significance (the stance of the regulator for a company operating in a regulated sector, for example). Analysts will focus on changes over time as well as the present situation, not just in terms of trends in a firm's financial situation and performance, but also in relation to other topics like shifts in the markets it serves or in the advertising media favoured by the company. They will also try to divine future changes in what the company does and the way in which these moves are executed. Such a considerable level of detail may not be needed and so a more limited version of it can be devised easily. It may be impossible or impracticable to obtain information on all of the items listed, but it should serve as a reminder of what can potentially be covered in a company profile.

Corporate description checklist

Contact details
- company's legal name and the name(s) it trades under
- registered office address and headquarters address
- telephone and fax numbers, website and email addresses.

Background
- company origins and history.

Activities
- description of products/services offered
- relative size of each line of business
- recent/forthcoming product launches
- strategic direction of the enterprise – staying close to traditional activities, branching out into new ones, downsizing or withdrawing from certain lines of business.

Markets
- sectors/market segments sold to and their relative size
- geographical areas sold to and the comparative importance of each
- market shares for each sector/segment
- key customers by market and level of firm's dependence on them
- upon what axis (price, differentiation, market focus) does the company compete in its chosen markets?
- strategic thrusts into new sectors and/or regions.

Financial condition
- total capital employed
- internal capital
  - shareholders' funds: issued share capital, retained profit, other reserves
- external capital
  - size of overdraft outstanding and overdraft limit
  - long-term bank loans – level and time structure
  - leasing and hire purchase
  - loans from other parties
  - bond and other capital market debt issues – level, coupon (that is, the rate of interest charged), terms and time structure
- financial strength
  - current ratio, acid test, working capital to sales ratio, gearing, interest cover, dividend cover
  - credit rating and payment record
- company valuation (while those involved in CI are rarely asked to assess the value of a business, an acquaintance with valuation techniques is useful – particularly when studying acquisitions made by companies they are interested in. A standard textbook such as Copeland and colleagues' *Valuation*[1] will provide a grounding in these)
  - book value, market to book value
  - price earnings ratio
  - consideration paid when similar companies have been acquired,
  - enterprise value
  - economic value added
  - market value added
  - enterprise value to EBITDA (earnings before interest, tax, depreciation and amortization).

---

1 Copeland, T., Koller, T. and Murrin, J. (2000), *Valuation: Measuring and managing the value of companies*, John Wiley and Sons, 3rd edition.

Financial performance

- sales
- overheads
- gross and operating profit margins
- return on sales, capital employed, total assets and equity
- interest payments
- pre-tax profit margin
- tax charge
- sales and profit per employee (and per square foot/metre for retailers)
- dividend policy
- cash flow.

Premises

- size of headquarters
- location of other premises
- what are they used for?
- are premises owned, leased or rented?
- value of real property owned
- lease or rental costs
- age and condition of premises
- recent or planned expansion/rationalization of premises.

Inventory

- amount of raw materials held and comparison with industry norms
- extent of work in progress
- level of finished goods held.

Technology, R&D and equipment

- hi-tech or low-tech
- stage of technological development – cutting-edge, typical for industry or technological laggard
- use of technology under licence
- research and development
  - nature and extent of R&D
  - success of research in terms of patents filed and subsequent commercial exploitation
- type and amounts of equipment available to company directly or through alliances and its age and quality.

Management and ownership

- names and personal profiles of senior management
- management structure – board of directors and its committees, senior non-board managers
- company mission and strategy for achieving this
- who owns the company? Structure of shareholdings.

Human resources

- total number of employees

- employees in each functional area, location and job grade
- demographic profile of workforce
- balance between full-time, part-time, contractors and temporary staff
- extent of outsourcing
- educational attainments, experience and skills of staff
- size, organization and form of compensation of sales force
- recent hiring activity
- employee morale
- collective bargaining/employee consultation arrangements.

Intangible assets and litigation

- intellectual property owned (patents, trade names, trade marks, copyright, brands) or controlled (licences and concessions)
- nature, organization and sophistication of knowledge management within company
- company reputation among
  - customers
  - those who are potential customers, but not actual ones
  - competitors
  - suppliers
  - industry experts and commentators
  - journalists
  - public at large, local communities
  - public relations activity including corporate involvement in the wider community
- litigation
  - results of past court cases
  - ones currently pending
  - penalties imposed by regulators.

Business processes

- value chain analysis including probing strengths and weaknesses in internal operations
- distribution channels – type and relative importance of each
- means of transporting supplies/finished products
- cash management
  - levels of cash held
  - debtor, creditor and inventory days.

Advertising

- total advertising spend
- spend by type of media
- form of advertising used
- purpose of advertising (to promote awareness of company, sell a range of products or services, introduce or sustain specific brands)
- pattern of advertising during a year, how much of estimated budget has been spent to date.

Alliances

- professional advisers – auditors, lawyers, bankers, financial advisers, registrars, financial public relations advisers, management consultants, technical consultants, lobbyists

- licensing agreements
- joint R&D
- joint production/distribution
- shareholdings in or by other companies, cross-shareholdings
- mergers, acquisitions and divestments activity.

Company's external environment (STEEP analysis)

- social and cultural
- technological
- economic
- environmental
- political, regulatory and legal.

SWOT analysis

- strengths
- weaknesses
- opportunities
- threats.

Firms can be assessed in terms of their present competitive strengths and weaknesses and the future opportunities open to them and potential threats menacing them.

A rare instance of a study commissioned by a business wishing to understand its SWOT better coming into the public domain was the leaked Cable & Wireless report summarized in the *Financial Times*[2] towards the end of 2002. This was concerned with the company's competitive position in the West Indies.

Examples of 'Strengths' included 'strong knowledge of local markets and culture', while among 'Weaknesses' were 'insecurity [among staff], low morale and rising sick days'. On the 'Opportunities' side 'roaming, business travellers, hotels and tourist sectors have considerable development potential', while 'loss of key staff and agents to competitors' was one of the 'Threats' posed.

SWOT is simple in concept and the results easy to understand, even if identifying all the individual strengths and so on may demand a lot of data gathering, powerful imagination and lengthy debate on the part of those assembling these profiles. SCIP members have rated it as the most useful analytical tool at their disposal. It stretches beyond the narrow confines of financial data or specific aspects of a company's performance to provide a comprehensive, forward-looking assessment of an enterprise. A SWOT analysis of a company is thus an excellent way to conclude a corporate description.

Corporate culture

One of the major weaknesses of a lot of CI output is that description is confined to basic facts such as activities, number of sites and names of directors, plus financial data drawn from accounts. The quality of subsequent analysis is thus lower because the profile leaves out key items such as a company's culture or interpersonal politics.

---

2   Murray Brown, J. (10 December 2002), 'It's warts and all', *Financial Times*, 28.

It is generally recognized that the works of Charles Handy are the best starting point for describing organizations (including commercial enterprises) and understanding their patterns of behaviour.[3] Handy has compiled a dictionary of the fundamental concepts used in characterising them, drawing upon a vast repertoire of ways of thinking about organizations. I shall follow his example by discussing a variety of approaches, which complement one another, to describing the culture of a business.

Corporate culture, like love, is intangible, difficult to define but still an immensely powerful reality. Definitions of *culture* abound in the management literature. The wider view of its scope embraces not only a company's internal rules and customary ways of working, but also the assumptions and priorities shared by those within the same firm. John Kotter and James Hesketh[4] see culture as being made up of four components:

- beliefs
- values
- norms
- behaviours.

As displayed in Figure 10, these form a hierarchy, but also overlap and influence each other.

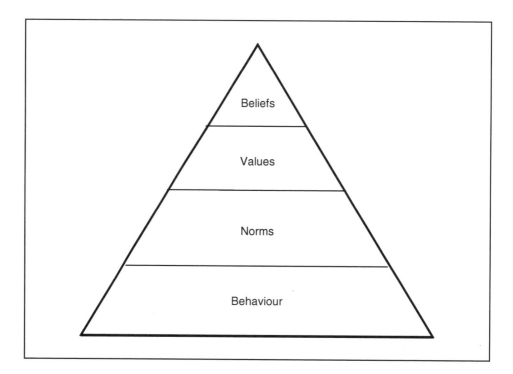

Figure 10 Components of organizational culture

3 Handy, C. (1993), *Understanding Organizations*, Penguin. Professor Handy has also written books on the special characteristics of schools and voluntary organizations.
4 Kotter, J. and Hesketh, J. (1992), *Corporate Culture and Performance*, Free Press/Macmillan.

Beliefs are the shared world view of those within the company. They are constructed from observations being generalized into theories and the fitting together of these provides a master model of how those in the firm perceive its identity, purpose and relations with the external world.

Values describe the relative priority given to different objectives – what *really matters* to a company is accorded high importance, other goals receive a lower priority and some alternative ones just ignored. Kotter and Hesketh place values first in their cultural hierarchy with beliefs following on from them. I prefer to see values as being formed and shaped by what is believed, although both are intertwined. Thus if someone has a more universalist attitude towards human relationships, this should dictate a different scale of values as against those held if they believe that these terms only apply to their actual siblings and immediate family – or extend to friends, members of the same nation or race or religion. The feedback to beliefs occurs when, in face of conduct from others that is decidedly non-fraternal, they refuse to change their previously held opinion.

In a corporate context this would mean an attitude of 'we don't rely upon the strict letter of the law or the small print of agreements in our relations with others, but will act fairly even though it costs us'. The other extreme would be represented by those 'businesses' run by the Mafia which place a high value on loyalty between 'family' or gang members (with a strict code of honour regulating internal relationships and behaviour and fearsome penalties for breaches of it) and complete disregard for the interests of outsiders.

Norms are those standards, policies and operational guidelines which govern how a firm actually carries on its business. They are based upon its beliefs and values. Examples would be 'we expect all employees to wear suits', 'we will always refund customers their money for unused goods returned with proof of purchase' or 'sales representatives are permitted to offer discounts of up to 15 per cent on their own initiative, larger discounts require approval from a higher level of management'. People joining the company are taught to accept and abide by its norms, whether these are overt and explicit – or not stated and merely implied.

Behaviours are what people belonging to the company actually *do*. They will usually conform to its norms. Departures from these are generally disapproved of and may lead to punishment. Those employees who refuse to abide by the enterprise's norms will eventually be removed either by persuasion, pressure or formal dismissal. Nonetheless, certain units or individual may be tolerated to act as 'laws unto themselves' if they have exceptional influence (children of the boss in a family firm) or value (maverick in terms of the company's prevailing culture, but brilliantly successful person or team).

Beliefs and values are often explicitly articulated in corporate mission statements, advertising slogans and other promotional efforts, public utterances by senior executives in speeches or articles and staff newsletters. Analysts need to treat these with some degree of caution as these communications with the world are intended to present the enterprise in the best light and may not accurately reflect its true beliefs and values. No company is going to publicly state that its actual beliefs include 'there are few repeat orders in this business, so we don't have to worry about customer unhappiness once they've paid' or that one of its values is 'as long as we don't get caught, we'll do anything we please'!

Furthermore, formal norms, such as those recorded in an operating manual, may be ignored in practice. An instruction from the IT department that passwords should not be saved, but entered every time an external database is consulted may be a dead letter in every other unit. Sales representatives may be briefed not to disparage competitors during pitches to clients – yet have no hesitation in running down their rivals when actually out in the field.

Consequently, studying the actual behaviours of a firm and its people is vital in trying to ascertain if the public face is the genuine one. This is also essential where there is little or no formal public expression of beliefs, values or norms and these have to be inferred from the way in which a company conducts itself. The universality of a corporate culture must also be probed. Does a single one prevail or are significantly different cultures found in its various divisions, functions or geographical locations?

SOCIOLOGICAL APPROACH

One path towards understanding and defining a company's culture, derived from sociology, has been expounded by Rob Goffee and Gareth Jones.[5] They point out that a firm is a community, just like a family, club, sports team or village and therefore the insights of sociology into how these other communities work can be properly applied to business as well. Sociologists position an organization's culture according to two axes: *sociability* and *solidarity*. The first is rooted in emotion and measures 'friendliness' within a firm. In a high sociability company personal relationships are very important, colleagues are also friends. Solidarity is based more upon rational calculation ('what do I get out of this?') and impersonality. In a high solidarity firm colleagues stand shoulder to shoulder, not because they have personal ties, but because success for the group benefits each of its members. This does not exclude emotional commitment. Like the famous Polish trade union of that name, solidarity can command tremendous fervour. It is distinguished from sociability by being centred on a common cause rather than personal relationships.

Depending on an organization's position along the scale of these two axes, Goffee and Jones describe it as having one of four types of predominant culture. This is represented in matrix form in Figure 11.

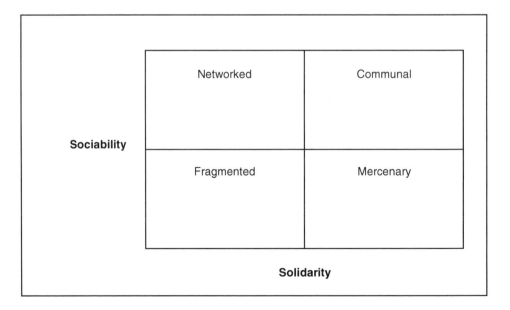

Figure 11   Sociological matrix of organizational culture

5   Goffee, R. and Jones, G. (November–December 1996), 'What holds the modern company together?', *Harvard Business Review*, 133–48.

They term organizations with both high sociability and solidarity as having a *communal* culture. Its people are bound together both by friendship and a strong identification with, and commitment to, the organization's success. Business start-ups often have a communal culture with the owners being close friends and everyone striving hard to ensure that the firm prospers. People in these firms are very clear as to who their competitors are and highly motivated in trying to beat them. Maintaining a communal culture in a company becomes more difficult as it matures and grows in size. Personal relationships tend to be diluted as the headcount increases. If the charismatic founders are no longer around both sociability and solidarity may weaken. Finally, the ongoing success of a mature company with a wider product range and perhaps overseas operations to manage may demand a shift towards emphasizing results at the expense of friendship.

Goffee and Jones describe a culture with high solidarity, but low sociability as *mercenary*. The focus is very much on achieving a common purpose, with 'getting on well together' assigned a low value in comparison. People are there to get results rather than enjoy themselves. Individual interests are subordinated to those of the company and underperformance will be firmly dealt with, ignoring sentiment. Those working for a mercenary company are prepared to accept this because its success will benefit their personal interests. There have a strong awareness of competitors and possess a powerful desire to beat them.

A third type of culture is the *networked* one where sociability is high, but solidarity low. The people in a networked environment place a greater value on loyalty to their colleagues, who are also friends, than to the firm as a whole. This does not mean such company cannot be highly successful. Goffee and Jones cite the example of Unilever as a networked organization. Executives from all parts of this multinational enterprise are encouraged to develop close personal ties by being brought together for internal conferences, training courses and social events and by frequently moving younger managers to other functions, divisions or countries. Unilever's high sociability enabled it to overcome the potential divisiveness of its staff being drawn from such a wide diversity of backgrounds and nationalities. It could operate well globally because its people had developed personal friendships with colleagues in other countries, while at the same time its low solidarity enabled it to stay close to local markets. By the mid-1990s, however, the firm was placing more emphasis on commitment to group goals as well as personal ones as it faced fierce competition from high solidarity companies like Procter & Gamble and L'Oréal.

Networked cultures will tend to be found where local market knowledge is a more significant factor for success than coordination from headquarters. Such companies, operating as federations, generally do better than those with uniformity imposed from the centre. They are also often observed in new overseas operations that will take a long time to bring to fruition. A company seeking to establish a presence under these circumstances needs strong personal bonds between its local team members to keep them motivated under difficult conditions and when the fruits of their labours lie in the distant future.

Finally, Goffee and Jones' fourth cultural form, the *fragmented* organization, which is characterized by both low sociability and low solidarity. 'Virtual companies' where there may be limited personal contact between staff members who work largely autonomously are an obvious example. In some law or consulting firms the partners may operate mainly on their own with little social interaction with colleagues and only a modest need for a company-wide strategy or management. There can also be unhappy situations in which 'fragmented' means 'torn asunder', where personal relations within a firm are so bad and solidarity so enfeebled that it has become a house divided.

'Organizations' here have been largely equated with companies. The model can also be applied to smaller groupings such as divisions, subsidiaries or functions within a firm (although finding data at these levels is more difficult unless one knows a business very well). It is also possible for these to exhibit different cultures. This will be particularly true in merger or takeover situations and can be the most difficult aspect of performing post-deal integration. Migrations between the cultural quadrants are always of great analytical interest, particularly when they are being undertaken consciously as with Unilever. Deliberate attempts to change corporate culture are notoriously difficult to achieve (so that boosting solidarity undermines sociability or an emphasis on relationships blunts solidarity). Efforts to do so are a 'moment of change' for a company, generating a large number of signals for analysts to interpret.

ANTHROPOLOGICAL APPROACH

Another way of describing a corporate culture is from the anthropological standpoint. This sees a firm's *artefacts*, its symbols, rituals and myths, as the outward manifestations of its culture. These three types of artefact are interlinked and self-reinforcing, as shown in Figure 12.

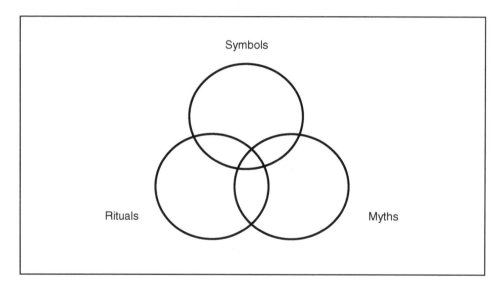

Figure 12 Anthropological model of organizational culture

Symbols can be images, words or physical objects. They include things such as logos, slogans, the layout and décor of offices. Bill Mackey, an insolvency expert involved in handling many British corporate failures in the 1970s and 1980s, compiled a light-hearted list of indicators that a company was headed for trouble. These included:

• company flag
• top of the range company cars with personalized number plates
• fountain or exotic fish in a tank in the reception area.

Visiting one client I saw they had their flag on a flagpole in their spacious and superbly maintained grounds. Referring to Mackey's list produced some wry smiles and one person told me privately that he believed that his job was in danger of being axed as a reorganization had been announced a fortnight earlier. A few weeks after my visit a series of redundancies and site sales was announced and the company subsequently came 'into play' as a potential bid target.

Rituals concern the customs and mores of corporate life. These are the ways in which day-to-day operations such as meetings are carried on, the degree of formality in how staff dress, their means of communication, the way they address each other, how meetings are conducted and after hours social events.

Myths, in an anthropological context, are not 'untrue tales' as in common parlance. They are stories intended to explain how certain things, such as the success of a firm, have come about. A corporate myth centres around heroes, either from the firm's past or still actively involved, who shaped its destiny. Henry Ford, Richard Branson, Giovanni Agnelli and Bill Gates are globally recognized examples. Another instructive case is Dave Thomas who founded the Wendy's fast-food chain. Thomas was brought out of retirement in 1986 to revive the company's fortunes. Although at least two other board members had shareholdings three times the size of his, Thomas wielded massive authority because of his role in founding and growing the firm and became its principal representative in advertising campaigns from 1989.

PSYCHOLOGICAL APPROACH

A third, more controversial, way of describing corporate culture is to view it through the lens of psychology. This standpoint asserts that, just as individuals have identifiable personality traits, so do organizations. Thus William Bridges in his *The Character of Organizations*,[6] applied the widely used Myers-Briggs classification of types of personality to associations, including businesses. He devised a questionnaire, the Organizational Character Index (OCI), to help uncover corporate personality. Some critics have dismissed this reasoning as confusing genuine biologically based, human personality with that of an artificial corporate body, whose immaterial existence is merely a jurist's fiction. An organization's persona in their view is merely an amalgam of the character traits of those working within it.

While Bridges readily accepts that there is a difference between individual and corporate personality and that analogies between them cannot be pressed too far, he contends that the psychological approach has considerable practical merit as a way of describing organizational culture. This view gains credence from the fact that people commonly use many of the same terms when discussing a company as those employed in talking about people.

Thus firms can be cautious, conservative and reactive or bold, adaptive and innovative. Their goals can be vaultingly ambitious and broad – or modest and limited. In their relations with external parties they can be aggressive, cooperative or isolationist. Some companies are pretty open, others highly secretive. Management styles can range from authoritarian through consultative to democratic. It is also true that those many of those working within an organization modify their behaviour and, to a lesser extent, their own personalities in response to its collective demands.

Like the Myers-Briggs system his model explores four key dimensions of personality:

6   Bridges, W. (2000), *The Character of Organizations: Using personality type in organization development*, Davies-Black, 2000.

1) *Introversion versus extroversion.* Introverted companies are inward-looking and derive most of their satisfaction from pursuing their own goals – regardless of outsiders' views – and abiding by their own procedures. Extroverted firms focus on the external world and are stimulated by their interaction with other parties. They seek to win favour with and influence these and in turn readily adopt their ideas and methods of operating.

2) *Sensing versus intuition.* This relates to how businesses acquire and use information. 'Sensing' is not a very good description because what is meant is actually the step-by-step gathering and evaluation of information and focusing on the present concrete reality of a situation. The opposite end of the scale is the intuitive method where the emphasis is more on its latent possibilities, thus taking a wider perspective and being directed towards the future.

3) *Thinking versus feeling.* While companies stress their rational, logical methods in reaching decisions, the extent to which this genuinely applies varies enormously. Some firms do operate with cold-eyed, systematic rationality, many others are more influenced by emotional considerations or inspirational events. Companies tending to the 'thinking' mode will prize orderly consistency in decision taking, while creativity and being prepared to make mental leaps are more highly valued among their 'feeling' counterparts.

4) *Judging versus perceiving.* Judging firms have a preference for order and structure, following a bureaucratic model, whereas perceiving ones lean towards a more spontaneous and free-wheeling business style.

Bridges uses these dimensions as the building blocks for a more elaborate model (again based on the Myers-Briggs original) whereby organizations are described according to 16 types of character. For example, a company might be characterized as ESTJ (extroverted, sensing, thinking, judging).

Provided the results of applying this scheme to specific bodies are treated as indicative rather than definitive, his methodology is another useful tool for analysts attempting to delineate organizational culture.

Role and status of individuals within a company and their interrelationships

One school of historiography minimizes the role of individuals compared with great impersonal forces and movements. While this was an understandable and healthy reaction to the hero-worship that marred some earlier historical writing it goes too far in regarding individuals as largely puppets incapable of having much influence on events. Government intelligence agencies do not make this mistake and devote a lot of effort to preparing profiles of political leaders and other influential people in foreign countries. This research is used to guide relationships with these individuals and to try and predict their reaction to certain events. Such intelligence is of equal value when analyzing competitors.

So as well as trying to understand a company's collective culture, analysts need to look at the key individuals working in it. A crucial issue in the life of any company is the internal distribution of power and influence. It has relevance even within a firm controlled and totally owned by a single dominant individual. The question of who would succeed the present boss is always of interest. The current leader may fall seriously ill, become incapacitated or die suddenly. Companies can rarely be left to run on a 'care and maintenance' basis for long and strategic decisions will have to be made even if the corporate leader is expected to regain control eventually. A sudden loss of a powerful chief is a 'moment of change' fraught with many implications, as with Robert Maxwell in 1991. The risk of this abrupt change of regime will be more apparent if the chief executive is known to have a potentially dangerous medical condition or (like Richard Branson and his daredevil ballooning) puts himself at risk in other ways. Trying to predict who will lead the firm in the future is also an important CI goal even when an orderly, long-term succession is expected or power within the company is more dispersed.

Formal job titles are not a reliable guide to the relative power of executives. An impressive name badge may mask a situation where nominal position does not translate into company-wide authority. Some company officers have certain rights and duties in law extending beyond those attached to other employees. In Britain the posts of director, secretary and chairman get statutory recognition in the 1985 Companies Act. This legal status may mean nothing in terms of actual influence within the firm. There have been many cases of non-executive directors being appointed for public relations or personal reasons rather than operational ones. Even executive directors may carry little weight when the CEO is pre-eminent in corporate decision making or until something occurs to undermine the leader's authority fatally.

An individual achieves influence within a company on the basis of several factors. One of these is the size of their shareholding. Despite the special case of Dave Thomas at Wendy (see page 203), a substantial personal stake in the enterprise (particularly in an environment in which institutional investors own most listed company shares) often denotes a position of power. Most listed companies expect their directors to buy some shares as a demonstration of commitment to the business, but a holding greatly in excess of the expected proportion tends to denote a heavier weight in strategic decision taking. In venture-backed firms the non-executive director representing the investing firm will have a notable voice in the investee company's strategy. On the other hand a relatively major personal holding may be owned by a passive investor who perhaps inherited the stake or acquired it when working for the company, but has now retired. The analyst thus needs other evidence to assess the significance of personal holdings correctly.

Company executives gain status within their organizations for reasons apart from their extent of ownership. Traditionally they gained a high rank by rising through the corporate hierarchy and this model remains valid in those many long-established firms who still tend to promote from within. In more bureaucratically structured companies the organization chart may be a good source for working out relative status. If the head of sales reports direct to the chief executive, this suggests greater influence than a manager reporting to someone else. Some also believe that more power is likely to be held by executives whose rectangle is nearest to the CEO's on the horizontal plane. However, Maurer and colleagues[7] point out this can be a false inference, as the order is often determined by other factors and may even be used to massage the egos of those with less actual influence.

The organization chart is less helpful in enterprises with a flatter hierarchy, while strategic decisions in younger, fast-growing entrepreneurial businesses are more likely to be taken by the founders. Companies with a longer pedigree often recruit outsiders to senior positions, with many CEOs coming from competitors or even other industries. An executive can also enjoy a position of greater power if hiring them gives an immediate boost to company size or growth. This is often the case in situations where a board judges it will be more likely to realize synergies following a merger or acquisition by retaining the other firm's chief executive.

---

7   Maurer, J.G., Nixon, J.M. and Peck, T.W., editors (1996), *Organization Charts: Structures of 200 business and non-profit organizations*, Gale Research, 2nd edition.

Another factor strengthening an executive's position is where they bring lucrative new clients along with them when they join. Starbuck[8] found that incoming partners in professional services firms who possessed this advantage tended to enjoy longer tenure and were more likely to play a top management role. Again those executives who can contribute unique knowledge or experience to a company will also tend to exercise greater sway than colleagues who are easier to replace. Individuals who can command this sort of client loyalty or possess distinctive qualities will usually have a higher public profile. This can be manifested in several ways such as receiving special mention in the company's own literature, representing it by being interviewed by the media, speaking at an industry conference, writing articles or playing a prominent role in a trade association. A high-visibility person will generally have a superior status within a firm to one with only a slight public presence.

In companies with a structure reflecting particular lines of business (as opposed to a functional one with directors for research and development, marketing, production and the like) an individual's place in the corporate pecking order will tend to reflect the fortunes of their division. Data on how divisions are faring can thus provide clues as to whether the internal stock of their head is rising or falling (this will not apply, of course, if a new chief has been given charge of a struggling unit with the task of reviving it). The diversion of resources to a division (indicated either overtly by a public announcement or indirectly by a stepping up of hiring or advertising activity relating to it) also suggests greater prestige and authority on the part of its boss.

Both direct and indirect evidence can be used in assembling personal profiles. The first category is information on the person themselves, while indirect data are other material that can illuminate their character.

Direct information includes such items as:

1) Basic personal and family details – age, nationality, country of residence, marital status (including data on spouses or partners), children, parents, siblings and other relatives.
2) Education, qualifications and special skills.
3) Career history including employers, posts held and geographical locations worked in.
4) Business activities outside the subject's company (non-executive directorships, advisory roles or major shareholdings).
5) Financial status.
6) Health.
7) Personality (the Myers-Briggs Type Indicator[9] referred to above is an effective tool for describing this).
8) Approach to business and working methods.
9) Beliefs, attitudes and values.
10) Reputation.
11) Non-business activities, interests and events (sporting, artistic, cultural, political, religious, local).

Indirect information covers:

---

8 Starbuck, W.H. (1993), 'Keeping a butterfly and an elephant in a house of cards: The elements of exceptional success', *Journal of Management Studies*, 30(6), 885–921.
9 A concise introduction is provided by Martin, C.R. and others (2002), *Quick Guide to the 16 Personality Types in Organizations: Understanding personality differences in the workplace*, Telos Publications.

1) Performance of other companies the subject has worked for (including before and after their period of employment) and any major corporate events during their time with them.
2) Extent of autonomy and authority in earlier posts.
3) Positions held or likely to be held by their associates outside the subject's own company.

Some data will emanate from the subject themselves or their company: material such as CVs and corporate biographical sketches on the firm's website or in its company literature, annual report or prospectuses. The subject may also write articles or books, give interviews or deliver speeches to industry conferences and other public events.

A caveat to be borne in mind here is that the pronouncements made by an executive in biographical entries, press releases or speeches may be a poor guide to their personality, interests and opinions. The higher the status of the individual and the larger the firm, the greater the likelihood that such pieces will be written for them by in-house public affairs staff, external public relations consultants or professional speech writers. A prominent person giving a speech in York reminded his audience that Constantine the Great had been proclaimed Roman emperor there in 306. It would have been wrong to infer he possessed a knowledge of the history of the city of York, ancient history or an interest in either of these from this reference. In fact his speechwriter, a classics graduate, had included it. Similarly, a description of their leisure pursuits may represent what an individual believes will be acceptable or impressive rather than revealing what they actually prefer to do in their spare time. One senior executive listed 'opera' as a hobby in the biographical entry she supplied to a reference source, when it later became clear that her operatic involvement was confined to having once enjoyed corporate hospitality at Glynbourne. As always, analysts should not place too much weight upon a single piece of evidence, but attempt to test it against other data.

Conclusions

- Sufficiently broad and probing descriptions of specific companies are a major contribution to management's understanding of the competitive environment.
- They also provide a springboard for other types of analysis.
- Corporate description needs to extend beyond basic facts and include material on a company's culture and detailed profiles of individual executives.
- This gives a much richer understanding of how a company operates and offers clues as to its future behaviour and performance.

21 *Comparing and Positioning Companies*

Compiling a dossier on individual companies, dealt with in the previous chapter, is the first step to making comparisons between them and determining their relative positions according to various criteria.

This chapter is devoted to the rest of this process and:

- looks at the problems in identifying competitors correctly, illustrating these by examples drawn from a wide variety of sectors
- examines the use of benchmarking to compare companies
- explores the application of techniques such as gap, conjoint and win-loss analysis in positioning firms.

Identifying competitors

Trying to define just who a company's competitors *really* are is often not a straightforward task. Consultants frequently find that clients fail to specify the market being contested and identify their rivals correctly. Specific instances of ignoring the threat from competitors from another industry entering the market or substitute products and services were noted in Chapter 3. Thus it will be helpful to briefly review research on who are perceived as market rivals.

Porac and Thomas[1] found that they were commonly identified as either:

- industry players offering the same kinds of products
- participants from other industries providing different products which nevertheless addressed the same customer needs. At the most elementary level a hotel group's industry competitors would be other hotel chains and its market rivals boarding houses, campsites, self-catering villas and other forms of temporary accommodation.

This categorization becomes less clear-cut when examined more closely, as Day, Shocker and Srivasta[2] emphasize. A five-star hotel is not really competing with a no-frills motel or a backpacker's hostel. Besides ambiguity in classification, they also point out that a product or service can be viewed from different perspectives. There will be big dissimilarities in approach when someone is assessing a hotel from the standpoint of a tourist compared with a corporate

---

1   Porac, J.F. and Thomas, H. (1990), 'Taxonomic mental models in competitor definition', *Academy of Management Review*, 15, 224–40.
2   Day, G.S., Shocker, A.D. and Srivastava, R.K. (Fall 1979), 'Customer-orientated approaches to identifying product-markets', *Journal of Marketing*, 43, 8–19.

customer judging its suitability as a venue for client entertaining or a conference or as against an individual merely seeking a good place to eat on a particular day.

Another difficulty is that various functional groups within firms might identify different types of rival. Anneli Pirtilla, in her study of the Finnish paper industry,[3] found when asked who were their competitors, general managers referred to companies. Marketing people, on the other hand, named opposing brands, production executives listed types of machinery, while research and development staff talked in terms of grades of paper.

The analyst should also remember that executives' mental maps of 'rivals' may be multi-layered. So they can also be placed in a hierarchical order, just as geographical maps cascade down from national through regional to town and then street by street. This attitude was evinced by managers in the clothing sector interviewed by Porac and Baden-Fuller.[4] They cited six categories running from 'textiles' at the top down to a particular fibre used in specific types of knitwear at the bottom of the hierarchy.

Subsequent empirical work by Porac and Thomas supported the earlier proposition of Rosch and colleagues[5] that the most heavily used mental map will be in the middle of the hierarchy. The top level will be too general for practical use, while the bottom will be too detailed. They interviewed grocery store managers in small towns in the American mid-west and asked who were the other stores selling groceries in their neighbourhood. The managers' hierarchy began with retailers at the top. These then split into segments comprising specialist grocers, supermarkets and smaller convenience shops, before further subdividing. Thus supermarkets, for example, were more precisely categorized into those operating as cash and carry warehouses as opposed to those with a wide range of customer service such as advice or help with packing. When asked to place their own outlets within this framework, most respondents chose the middle category. A diagrammatic representation of this psychological classification is given in Figure 13.

The definition of competitors is another instance where diligent analysts, just as they probe more deeply to ensure they understand the precise nature and purpose of a CI project, need to ask further questions. The mental maps used by management may be too simplistic or have significant lapses in coverage. Merely accepting a client's list of rival firms as accurate and complete can lead to an intelligence perspective marred by serious omissions. Their clients may have an accurate picture of their competitors, indeed they should have this and certainly need to possess it. If they do not then one of the most useful services a CI analyst can render them is to supply one.

3 Pirtilla, A. (1998), 'Organizing competitive intelligence activities in a corporate organization', *Aslib Proceedings*, 50(4), 79–84.
4 Porac, J.F. and Baden-Fuller, C. (1989), 'Competitive groups as cognitive communities: The case of Scottish knitwear manufacturers', *Journal of Management Studies*, 26, 397–416.
5 Rosch, E., Mervis, C., Gray, W., Johnson, D. and Boyes-Braem, P. (1976), 'Basic objects in natural categories', *Cognitive Psychology*, 8, 382–439.

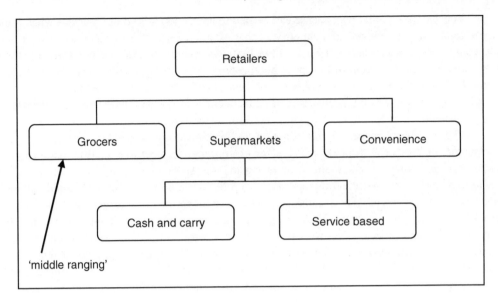

Figure 13   Mental map of who competitors are (after Porac and Thomas)

Benchmarking

The British company and market information firm ICC (now part of Bonner Hoppenstedt[6]) was originally called Inter-Company Comparisons and its services enabled a firm to see how it matched its competitors in terms of those financial ratios which can be used to measure relative efficiency. These enable rapid comparisons to be made between firms and stimulate the search to find explanations for superior performance. A key measure of the efficiency of many enterprises is how rapidly they turn over their stock. Thus supermarket profit margins are low, but very fast stock turns yield high absolute levels of profit (the opposite obviously applies to luxury or similar goods where stock turnover is slow, but margins very high). In the late 1990s Dell Computer were achieving a stock turn of around 3, whereas Apple Computer only managed a ratio of about 1.5, sliding in 1999 to 1. Dell's expenses for overheads ('sales, general and administrative' costs in US accounting terminology or 'administrative and distribution' expenses in British parlance) fell from around 12 per cent of revenues in 1996 to only ten per cent over the rest of the period. Micron never reduced this burden to less than 15 per cent (it hit 22 per cent at one point) and ended the period with it at almost 18 per cent.

Dell outperformed other computer manufacturers according to these ratios and others such as its efficiency in maintaining levels of net cash inflows, the reliability of its operating income and return on capital employed. The key to this superior performance lay in Dell's leaner business model. Other firms owned large warehouses, scattered manufacturing over numerous sites and sold their machines through complex distributions channels. Dell slashed storage costs by inducing the retail outlets it supplied to hold minimal stocks, replenished stocks on a 'just in time' basis, concentrated production on a few sites and simplified distribution by developing its own direct sales force. The economies flowing from these policies were reflected in rapid turnover of stock and low overhead costs.

---

6   www.icc.co.uk.

Benchmarking in its wider sense can be said to have commenced in the 1980s when Rank Xerox found that its market domination was sharply diminished due to Japanese competition. The company's return on assets, 19 per cent in 1980, was slashed to just over eight per cent three years later, when 80 per cent of European photocopiers were being supplied from Japan. Urgent action had to be taken for Rank Xerox to compete effectively and an important element in its recovery programme was the comparison of all its operations against the best practice elsewhere. The company then worked to catch up or outperform on these measures.

The involvement of the CI function in benchmarking varies enormously between companies. In Proctor & Gamble the director of corporate competitive analysis organizes the firm's benchmarking activities aimed at increasing the speed with which new products are brought to market and that P&G internal business processes are nimble and yield good value for what is spent on them. The Motorola intelligence department 'engages in some formal benchmarking for the company. They are not the benchmarkers for the company, but they do very special benchmarking when we have identified a certain target.' Other firms create teams drawn from one functional group or made up of staff chosen from several functional areas. Some involve CI people either as part of the team or to help choose which firms the enterprise should benchmark itself against. A number of businesses hire external consultants to conduct a study or contribute to one undertaken by an in-house working party. Whatever approach to benchmarking is adopted, the CI unit should get hold of the results of these studies and sift them for clues as to wider competitive issues than those directly addressed in them.

Once a business process to be examined is decided upon, the benchmarking squad will begin by understanding how it is presently carried out in their own organization. They will then review the literature relating to the process and visit other companies to see how they perform it. Zairi[7] provides thorough practical guidelines on how such projects should be planned and executed along with detailed case studies of their use by companies such as American Express, Texas Instruments and Unilever.

Although the most prominent exemplars of good benchmarking are large companies, it would be wrong to believe that its benefits are confined to those businesses that have ample resources. Modest amounts of staff time and money can still yield useful results. Rather than attempting benchmarking across all operations, a smaller firm will be able to improve its competitive position by carrying out more narrowly focused comparisons. Although company visits yield richer and more directly applicable knowledge, quite a lot can be learned about how to improve a firm's business processes from a literature search or by drawing on the expertise of consultants. Smaller enterprises can often derive instructive analogies from giant ones, even though they cannot directly imitate the multinationals because they lack their resources. Larger companies can also learn from smaller ones in trying to remain agile and avoiding the ponderousness that often accompanies greater size.

Some firms confine themselves to benchmarking against companies in the same industry. This runs into the immediate obstacle that competitors are reluctant to share information with their rivals. Vermeulen's[8] survey of benchmarking in the South African financial services sector showed that this was limited to making comparisons from annual reports and informal visits to the public areas of other banks' branches. Poulson[9] found that that British retail banks did little internal benchmarking and relied on the financial results of their peers to assess relative

7   Zairi, M. (1998), *Effective Management of Benchmarking Projects: Practical guidelines and examples of best practice*, Butterworth-Heinemann.
8   Vermeulen, W. (2003), 'Benchmarking as an enabler of business excellence in the South African financial sector', *Benchmarking*, 10(1), 65–72.
9   Poulson, B. (1996), 'Process benchmarking in retail financial services', *Management Services*, 40(6), 12–14.

performance. Apart from being harder to find benchmarking partners among one's peers, confining comparisons to the same sector also risks inducing 'marketing myopia'. Thus a theatrical ticket booking agency may find the lessons learned from airline seat reservations systems provide more insight than merely observing its direct competitors. A classic example is photocopier manufacturer Rank Xerox including a warehouser, L.L. Bean, among its benchmarking partners. When Motorola sought to reduce the time between receiving an order for a mobile phone and delivering it to the customer, it studied the Domino Pizza company to gain insights from the latter's speedy home pizza deliveries.

Making comparisons with the best of the best is often how the choice of partners is conceived. This represents the ideal, but the gap in the performance between a company and the global top of the class may be so great that the exercise spreads demoralization instead of sowing inspiration. Much can be learned from partners that are 'better than us' even if they are not world leaders. It is also easier to get such partners, as the best in the class tend to attract excessive requests for benchmarking visits to their facilities (hence L.L. Bean are reluctantly forced to turn away many of the companies who approach them or they would be inundated with visitors).

Gap analysis

The SWOT methodology ('strengths, weaknesses, opportunities and threats') was mentioned in the previous chapter in the context of assessing individual companies. It can also be fruitfully employed when making comparisons between firms.

Aggregated, generalized SWOT can usefully be extended, as Paul Dishman[10] argues, to the appraisal of firms on different dimensions of performance such as their capacity to increase market share or break into new markets or, in another context, the case for and against buying a competitor. In the first instance the opportunity might reside in a rapidly growing market for a product, but a weakness could be that what is offered may be too over-designed, providing many superfluous features customers are not interested in. In the other one an acquisition could give access to strong and enduring cash flow, yet may place a heavy burden on its management team by distracting them from running their existing business.

He relates extended SWOT to strategic *gap analysis*. This compares the present situation of a firm with the state it would like. So a business with erratic cash flow that wishes to reduce the volatility between its receipts and outgoings might consider closing the strategic gap by buying a cash-generative company. The assessment is concluded by weighing the benefits of closing the strategic gap (reduced borrowing and interest charges for instance) against the costs (such as the management time need to negotiate the deal, the heavy immediate expense of paying for it and the potential problems of integrating the two businesses).

A sales-orientated approach to comparing firms can start by examining product features. The table overleaf explores the relative position of four hotels.

---

10 Dishman, P. (2001), 'Two tools for M&A analysis', *Competitive Intelligence Magazine*, 4(1), 23–26.

Table 11 Hotels – comparative features

Features	A	B	C	D
Location	Excellent	Good	Excellent	Very good
Facilities	Excellent	Good	Fair	Good
Service	Excellent	Very good	Very good	Very good
Catering	Very good	Excellent	Poor	Good
Accommodation	Very good	Very good	Very good	Fair
Price	Slightly lower	High	High	Much lower

Creating a feature grid is a means of making rapid (albeit fairly superficial) comparisons between what the rival companies are offering. The scores used could be made more precise by using numbers 'C scores 5 for location, but only 2 for catering' or actual data 'We are charging £125 per night, two of our competitors charge £135, while D only charges £85'.

Even this very simple assessment yields actionable insights. If our hotel is A there is a performance gap compared with B in terms of catering. Is this gap worth closing? Perhaps not if the extra cost fails to generate more business or forces us to reduce or eliminate our slight price advantage. It is extremely unlikely we could cut prices enough to seriously undermine D's superiority in offering cheaper, though modest quality accommodation. The lesson for our hotel's marketing team would be to emphasize to appropriate audiences its slight edge in terms of price while being well matched against its rivals in terms of quality across all dimensions with exception of catering. The market player that needs to take strong action is C, which has notable competitive disadvantages as regards its facilities and catering despite being a costly place to stay.

Conjoint analysis

A more sophisticated variant on this method is to assign weights to the different features depending on how important they are to potential customers under varying circumstances. Thus the relative value of legroom as against price to an airline passenger will rise on long-haul flights as opposed to short trips. This *conjoint analysis* allows useful inter-company comparisons to be made and enables an airline to boost revenues by adjusting the kinds of planes used on different routes and its fares to meet customer preferences more exactly.

Win-loss analysis

Examining why one firm won a contract and the others failed can also yield revealing comparisons. While sales teams often conduct some form of *win-loss analysis*, there are good reasons for the CI unit and other functional areas to be involved in this. Many companies believe that is it sufficient to track their sales successes and failures or to conduct post-mortems when they take place. These are not enough to capture the full benefits of reviewing the factors that result in a competitive victory or defeat. Their perspective is limited to the sales team's outlook and the results are rarely shared with other functional groups, except perhaps top management. Many post-mortems are prompted by an ad hoc occurrence, typically the unexpected loss of a major account, rather than being periodic and ranging across the client base. Furthermore the lessons learned are often not recorded or generalized, so they get forgotten over time or are seen as purely specific to an individual client.

More effective win-loss analysis is directed towards customers or potential customers. Sales teams mostly lack the objectivity to conduct this themselves, being too emotionally involved with clients and the selling process to approach the task dispassionately. Hence firms that take this kind of study seriously use staff from the marketing, the CI team or external consultants to conduct the interviews with clients, with the sales people contributing their specialist knowledge to guide the other researchers. The customers selected for interviewing are generally those making the largest contribution to sales revenue, although there may a particular interest in certain market segments that are perhaps growing exceptionally quickly or seen as especially vulnerable to competitors. A decision also has to be made as to the frequency of carrying out this analysis (many companies adopt a quarterly cycle for undertaking it, as against annual or six-monthly surveys of customer satisfaction and loyalty).

The topics covered in these interviews will be company reputation, its sales approach, the attributes of the product and standards of service:

- *Company reputation* includes its image as against those of its rivals, the perception of the quality and reliability of its product range and the assessment of its financial stability.
- *Sales approach* covers the professionalism of its sales team (such as product knowledge and understanding of customer needs), the closeness of the relationship between the company and its client (including level of trust and whether it is the sole supplier or one of a group of firms selling to the customer) and the distribution mechanism (whether sales are made directly, through third parties or a mixture of the two and whether they are achieved via personal visits, mailshots, telemarketing, the Internet or any of the other promotional options).
- *Product attributes* deals with the features and specifications of the company's market offering, the quality of its technology and its pricing policies (including terms and conditions, special offers and other aspects of making its goods or services financially attractive to customers).
- *Service standards* relates to speed and reliability of delivery, the extent of disruption caused to the customer by installation, levels of maintenance provided by the supplier, customer training and quality of communications on service issues.

Well-conducted win-loss analysis is a powerful tool for understanding customer needs and their perceptions of how a firm compares against its market opponents. It provides both tactical and strategic benefits. On the tactical front the results obtained from it should enable the sales team to base their activities on a more profound understanding of what the client is seeking and to fine-tune their sales campaigns to achieve better results. Sales staff tend to place too much emphasis on price in explaining selling failures: 'We just couldn't compete with our competitor's price offer.' This can panic management into price cuts and special offers which reduce profit margins without an offsetting rises in revenues. By taking a multidimensional view, these kind of studies offer a more comprehensive view of the market battlefield. For example, the product on offer may be superior in quality and could command a premium price, but poor reliability in delivering on time leads the customer to choose a rival instead.

In terms of strategy, win-loss analysis is an excellent means of uncovering a firm's strengths and weaknesses – as perceived by the client. If these perceptions are incorrect, so that the reputation for unreliable delivery is undeserved, then the company has to communicate with its sales targets and demonstrate their unfairness. Should this reputation be well merited, then management must give improving delivery a high priority. Shared beyond the confines of the sales force the results can be used to guide new product development, the enhancement of existing products, changes in the way they are marketed and to aid the anticipation of competitor moves.

Conclusions

- A sound understanding of a firm's competitive situation demands comparison against other companies on a wide range of aspects of performance.
- Accurate and complete identification of competitors is vital for fully effective CI. Analysts should never assume that those named by clients or other parties provide them with a comprehensive and reliable list of rivals.
- Where management are operating with a faulty or incomplete knowledge of their existing or potential competitors, filling this gap is a major benefit of creating a CI function.
- Proper benchmarking generates extremely valuable corporate self-knowledge by comparing a company with others. If not directly involved in benchmarking exercises, CI analysts should obtain reports on these and sift them for material that yields actionable intelligence.
- They should also be aware of the results of strategic or marketing projects using gap or conjoint analysis, while it is desirable for them to participate in win-loss studies.

22 *What does the Future Hold?*

CI professionals use their knowledge of the past and understanding of the present to submit findings (and perhaps tender advice) that guides future decisions. This chapter is concerned with:

- qualities to be developed for fruitful understanding of the future and the types of study involved
- forecasting techniques and alternative approaches to exploring the future
- technology forecasts
- ways of attempting to gauge future competitor moves.

When it can be so difficult to discover what really happened in the past – not to mention what is actually happening at present – trying to discern the shape of the future is a daunting task for an analyst. To do well at it they must mobilize and develop certain essential skills and qualities:

- While dealing with very specific, narrow issues and handling fine detail they must never lose sight of the broader picture. Throughout this book I have stressed the vital need for them to take a wide view.
- This contextual background is based upon their knowledge of their industry, the key factors influencing it and the players involved in a particular market. Analysts must strive to maintain the currency of their sectoral knowledge and ever deepen it.
- At the same time, when endeavouring to provide management with enlightenment about the future, they must have a wider field of vision, extending beyond their industry. Every specialist profits from the insights offered by other disciplines and the whole spectrum of human experience and knowledge. Without this they become blinkered and risk being unprepared to challenge conventional industry wisdom. It is very beneficial for analysts to have an interest in subjects outside their own vocational concerns.
- Because the future grows out of the past, projections enriched by a historical perspective have a greater likelihood of being accurate. Good analysts never just start with the present and ignore the past. Instead they will be conscious of long-term trends, receptive to the immense variety of human experience at different times and in different places and appreciate the value of what the past can teach us. They will seek to uncover the historical roots and trace the evolution of the present situation when pondering its future development. The study of history also accustoms the analyst to handling incomplete or unreliable data.
- Thinking about the future is an exercise in imagination. Analysts have to try and envision all plausible possibilities, hence the need to nurture their creativity (as discussed already in Chapter 15).

- Finally, analysts must cultivate sound judgement. Without this quality no breadth and profundity of knowledge or vividness and richness of imagination will yield effective results. The definition of what constitutes judgement is a deep philosophical question, but it certainly encompasses the following attitudes of mind:

  - unprejudiced: a constant struggle against tacitly accepting unexamined assumptions and coming to a decision before properly considering the evidence
  - open-minded: being prepared to change viewpoint in the light of new data
  - balanced: giving each piece of evidence its due weight
  - insightful: getting to the roots of an issue and not being deflected by superficial aspects
  - incorporation of experience: reflecting on past situations and being able to draw correct lessons from these. Hence a more experienced analyst should be able to arrive at superior judgements than one who is relatively inexperienced
  - logical: constructing and testing an explicit chain of logic upon which an assessment rests.

  The forecasting component of CI involves three forms of study:

- Short-term, targeted projects to answer specific questions such as 'When will our competitor's new drug be launched?', 'Is one of our major suppliers going to collapse' or 'Which towns have the highest projected population growth?'.
- The ongoing 'radar screen' surveillance within the boundaries of the normal competitive environment, where the analyst keeps a lookout for anything interesting rather than searching for particular answers.
- 'Horizon scanning', trying to identify developments outside the usual frame which could have potential significance. The latter is the more difficult because of its unlimited scope and is less commonly performed. Yet its value in alerting management to new areas of opportunity and avoiding bolts from the blue from an unexpected direction can be immense.

Forecasting techniques

Several techniques of economic and business forecasting, ranging from the simple and inexpensive to sophisticated and costly methods such as war gaming, are available to analysts. Which they use will depend on their circumstances, but they need to be aware of these even if they are unable to apply all of them.

EXTRAPOLATION

Perhaps the most common is simple *extrapolation*, taking an existing trend and projecting it forward. This sometimes works well, but involves two major difficulties. The first is correctly distinguishing between the start of an enduring trend and a one-off aberration. Trends are more accurately discerned when they have been established for some time. However, this inevitably means the analysis is somewhat dated. Second, it assumes the trend will persist; in reality trends often fade in strength or are even reversed.

The crude use of extrapolation is often the downfall of lazy analysis. An aberrant event is wrongly seen as an entrenched feature or a trend simplistically run forward in a straight line. A press forecast that the explosive growth in the number of professional Elvis Presley lookalikes meant that most of the population would be earning its living donning rhinestone spangled suits in coming years was widely ridiculed. Yet much expert prediction is almost as crass. Share prices in the late 1990s, based on the assumption that US corporate profits could continue to expand by ten per cent each year, looked excessive when the secular trend rate of economic growth was under three per cent. As Friedman and colleagues have argued, analysts need to think in terms of curves rather than straight lines.

Much forecasting at the industry level produced by market research firms is based on extrapolation with some adjustments made to allow for the special features of a particular sector. Extrapolation is quick, easy and cheap to perform and can be profitably used for short-term forecasts, but should be used in tandem with other techniques and avoided for longer-run forecasting.

SURVEYS

An alternative, marketing-based approach is to undertake *surveys*. These are a useful way of finding out about present conditions and generally work well for very near-term forecasting. On the other hand they are too expensive for smaller individual firms to conduct and rarely valid for periods beyond about three to six months.

Numerous nationwide surveys are produced by business organizations such as the Confederation of British Industry or the Engineering Employers Federation. Some of these relate to the whole economy and others to particular sectors such as retailing

A description of the various surveys is given in an article I co-authored,[1] while Simon Bristow contributes some valuable guidance on their merits and drawbacks in his *Interpreting the Economy.*[2]

ECONOMETRIC MODELS

Macroeconomic forecasts are based upon *econometric models* where equations derived from statistical data are used to quantify the relationships between the different components of the economy. As well as the government's economic forecast compiled by the UK Treasury, many other institutions such as investment banks, academic economic research bodies, international organizations and private sector forecasters offer predictions of the outlook for the British economy. The Treasury publishes a monthly summary, *Forecasts for the UK Economy*, of all of these on the Economic Data and Tools page of its website (www.hm-treasury.gov.uk).

International bodies like the International Monetary Fund and OECD present forecasts for the world economy and for individual countries. A very useful set of links to these and other organizations undertaking forecasting is available on the Society of Business Economists website (www.sbe.co.uk).

Although econometric techniques are more powerful and accurate for longer-run forecasting than extrapolation and surveys, they are still far from reliable. In the 1960s and 1970s very complex models were used (the UK Treasury one had over 1200 variables). Later it was realized that just as a machine is more liable to malfunction as the number of parts in it increase, so the greater the sophistication of a model the higher the risk of it going wrong. Individual pieces of poor data or instability in the relationship between different parts of an economy could seriously upset the accuracy of the forecast. Michael Clements and David Hendry[3] list nine sources of error in econometric predictions. Contrary to a widely held view they argue that it is

1   Murphy, C. and Ng, S.L. (July–August 1998), 'Discover: Business surveys', *Managing Information*, 27–30.
2   Briscoe, S. (2000), *Interpreting the Economy: An essential guide to economic statistics*, Penguin, 187–99.
3   Clements, M. and Hendry, D.F. (1999), *Forecasting Non-Stationary Economic Time Series*, MIT Press.

changes in the relationships between the basic building blocks of models, rather than shocks resulting from the random, 'stochastic' element, which are the gravest cause of forecast error.

Former UK Government chief economic adviser Lord Burns suggests[4] that all the gains in computing and model building of the last few decades have failed to improve forecasting accuracy significantly because the economy has grown so much more complex in the same period. A more profound reason for this disappointment is pinpointed by John Walker,[5] who reminds us that governments, businesses and consumers *respond* to forecasts and thereby falsify them. Hence a predicted recession is headed off by cuts in interest rates and budget deficits or weakening demand for a company's products revived by steps such as rebranding and repackaging them, arranging special promotions and an advertising blitz. Walker convincingly argues that better forecasting should embrace both the contribution of efforts to improve its statistical base *and* the incorporation of qualitative judgement.

CI analysts thus have a considerable body of macroeconomic data and commentary available to them, but should use this to guide their view of the economic outlook rather than rely too heavily on the apparent precision of the predictions.

DELPHI TECHNIQUE

One way of leveraging the qualitative dimension is the *Delphi forecasting technique*. Named after the ancient Greek oracle located in the temple of Apollo at Delphi, this involves the distribution of a questionnaire canvassing views as to what the future holds. Its key virtue is that the respondents enjoy anonymity. Using the Delphi technique overcomes the drawback that can arise in meetings, when participants may be inhibited from challenging a dominant individual or clique – or junior/less experienced people hesitate to venture an opinion that may be ridiculed by those enjoying higher status. The organizer collates these responses and the questionnaire is circulated again along with a summary of the initial responses. The first set of questions may also be amended or new ones added in the light of the initial replies. Respondents are then invited to answer again, this time taking the views of the other people into account. This process continues until a consensus emerges.

As a way of generating forecasts the Delphi method has several weaknesses. First, the respondents may have such divergent views that no general ground of agreement can be reached. Second, it takes longer and involves more effort than a simple round table meeting, conference call or videoconference. Finally, a consensus may simply be wrong! Against this it has the considerable merits of ensuring that everyone has a chance to air their views, nonconformist opinions are considered as well as the conventional wisdom and important issues are less likely to be overlooked. There is also experimental evidence that groups generally produce better decisions than individuals.[6]

---

4   Burns, T.J. (2001), 'The costs of forecast errors' in Hendry, D. and Ericsson, N.R. (eds), *Understanding Economic Forecasting*, MIT Press.

5   Walker, J. (2003), 'Does forecasting have a future' in Hurst, J. (ed.), *The Challenge of Change: Fifty years of business economics*, Profile Books.

6   For the results of an experiment using London School of Economics students see: Lornbardelli, C., Talbot, J. and Proudman, J. (Autumn 2002), 'Committees versus individuals: An experimental analysis of monetary policy decision-making', *Bank of England Quarterly Bulletin*, 262–73, and outlining similar research at Princeton University in the US: Blinder, A.S. and Morgan, J. (September 2000), 'Are two heads better than one?: An experimental analysis of group vs individual decision making', *NBER Working Paper No. 7909*.

NEURAL NETWORKS

Some technological support in trying to predict quantitative dimensions of the future such as sales or costs is now available in the form of neural networks.[7] People learn through rearrangements in the connections between their brain cells (neurons) and this type of software tries to imitate the way the human brain works. It uses trial and error to refine its predictions and is claimed to be superior in accuracy to statistical techniques such as linear regression[8] and to have produced a better forecast of US Treasury bill rates one year ahead than either the futures market or leading economists.[9]

A number of packages are available. A popular one used in CI is California Scientific's BrainMaker (www.calsci.com) while NeuroXL Predictor is inexpensive and easy to learn to use (www.neuroxl.com).

Alternative futures

For decision making the most fruitful avenue is to go beyond making a single prediction for the future and instead examine alternative versions. Thus government economists and planners will produce best case, central and worst case versions of their forecasts. In corporate planning this typically takes the form of *sensitivity analysis* where the vulnerability of a project to environmental changes is explored. This will result in questions being posed such as: 'What will be the effect on our sales if the economy only grows by one per cent instead of the two per cent expected?' or 'Is this product line viable if it achieves less than five per cent market share within a year?' This broader approach offers a richer learning experience by forcing decision takers to consider the consequences of different outcomes and how they might respond to these. It also reduces over-dependence on forecasts and the resultant damage if they are inaccurate.

SCENARIOS

However, there is still the difficulty that the future may assume more than just three shapes and the tendency of most people to seek shelter in 'the comfortable middle' case situation. Thus an even broader range of possibilities can be explored by creating scenarios. It is important to stress that these are not predictions of what *will* happen, but what might happen. For instance, the CI team may have learned that a competitor is planning to replace its existing IT configuration with enterprise software. This means that there will now be a single company-wide IT platform instead of the production, warehousing, accounts and other departments using their own specialist software. Reviewing the experience of other firms who have made this switch shows that it offers considerable long-term efficiency and cost-saving benefits (thus making the competitor more dangerous). However, a project of this nature is fraught with difficulty and there have been several cases where serious harm has been suffered when it has been botched.

A scenario could be imagined in which the rival's supply chain is disrupted by failings in the new IT system and they are unable to fulfil customer orders for some time. The actionable issues would then be 'How well placed are we to seize business from them during this period and what steps can we take to prevent the new clients going back to their old supplier when deliveries

---

7   Zhang, G.P. (2003), *Neural Networks in Business Forecasting*, Information Science Publishing, is a good introduction to the applications of this software.
8   Aiken, M. (1996), 'Using a neural network in business forecasting', *American Business Perspectives*, 192, 1–3.
9   Aiken, M. (1995), 'Forecasting T-bill rates with a neural network', *Technical Analysis of Stocks and Commodities*, 13(5), 85–89.

return to normal?' This is not based on expecting the project to go wrong – it is actually more probable that it will proceed smoothly. The scenario's contribution is to prepare the ground for contingency planning so to grasp this opportunity should it arise. In its absence there may not be enough time to pull together plans hurriedly and rearrange production or sales activity to exploit the rival's temporary weakness.

Devising scenarios demands both unchained imagination and rigorous logic. An analyst who is afraid to stray too far into speculative territory will create scenarios that are closer to the probable than the possible. This risks – as has so often happened – being caught flat-footed by 'the unthinkable'. At the same time scenarios are grounded in plausibility. Creative exploration inspires them, but they are not pure fantasy. An operationally useable scenario has to be *possible* in terms of contemporary knowledge even if it seems highly unlikely. This means it has to have an undoubted substratum of fact and a robust logical chain linking this with the conclusions. Two invaluable tests of the strength of that chain are:

- checking for internal consistency (something elaborated in the next chapter)
- putting each link in the chain to the proof by applying linchpin analysis (as discussed on page 80).

SIMULATION

Scenarios are a powerful means of trying to anticipate the unexpected. A related, but more narrowly focused technique (because it does rely upon prediction) is to simulate the likely outcome of a new corporate initiative. Simulation goes beyond mere marketing projections by also factoring in competitors' responses to it. One major oil company considered building 24-hour filling stations in rural areas, reasoning that this was an underserved market and would appeal to country motorists because of the added convenience. The project was estimated to produce a significant increase in revenues. However, management realized that their competitors were not going to allow them uncontested control of this new market, but would hit back by building their own chains of filling stations. An initial spurt in profits would be dissipated as rivals started taking their share of the rural market and trimming margins. Once the high capital cost of constructing these stations was taken into account, the simulation indicated total future profitability would actually be lower than if the project was abandoned and the resources provisionally assigned to it invested in other areas of the business.

Simulation thus enables a company to try out a new initiative and gauge the impact of competitor countermoves on its eventual gains or losses. It has something in common with the flight simulators used to train pilots before they are entrusted with actual planes. Where it differs in business is the grave uncertainty over revenue and cost projections compared with the known laws of avionics.

WAR GAMES

The most sophisticated form of simulation is the war game. Military planners try to improve their understanding of what will happen in actual campaigns (and hone commanders' skills in responding to changing circumstances) by forming teams and then role-playing in particular situations. In business war gaming there will usually teams representing:

- customers
- existing competitors

- potential future competitors
- the 'X team' playing the role of macro factors like the state of the economy, regulation or technological change.

Depending upon resources many other teams may participate representing parties such as suppliers, distribution channels, strategic allies, analysts and media commentators, employees, shareholders or civic lobbying groups.

As well as the players there will also be:

- umpires who ensure compliance with the rules of the game and make rulings on the acceptability of unconventional moves
- market judges who produce assessment of changes in market share/profitability at the end of each round of the game (these may be people, more often computer-generated scoring will be used)
- game overseers who devise the contest, are responsible for its administrative support and write up the conclusions reached.

This list of dramatis personae highlights the practical drawback of war gaming. In its fullest version the technique requires the commitment of a lot of time from many highly pressured executives who are probably dubious about the business value of playing games. However, it is possible to run less elaborate versions. The essence of war gaming is role-play and this can be conducted effectively among even a few people.

At the beginning of the game, having been briefed on the market situation and their resources, the competitors decide their first moves. These are then scored by the customer's team in terms of how well the new initiatives meet their needs and the market judges award increased or reduced market share to each competitor.

The game goes on for perhaps three or four rounds with each player responding to the moves made by the other parties. When it ends each team produces a summary of the lessons learned. These are then presented before all the participants and the game masters summarize them into a series of conclusions which form the basis for a plan of action.

War gaming not only provides a far broader and deeper understanding of the competitive environment, but is also a superb means of developing the skills of managers. Like simulation it gives them the chance to learn through making mistakes – without incurring the risk of inflicting damage on their firms.

Technology forecasting

CI analysts are concerned with technological developments in two ways. First, by being aware of the more profound technical advances that will affect their industry as a whole, perhaps completely transforming the options available to producers and customers. Second, through their need to track tactical changes where incremental technological improvements are made by their suppliers or rivals (although, as argued in Chapter 1, responding to these should not be at the centre of a firm's competitive strategy).

Hence they are concerned that forecasts of future technology are usually so inaccurate. Ringland, Gill and colleagues[10] tried to pin down the reasons for this. One problem is the human tendency to base their projections on far more powerful versions of existing technologies (extrapolation once again). Thus Jules Verne in *Five Weeks in a Balloon* imagined the earth being destroyed by the explosion of 'some colossal boiler', while H.G. Wells foresaw the use of atomic weapons in *The World Set Free* – in the form of grenades thrown from the open cockpits of aircraft. Even people as extraordinarily imaginative as these could not escape the mental limitations imposed by the familiar (and at the time highly impressive) contemporary technologies of steam power and bi-planes. Likewise the obsession with imagining robots that walked and spoke like humans lead to the potential of electronic computers being underestimated or misunderstood. In Robert Heinlein's *Starman Jones*, while the astronauts do have computers aboard, they spend a lot of time using logarithmic tables to process the data manually *prior* to entering it into their machines.[11]

The opposite obstacle to accurate technology forecasting is an exaggeration of the potential of exciting new technologies or the speed of their adoption. Forecasts of nuclear powered buses running on city centre streets ignored issues of safety and acceptance. James Watt invented a mechanical copying device in 1780 that was used for many years to make copies of legal documents, yet mass copying was not to become a reality until long after his time. A form of facsimile transmission was patented as long ago as 1843 and even when fax machines of the modern type were developed they were slow and expensive and it would take some 20 years for them to be fully diffused.

Ringland and colleagues also allude to the ease with which experts in a field can become blinkered and fail to perceive or accept 'wider field' possibilities. At the same time their undoubted knowledge and expertise ensures their views are treated with respect. Once a fully developed conceptual framework, a *paradigm*, is in place and represents the consensus view, it is very difficult to dislodge. Alternative viewpoints tend to be marginalized, dismissed or even ridiculed. It is hard for lone or minority voices to get a hearing and receive serious consideration. That those who depart from the accepted wisdom are regarded as mavericks (a word originally applied to stray cows) and this may harm their careers creates a strong disincentive against disturbing the consensus.

Apart from trying to identify strategic shifts in technology, CI analysts are also concerned with tactical technology intelligence. A good example of this was a case study presented by Wayne Rosenkrans at the SCIP symposium on 'The Value of Technical Intelligence' in 1997.[12] This concerned the development of an anti-cancer drug by SmithKline. Marketing plans for the product had to take into account when a rival compound from Bristol-Myers Squibb (BMS) would be launched. SmithKline's CI team saw growing evidence that the competing drug would be released much earlier than originally believed. BMS was dedicating substantially more money and scientists than previously to its development, while Congressional testimony revealed that production of the compound was being stepped up. Their conclusion was correct, the application for regulatory approval of this preparation being brought forward by 18 months. This early warning enabled SmithKline's management to formulate a new marketing strategy in time to respond to the far earlier launch of the rival drug.

---

10 Ringland, G. and others (1999), 'Shocks and paradigm busters (why do we get surprised?)', *Long Range Planning*, 32(4), 403–13.

11 Nicolls, P. (ed.) (1983), *The Science in Science Fiction: Does science fiction foretell the future?*, Michael Joseph.

12 Rosenkrans, W.A. (1998), 'Past, present and future directions for technical intelligence', *Competitive Intelligence Review*, 9(2), 34–39.

Gauging future competitor moves

Anticipating the future actions of business rivals is vital in a competitive environment. This contest has been given more abstract, mathematical expression in *game theory*. Thus the term 'zero sum game' has entered common parlance to describe a situation where (in the business context) a competitor seizes market share from a rival, but the total size of the market remains the same. While I noted the dangers of an excessive concentration on what competitors are doing back in Chapter 1, not giving them adequate attention is also to court disaster.

Accurate anticipation has two components. First, detecting indications of change in a competitor's intentions and actions. This requires a comprehensive and continuous search for evidence of these, hence effective scanning by the analyst is essential if these indications are to be picked up. Second, the evidence has to be interpreted using hypotheses. These have to be judged in the context of the industry in general and the particular circumstances of the competitor.

If a competitor announces a price reduction there can be many reasons for this decision. For example:

- The company is simply following an already established trend for players in the market to trim prices.
- Lower industry-wide prices were expected and a competitor is the first to implement this.
- The price cut may be across the full range of the firm's products or restricted to part of its offering or even just a single product.
- This decision could be a long-term strategy or just a short-term move that will be reversed fairly soon.
- The firm's management might have decided to capture market share rather than maintain profit margins.
- A financially strong competitor may be trying to drive less prosperous rivals out of the market by launching a price war.
- On the other hand it could be prompted by the competitor's marketing or financial weaknesses such as an accumulation of unsold stocks or an urgent need to boost cash flow even at the expense of profitability.

Without this contextual knowledge numerous hypotheses can be tabled, but no judgement can be reached because any of them are plausible in themselves.

The signal may be sufficiently convincing for an analyst to form a rapid conclusion, but in many cases the evidence will be too ambiguous or too unreliable for a firm judgement to be reached. Here they must look out for other data that support or contradict a hypothesis. For instance an original conclusion was that the price cut was a short-term move to boost market share would have to be revised if new information suggested that the firm was in fact intending to exit this particular market and wanted to sell off its remaining stock quickly.

Shifts in a rival's general strategy are easier to detect because they involve the whole company, are executed over time and are more likely to be communicated publicly either directly in management statements or indirectly through its dealings with customers, distribution channels or suppliers. Changes in the components of that strategy such as output (an expansion of productive capacity, for instance), R&D (a project to develop a different product line) or marketing (plans to launch a new service) are more elusive. They are often deliberately shrouded in secrecy, which can sometimes even be used as marketing tool. Thus the motoring press have their curiosity piqued by manufacturers giving tantalizing hints about new models while keeping the vehicles carefully hidden as so to maximize the impact of their actual launch.

However, there are a number of keys to such mysteries. It is extremely difficult to avoid leaving some clues. An expansion of production may require extra machines to be bought and workers hired or the extension of premises. This may be reported in the media, revealed in recruitment advertising or through filings for planning permission or to meet environmental regulations, detected by direct observation (for example, building work at a site or an increase in the workforce or number of shifts they work) or simply become a subject of industry gossip. R&D projects may be referred to at scientific conferences and in publicly available regulatory documents or indicated by the filing of new trade marks and patents. Using industry experience it may then be possible to estimate a timeline for when they will be ready to come to market. Preparations for new product launches such as arranging advertising campaigns, hiring new ad agencies, booking venues to unveil the new offering and inviting the press and others to attend them are all activities that may come to the notice of rivals.

In trying to divine the future analysts need to make judgements as to the speed and characteristics of change. The index of environmental turbulence developed by H. Igor Ansoff is a helpful way of trying to gauge how well a company is placed to manage change. There is only space here for a brief description of his matrix, but it is well worth exploring further in the influential book he co-authored with McDonnell.[13]

A slow moving company in a rapidly changing environment will not succeed, neither will a firm who puts a huge effort into research and development and frequent new product launches if the pace of technological development in its sector is leisurely and product life cycles long. Ansoff's approach is to assess the degree of turbulence in a sector in terms of several features (like the rate of change, intensity of competition or length of typical product life cycles). The next stage is to profile an individual player in this market according to eight critical characteristics such as its marketing, culture and style of strategic planning.

Table 12   Ansoff Turbulence Index

Turbulence rating	1	2	3	4	5
Rate of change	Slow		Fast		Chaotic
Complexity of change	Low		Moderate		High
Intensity of competition	Slight		Moderate		Ferocious
Predictability	High		Moderate		Unpredictable
Length of product life cycle	Long		Moderate		Very short
Value chain	Multi-level		Compressed		Vertical integration
Pace of technological change	Slow		Fast		Discontinuous

Ansoff contends that when a company's rating on any of its critical characteristics lags over one scale point behind the general level of turbulence in its chosen market then its profitability is markedly reduced. Once the gap exceeds one and a half points the damage to profitability will be severe.

Ansoff and Underwood[14] used the failed AT&T acquisition of NCR as a case study. They rated turbulence in the computer sector following the deal as very high (4.3 per cent). The

---

13 Ansoff, H.I. and McDonnell, E. (1990), *Implanting Strategic Management*, 2nd ed., Prentice Hall.
14 Underwood, J. (1998), 'Perspectives on war gaming', *Competitive Intelligence Review*, 9(2), 46–52.

industry was changing very rapidly, these changes were highly complex and future developments extremely unpredictable. When they assessed the post-deal NCR they found serious mismatches in marketing, innovation and management and critical deficiencies on the other five dimensions. They concluded that the failure of the acquisition arose from AT&T imposing a corporate profile on NCR more suited to a low turbulence sectoral environment.

In over one thousand studies, Ansoff found a positive correlation between the degree to which an organizational profile matched the market environment and its profitability. Underwood has also used the model in assessing large US corporations in the Fortune 500 group and reports that the predictions for industry changes it generated were highly accurate.

Conclusions

- An analyst's ability to project the future is enhanced by them:
  - gaining knowledge through study, interacting with others and observation
  - the stimulation of their creativity
  - cultivating good judgement, which is a bundle of attitudes of mind rather than a set of techniques.
- Technology forecasting is improved in a strategic sense by stretching the imagination beyond the limits of the familiar and in a tactical context by being on the alert for signals of technological moves.
- This also applies when monitoring competitors for signs of change in intent or action. When detected the implications of these indications should be explored. The hypotheses they provoke must be assessed for plausibility in the light of industry and competitor knowledge and tested against new signals which confirm or undermine them.
- The late James Morrell wrote a splendid guide to business forecasting, *How to Forecast*,[15] which analysts will find of great help in tackling this most difficult aspect of their work.
- An excellent introduction to developing scenarios is *The Art of the Long View* by Peter Swartz.[16]
- They should also consider joining the World Future Society: 'an association of people interested in how social and technological developments are shaping the future' which now has 25 000 members in over 80 countries (www.wfs.org).
- The Wharton business school provides a comprehensive description of forecasting methods on its 'Principles of Forecasting' website (to be used in conjunction with a book of that title): http://morris.wharton.upenn.edu/forecast/.

---

15 Morrell, J. (2001), *How to Forecast*, Gower.
16 Swartz, P. (1996), *The Art of the Long View: Planning for the future in an uncertain world*, Currency.

23 *The End Crowns All – Disseminating Competitive Intelligence*

This chapter is devoted to the final stages in the intelligence cycle – the dissemination of the analyst's conclusions. Its first section considers the accuracy, credibility and timeliness of their content and the second the way in which they are presented.

Content accuracy and credibility

CI conclusions must be both accurate and accepted as such by the consumer of intelligence. So analysts:

- must take care to avoid contradicting themselves
- should unbendingly reject the temptation of unjustifiably manipulating, ignoring or concocting data in order to make them agree with their conclusions
- nevertheless they have to avoid any failure, due to an excessive desire for accuracy on their part, to produce conclusions in time for them to be of use to their end-users.

    The appropriate level of accuracy:

- depends upon source quality, the analyst's skill and the importance of the issue involved
- is more likely to be achieved when methods and conclusions are scrutinized *before* presenting their findings.

CONTRADICTIONS

Some CI reportage is marred by self-contradiction. For example, a statement that 'strengths include rigorous financial discipline' cannot be reconciled with the later observation that 'weaknesses include poor cost control'. Regardless of the excellence of work that has gone into preparing the report, it counts for nothing if the analyst lacks credibility owing to self-contradiction.

    Now contradictions may be merely apparent. For example, the characterization of a market as 'fast growing and broadly based' sounds attractive. The reader is then bemused by the observation that: 'several competitors have recently withdrawn from this market'. In fact both conclusions were true. The market environment was favourable. However, to exploit the opportunity effectively demanded a substantial commitment of resources and some of the players lacked these. Recalling that strategy must balance opportunity *with capability* explains the seeming paradox. These companies acted rationally in pulling out because they did not possess the means needed to take advantage of this growing market without having to divert them from their core operations.

The lesson here is to be on the alert for apparent contradictions, for the analyst to show that they are aware they sound paradoxical and to explain why they are consistent in reality.

FACT-FITTING

While self-contradiction is a potentially disastrous blemish in a CI report, it is inevitably committed unconsciously. *Fact-fitting*, on the other hand is a deliberate act of deception (although, perhaps, of the perpetrator as well as the person reading the report). Here data are twisted, ignored or even invented to support conclusions. It is a huge temptation because the real world is so untidy, confusing and baffling, whereas the report has to be a logical, coherent and persuasive submission. Analysts need hypotheses in order to drive forward their enquiries. The danger lies in them becoming so committed to their theories that they deny evidence incompatible with them. Awkward facts or views can then be massaged or just allowed to fall by the wayside when the final report is written.

Even more serious is when an analyst simply concocts evidence.

CASE OF THE LAZY ACADEMIC

When doing a market sizing exercise I found a working paper produced by a faculty member in a business school that provided a suspiciously exact looking figure of £65 million. No source was given and so I phoned the academic to probe further. His response was vague and unconvincing: 'It's based on interviews I've conducted with people in the industry.' After this conversation enlightenment came to me. For various reasons the potential maximum market size of the sector was known to be around £120–£140 million. He had taken the mid-point of this range at £130 million and then simply divided by two. An extravagant example of sheltering in the 'safe middle'!

If academics resort to this kind of thing, it is no surprise that there is an even stronger temptation for CI staff, as well as journalists, market researchers, security analysts – who have a much more powerful financial incentive – to indulge in fact-fitting.

EXCESSIVE DESIRE FOR CERTAINTY

Clearly such dishonesty is unethical and, if an analyst indulging in it presents their conclusions to a shrewd person, they will be in serious trouble when their efforts to bend the truth are exposed. The other side of the coin is that too fervent a search for accuracy and completeness can also be a vice. It may be a wasteful use of time, energy and other limited resources and fail to align with the need for CI to be delivered in time for it to be acted upon.

While some of the data presented may be reasonably reliable, many conclusions analysts arrive at are uncertain, *of their nature*. Business decisions cannot be postponed in a misguided search for greater certainty, more thorough coverage or closer accuracy. Some executives fail in their jobs because they lack the self-confidence and realism to make decisions based on imperfect information. The tide of business needs to be taken at full flood and dithering and delay are often more dangerous than a bolder approach. So analysts have to balance their natural – and commendable – commitment to attaining the highest level of accuracy against the need for producing CI in time for it to still have value in influencing management decisions.

APPROPRIATELY ACCURATE INTELLIGENCE

The reliability of conclusions and the degree of accuracy required depend on several factors:

- The quality of the sources used. Here analysts may have to make do with what they can get. However, the more they are able to cross-check them, the greater can be their confidence. Being able to compare a secondary source with the original it is derived from can help establish if the first source has been accurately reported and interpreted.
- The analyst's skill in drawing conclusions from the evidence also has a significant impact on the accuracy of their recommendations. This skill has to be honed through experience, education through courses, reading and exchanging knowledge with others and seeking their advice.
- Finally, they must ask 'What's at stake?' A report that will influence a major strategic departure demands a higher level of exactitude than an exercise where relatively small stakes are being hazarded.

TESTING THE ROBUSTNESS OF CI CONCLUSIONS

In defending their research methods and findings CI professionals need to justify them to themselves before releasing them to others. Have they been diligent in ensuring that all systematic sources have been thoroughly mined? Did they demonstrate mental energy and ingenuity in identifying and using creative sources? Is the analysis sound? These vital procedures are often skimped because the end of the intelligence cycle has been almost reached (as shown in Figure 14) and the analyst is impatient to present their conclusions (and is perhaps being pressed by management to supply them).

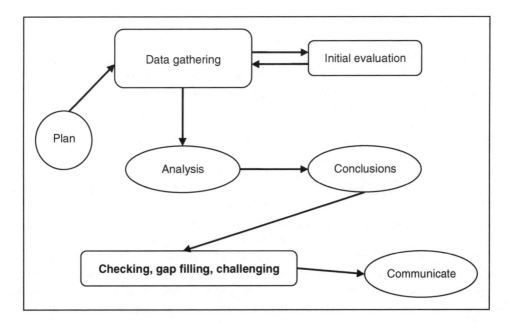

Figure 14   Checking, filling gaps and challenging conclusions

The most rigorous way of testing CI conclusions to destruction is to have a separate 'B' team of analysts not involved in the project examine them with a view to detecting weaknesses in the data and their interpretation. Where this is impracticable, those specializing in CI should try and get a colleague from another functional area to review their evidence and findings. Whoever is probing the individual components of the analysis, a number of general tests can be applied.

Organizational impediments

- Have the ideological leanings of the organization been allowed to override the personal judgement of the analyst?
- Do bureaucratic procedures inhibit 'china breaking' analysis? So if the results have to receive approval from a department head before being disseminated this may discourage the analyst from straying too far from the 'safe middle'.
- What has been the impact of resource limitations on the quality of the analysis?

Systemic weaknesses of the analyst

- Is the analyst too knowledgeable about a topic? They can be so closely connected with it that they complacently rely upon accepted industry wisdom, ignoring other factors outside its traditional frame of reference.
- Perhaps the problem is the opposite one where they have made superficial assessments because of lack of knowledge.
- Has the analyst a preference for certain types of data, financial statements for example, which receive greater attention than others?

Flaws in a specific piece of analysis

- Are assumptions being treated as facts?
- Has what was initially expected had too much influence on the outcome?
- The opposite problem – are the most recently collected data given excessive weight compared with that obtained earlier?
- Small, successive changes in the data being collected may add up to a significant shift over time, yet the analyst fails to notice this incremental process.
- Are there significant gaps in the coverage?
- Is the chain of logic supporting the findings intact?
- How well do the conclusions stand up to linchpin analysis (discussed earlier on page 80)?

CI analysts are expected to do their job in a dispassionate, objective way. They must constantly battle against their own preconceptions, unchallenged assumptions, prejudices, wishful thinking and pet theories (before even beginning to struggle against these vices among their colleagues). A good CI person has the emotional humility and intellectual flexibility to change their mind in the light of the evidence. None of this means they are bloodless machines – the best analysts care passionately about doing their job well, coming up with correct interpretations and delivering results that make a difference. Only such a powerful emotional commitment to their discipline can give them the psychological strength to put forward and defend their case (based as it usually is on imperfect data and clouded by uncertainty) in the face of scepticism, vested interests and more senior colleagues who disagree with it. As Friedman and colleagues succinctly express it: while many people prefer to be wrong than to be the odd one out, the exemplary CI analyst 'has to be indifferent to whether he is alone or in good company ... [and] more obsessed with whether he is right than with whether his boss likes him'.[1]

KEY POINTS

- The content of CI end-products needs to be checked and challenged before submission to users.

- A 'B' team of analysts not directly involved in a project is the ideal way to do this.

- Alternatively a colleague from another discipline or department should be invited to review the findings.

- Analysts may end up having to perform this exercise on their own.

- In all of these cases the tests mentioned above should be applied.

Means and styles of communication

Actually presenting the findings is the final leg in the long journey which began with planning the CI project and thus the last stage (as shown in Figure 15) of the intelligence cycle.

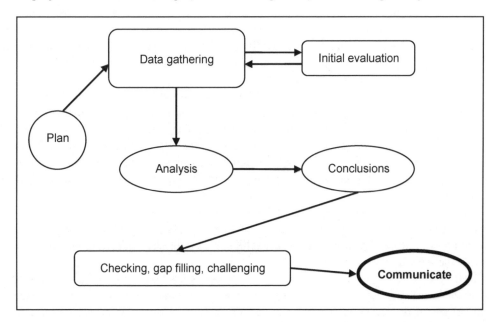

Figure 15   Dissemination – the final stage in producing intelligence

The method of disseminating findings will vary greatly between organizations depending on their culture, operational structure and the preferences of individual managers. This can range from a short conversation held in the lift to a formal presentation with slides and hefty volumes

---

1   Friedman, G. and others (1998), *The Intelligence Edge: How to profit in the information age*, Century, 194.

of supporting documentation. Analysts must tailor their methods and manner of communicating results to meet the particular needs and tastes of the audience(s) they are addressing.

GETTING THROUGH TO THE INTELLIGENCE CONSUMER

They also have to get their message through before trying to get it across. One practitioner discovered that her emails to a senior manager did not reach him because his secretary vetted incoming messages and deleted any (like the unfortunate analyst's) she considered low priority. However, he did listen to voicemail messages himself and using this approach ensured the CI reached its recipient. If an analyst is getting no response from an end-user they should check to see that it actually being seen by them.

METHOD OF COMMUNICATION

The medium selected by analysts for reporting intelligence is ultimately determined by the needs of their audience and the resources available to them. However, the various types of CI output tend to be communicated through particular channels:

- *Basic intelligence* supplies the foundations for a CI function. This is the knowledge bank created and maintained by analysts containing background data on topics such as industry structure and trends, competitor profiles and details of information sources. It enables answers to straightforward factual questions to be supplied quickly and shows where to seek further material. This resource must be updated and extended as soon as fresh information becomes available. It can be made directly available to executives through an intranet, although some material may be excluded from this on the grounds of commercial sensitivity or the need to protect source confidentiality.

- *Current awareness services* providing short-term (daily or perhaps weekly) intelligence. As speed of delivery is essential these are usually mounted on intranets or distributed via email or as printed sheets and contain little or no analysis. They may also mention relevant CI already created. For example, a report that a competitor is scrapping its direct sales force might be accompanied by a reference to an intranet document detailing earlier instances of switching to distribution though intermediaries. They can assume both a standardized form and also be refined to meet the specific needs of teams or individual executives. These alerting services stimulate the demand for further intelligence as recipients see items on which they would like more information or some analysis performed. They are also a common way of disseminating technical intelligence, the results of ongoing monitoring of a particular topic or early warning material.

- *Targeted intelligence* is created in response to responses from end-users. It can be short term and consist of data gathered quickly from internal and external sources such as existing CI, the results of database and internet searches or an account of a conversation with a trade association. The level of analysis will vary from none being undertaken to the analyst structuring, summarizing and commenting on it. It is typically delivered by email.

- This type of CI can also be longer term which generally demands a considerable amount of data collection and analysis. It may be limited to a detailed background description of a topic, but will also often involve the creation of projections and scenarios of the future. The end product is usually a presentation or written report.

BREVITY

Whatever mode of communication is chosen analysts have to strive to report their findings succinctly.

It has already been seen that many consumers of competitive intelligence do not want the whole story – they prefer a few key points. In contrast, researchers and analysts often believe that a lengthy and elaborate report is the best illustration of their value. Such a mismatch between what is wanted and what is provided is a massive weakness in a CI programme. A great deal of research and analysis may be needed to produce a few salient points, but there is no need to report all of it. The great philosopher and mathematician Rene Descartes famously apologized for writing such a long letter. Descartes explained that he was too pressed for time to write a shorter one! What he meant was that if he had been less busy he would have drafted a briefer, more considered and pithier epistle. So analysts should review their work to see if it can be distilled further without omitting relevant points before submitting it.

Concise intelligence is not only easier for users to absorb, the discipline of condensing their mass of material into a compact finished product helps analysts distinguish those items which carry greater significance and also clarifies and tests the line of argument they intend to advance.

SHOULD ANALYSTS MAKE RECOMMENDATIONS AS WELL AS PROVIDING ANALYSIS?

There will also be major differences in this aspect of content depending on organizational culture and individual managers' tastes. In some cases analysts will be expected to outline the present situation or explore the most likely future outcome rather than a set of choices for management. Here the analyst should generally emphasize that this represents their best judgement, but that other outcomes (which should be outlined and assessed in terms of probability) are possible. The degree of prescription will also vary considerably. As the ultimate responsibility for a decision rests with those actually taking it, some practitioners take the view that CI professionals should only provide analysis. They fear that to be seen advocating a particular course may cloud their objectivity and offend management by appearing to usurp their role. In other situations, especially when the analyst is a consultant working on behalf of a client, a greater willingness to make recommendations will be expected.

STYLE OF WRITTEN MATERIAL

Such divergent views are also reflected in writing styles, a number of practitioners believing that displaying emotion suggests lack of objectivity. Constance Thomas Ward, on the other hand says that by showing 'passionate conviction of truth in your writing, you will be more convincing'.[2] I incline towards the latter viewpoint – after all if the analyst does not argue their case vigorously why should anyone else take it too seriously – so long as passion does not displace professionalism or lead to the use of theatrically exaggerated language. Indeed, making statements with words such as 'surveillance' and similar terms associated with spying could prove highly embarrassing if allegations of unethical or illegal conduct were made, while over-dramatic phrases like 'smashing the competition' might be construed as evidence of unlawful anti-competitive activity. Provided this kind of excess is avoided there is no reason why CI reports should not be written in a lively and attractive way.

---

2   Ward, C. (1999), 'Myths about CI report writing', *Competitive Intelligence Magazine*, 2(1), 35–36.

An analyst's writing skills can be honed by studying handbooks on effective written communications like the classic *The Complete Plain Words*.[3] Reference works such as newspaper style guides can also help avoid errors and inconsistencies.[4] For advice on ways of presenting numerical and graphical data Peter Sprent's *Understanding Data*[5] or Edward Tufte's *The Visual Display of Quantitative Data*[6] are excellent textbooks.

Just as it is highly desirable to have someone else review the content of a presentation or report before it is submitted, getting another person to proofread the text is very beneficial.

GIVING BRIEFINGS RATHER THAN WRITTEN REPORTS

Although much material is delivered in written form, there can be occasions when a face-to-face briefing is called for. Where the analyst is not in physical proximity to the end-user this may take the form of phone and conference calls or videoconferencing. Such direct briefings are clearly appropriate during periods of organizational crisis when the issues involved carry serious consequences and the time available to deal with them is very short.

Bill Fiora also recommends them as probably the best way to deliver early warning intelligence.[7] A personal encounter may be a better means of conveying the potential significance of the opportunity or threat when the evidence for it is usually vague and tentative. A briefing can also be useful in advance of meetings with existing or possible business partners, a major industry conference or trade show or an executive's media appearance. Additionally, it can be included as part of an acclimatization programme when a new manager is appointed.

From the analyst's viewpoint, briefings are also an excellent way to get a deeper insight into managers' thinking and preferences. As it involves two-way communication they can also learn, whereas other types of CI delivery are a learning experience only for the recipient. Fiora warns analysts to be prepared for questions that range beyond the immediate issue and believes a formal presentation with slides tends to inhibit inter-communication (although he accepts that a picture or chart drawn on a whiteboard or flip chart can be a useful visual aid).

APPLYING THE PYRAMID PRINCIPLE

Given the complexity of business, how can analysts come up with terse, compelling findings? Short-term memory is confined to between five and nine items, as George Miller has demonstrated.[8] If we try and remember more items, we simply forget them. A means of coping with this limitation has been applied to reporting conclusions by Barbara Minto in formulating her pyramid principle.[9] She was invited to produce a methodology for consultants at McKinsey & Co. to make effective presentations of their recommendations to management. Minto's approach was to display the findings in a pyramid structure rather like an organization chart. An example of this is given in Figure 16.

3 Gowers, E., Greenbaum, S. and Whitcut, J. (2002), *The Complete Plain Words*, David R. Godine.
4 Some key examples: The Economist (2003), *The Economist Style Guide*, 8th edition, Bloomberg Press. Inman, C. (2000), *The Financial Times Style Guide*, Financial Times Prentice Hall. Austin, T. (2003), *The Times Style and Usage Guide*, Harper UK.
5 Sprent, P. (1998), *Understanding Data*, Penguin.
6 Tufte, E.R. (2001), *The Visual Display of Quantitative Information*, 2nd edition, Graphics Press. See also his (1990), *Envisioning Information*, Graphics Press.
7 Fiora, W. (2002), 'The lost art of briefing', *Competitive Intelligence Magazine*, 5(3), 35–36.
8 Miller, G.A. (1969), *Psychology of Communication*, Penguin.
9 Minto, B. (1996), *The Pyramid Principle: Logic in writing, thinking and problem solving*, Minto International.

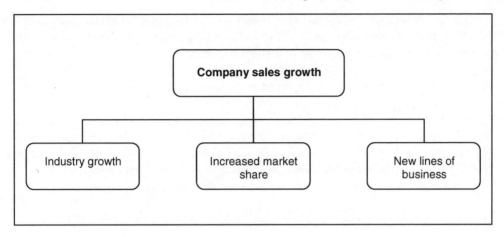

Figure 16 Pyramid principle – a logical chain to make sense of complexity

For example, we want to know the sources of sales growth for a company. This can arise from three causes. First, the industry expands, bringing extra sales to the players operating in it. Second, our company increases its market share. So the sales of the individual enterprise rise, even if the industry size remains static. Third, the firm can develop new lines of business outside its original sector.

We can carry on this progression (as illustrated in Figure 17). Where does industry growth come from? Either an increased volume of sales or the ability to achieve higher prices for an unchanged level of sales. The pyramid principle enables even the most complex progressions to be easily traced as they cascade down the chain in logical order and converts the seemingly bewildering ramifications of a business situation into something easy to grasp.

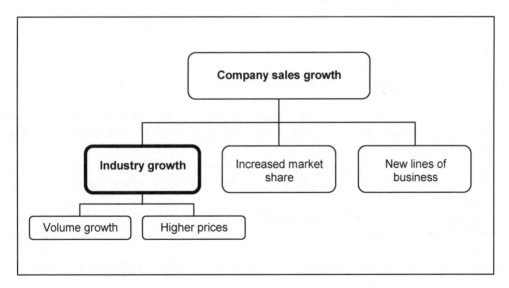

Figure 17 Progressing further along the chain

Serving up a handful of useable conclusions may be sufficient for management to decide what action should be taken. For example, one of our assignments was focused on a privately owned publishing house. In presenting our findings to clients:

- We described a firm as a 'well-regarded niche publishing business' which would be an attractive prospect to own.
- 'However, management lacks the desire or the capital to expand.' The present owners had built a successful company, but were 'lifestyle' managers who had no wish to stretch themselves in a frantic drive to maximize profits considerably. Even if they had been more ambitious to grow the company, their lack of capital imposed a severe constraint.
- We predicted that the existing owners/managers would soon retire.

The action conclusion for our client's management was that they should consider buying it.

This business had a good reputation and occupied a defensible niche in the market. Backed by our client's commitment to growth and ample capital, the new owner should be able to considerably develop this company's sales and profits. Although our client could offer it a more exciting future, its owners might have rebuffed its offer if they had been content to maintain their independence and a quieter business ethos. Hence our prediction that they were planning to retire was crucial because it showed that they are more likely to be prepared to sell it.

SUMMARIZING THE EVIDENCE THAT UNDERPINS CI CONCLUSIONS

A shrewd manager, while being pleased to receive a punchy and action-centred set of CI findings, is going to want to have a clearer idea of their foundations. Thus we needed to outline the evidence supporting our conclusions. We predicted that the owner/managers intend to retire soon. What was the basis of this forecast?

Evidence for the predicted retirement:

- The annual return filed by the firm at Companies House revealed that the two directors are aged 63 and 65 respectively.
- One of the firm's customers said the older director had been in poor health in recent months.
- The annual return and the annual report and accounts revealed no other family members to be either shareholders or directors. It is thus unlikely that their children will succeed the founders. However, sometimes family-owned firms are transferred to the control of a son or daughter even though they hadn't hitherto held shares or sat on the board.
- A more exhaustive enquiry established this couple had two children, both long established in unrelated professions and living with their own families at considerable distances from their parents.
- These publishers have added some new titles to their product line each year for 13 successive years, yet no further ones have been commissioned in the last couple of years, suggesting a degree of winding down.
- Once inveterate attendees at the main annual industry exhibition, neither of the directors had gone to it for several years according to its organizers.

We provided full documentary support for each of these pieces of evidence – but relegated them to exhibits following our one page set of findings.

Supplementary conclusions

It may also be helpful to add some further points that did not form part of the central thrust of a project, yet are interesting enough to be worth reporting. As an incidental part of our assessment of the publishing company we discovered that 'several similar companies wanted to retain their independence, but would benefit from an injection of capital'. While these are unlikely candidates for our client to approach with a view to purchase, this intelligence was attention grabbing. Our client had capital and they lacked it, so there should be mutual advantage if it could negotiate partnership agreements with them. They would obtain the capital they needed to expand while retaining their independence and our client would then enjoy a share of their enlarged pool of profits.

Our action conclusion for management was thus: 'consider approaching them with a view to partnering them, perhaps by taking a minority stake'.

'Unchaining the mind' intelligence

Aside from adding supplementary conclusions, analysts may also table those that widen the scope of executive thinking. In this example, when assembling a description of the publishing company we discovered that it had been able to enter the US market with substantial success. This achievement was grounded in persuading American academics to collaborate with editors in Europe to produce 'European' versions of their textbooks. These retained the structure and essence of the original tomes, but with 'English' English being substituted for 'American' English, some of the US examples given replaced with European ones and the inventory of key resources refocused to reflect what would be used in the 'Old World'. Building these relationships with American academia ensured their other publications enjoyed greater recognition and a more favourable reception when being marketed in the US.

The action conclusion here was for our client to investigate using this approach themselves.

Conclusions

- The method and style of CI submissions must be aligned to the needs and communication preferences of the audiences being addressed.
- Revising the draft material to shorten and sharpen it enhances the analysis as well as benefiting the recipient.
- Complicated findings can be made easier to impart using the logical tree method of the pyramid principle.
- Analysts should present not only their conclusions on the specific intelligence sought, but also report any other findings that are likely to be of value to their clients.

24 *Intelligence Countersteps*

Many CI professionals see their job as confined to 'obtaining intelligence' and, given the daunting nature of this task, the thought of getting involved in protecting their organizations or clients against penetration by outsiders will often seem an unwelcome additional burden. The very nature of their role, however, makes them well placed to make a substantial contribution to defensive countermeasures against the intelligence operations of others, whether these involve legitimate CI or industrial espionage. The actual implementation of many of these may be undertaken by security or IT specialists, but CI analysts can bring a breadth of perspective and particular forms of expertise to the task of building a protective shield. This is especially valuable when an organization has major gaps in its defences owing to 'security concerns' being too narrowly defined.

This chapter deals with:

- preserving security without losing the benefits of openness and active communicating
- the steps to creating stronger information defences using the Operational Security model
- physical aspects of intelligence countersteps
- preserving confidential information through sensible management of paper and electronic documents
- guarding against espionage and leaks by employees and others having access to the firm's premises
- taking security into account in relations with external partners
- maintaining it in activities away from the office and when sending out information.

Strong security does not entail unreasonable secrecy and refusal to communicate

In discussing corporate intelligence countersteps a sense of proportion must be kept. I am not advocating a stultifying excessive focus on defensive measures, paranoid anxiety or communicating as infrequently and minimally as possible. That type of attitude will do far more harm to a company's bid to achieve business success than any rival could inflict. A shield that is too large and heavy becomes an useless burden rather than an effective defence. Just as Chan Kim and Rénee Mauborgne have shown the general danger of becoming fixated with competitors (page 5), so fretting too much over rivals' CI efforts distracts management from the truly vital aspects of running an enterprise. It is impossible to do anything that involves other people without trusting at least some of them and operating a company of more than minimal size demands that a large number are confided in. A climate of suspicion and mistrust is not conducive to efficiency, dynamism or creativity. Moving from exchanging information within a firm from 'on a need to know' basis to sharing knowledge, while increasing the risk of leaks, brings gains that heavily outweigh this drawback. For this reason I have avoided using the term 'counter-intelligence' as governments and armed forces engaged in this are able to operate on very different assumptions regarding secrecy compared to business enterprises.

For the latter, non-communication with the outside world is a disaster not prudence. The best companies are very active communicators in terms of both frequency and extent of information provision. Again the loss of corporate privacy is of slight import compared with the benefits derived. Keeping customers, suppliers, allies, investors, the media and other groups in the dark is not the way to maintain their confidence in a firm and cooperating with it for mutual advantage. Indeed an unreasonable degree of secrecy (as in the case of the Bank of Credit and Commerce International quoted on page 124) is self-defeating in that it actually provokes closer, and usually suspicious, scrutiny than a more open enterprise would face.

Total information security is impossible and too much effort to get near it is extravagantly costly and is a powerfully effective way of hamstringing a company's competitiveness. Instead of this illusory goal, I am advocating an integrated framework for functioning in an open and trusting manner while still possessing a keen sense of the need to keep certain things secret and employing sensible precautions to do so. CI countermeasures are largely a mixture of a good general corporate security practice, awareness of the nature of the intelligence threat and common sense.

Operational Security model

All businesses need to protect their premises from thieves and vandals, as well as fires and other accidental hazards. The defensive system used to deter, foil, detect and handle these menaces can also serve to safeguard information. Unfortunately, as long as measures to protect physical security are in place, security of information is often assumed to have been taken care of. Subtler precautions are needed to achieve this in reality.

A shield more specifically intended for corporate data cover can be fashioned using the Operational Security (OPSEC) model taken from the armed forces. This consists of five stages:

- grading types of information to determine which, if disclosed, are:
  - critically important
  - significant but less vital
  - moderately sensitive
  - harmless
- reviewing the threat posed by rivals in terms of their CI capabilities and operating methods
- determining where the company is vulnerable to CI probing or industrial espionage
- assessing the extent of the risks posed in the light of the previous exercises
- devising countermeasures to buttress areas of vulnerability.

Physical security

A company's premises should be its stronghold and a safe repository for corporate secrets. So I shall take it for granted that the reader's firm has an adequate defensive perimeter with a limited number of properly protected access points. This should take care of unauthorized entrants, but many other people are likely to be visiting by invitation. Again I shall assume that a sensible policy, including a security component, is in force for handling them. Some firms have their meeting rooms placed outside a secure area (or even on a different floor) so that outsiders do not have to enter the operational parts of the premises, although this may not be practicable because of limited space or the layout of the building. Plant visits are an obvious source of risk (particularly when small devices like camera phones, USB data sticks and iPODs can be used unobtrusively to take pictures and download data from PCs)[1] and care must be taken not to make unintentional disclosures. A good security discipline, as well as being tidy, is for whiteboards to be cleaned at the end of meetings and all papers removed from the room. Apple Computers has a prominent sign in its meeting rooms warning: 'Spies have booked this room after you. Please erase the board and dispose of any confidential papers into a confidential bin.'

Paper and electronic documents

Apple's sound advice also applies to document handling and disposal. Some companies maintain good security practice such as insisting all sensitive papers are locked up when not being used – only to fall down on the final stage of document disposal. Shredding of confidential papers that are no longer required is essential if an enterprise is to avoid 'garbage archaeologists' finding nuggets of competitive gold among its wastepaper. Likewise fax machines should be located, as far as possible, in secure areas so that incoming or outgoing faxes cannot be read by unauthorized eyes. Notice boards can be a very rich source of intelligence, so discretion should be exercised as to what notices are allowed on them, especially on those located outside a secure area.

Digital documents present special dangers because of the ease of retrieving, copying and transmitting them. Password protection is often rendered nugatory by the codes being displayed on a sheet of paper close to the computer (sometimes actually stuck to it), failure to change passwords frequently or by saving them rather than having to re-key them. Tighter procedures need to replace this sort of laxity. Because a computer file can be copied far more quickly than a sheaf of papers be photocopied, there is a tendency for multiple copies to be scattered across numerous locations – on the hard drives of PCs, CDs and similar recording devices, in paper print-outs and in other media forms. This in turn multiplies the risk of security breaches.

Good hard disk housekeeping also reduces the likelihood of information leakage. Highly confidential information may be retrieved using temporary files, DOS directories and Internet caches and cookies. As deleting a document merely removes the file name and does not scrub its contents, it can often be restored. In one case I know of a very sensitive file that had been deleted, but was still in the recycle bin and thus restored with a couple of mouse clicks. Such dangers can be avoided or least reduced with sufficient awareness and care in ensuring discarded files are scrubbed from PCs and all portable media. Running a disk defragmentation program reasonably frequently not only increases the speed of the PC, it also overwrites such files.

Internet communications are another key point of vulnerability transmitting viruses and presenting opportunities for hacking into an organization's computers. External access must be kept separate from the internal network and vaccine programs installed to screen for viruses. Employees should know the dangers of downloading freeware, downloads made to portable storage media rather than to hard drives, messages encrypted and log-ins analyzed for unusual

---

1   In one extreme case a group of visitors even had special pads on the soles of their shoes to collect residues of material on the factory floor for subsequent laboratory analysis.

traffic. Internet surveillance software packages like WEBsweeper, Disk Tracy, SearchView and Telemate.Net can be bought to perform this.

Employees

For security purposes this includes not only permanent staff, but also temporary workers and external contractors. Although the great majority of companies get employees to sign confidentiality agreements, there are often major weaknesses in this area. Some firms do not get temporary staff to enter into non-disclosure agreements as their checklist of documents required from workers only relates to permanent employees. When engaging temporary labour or admitting contractors to its premises the security-conscious enterprise does not just rely on the confidentiality clauses in overarching contracts with employment agencies or other external suppliers. It insists that the individuals concerned sign *personal* non-disclosure agreements to emphasis the seriousness of the issue. Careful enquiries should also be made about the firms supplying these people, who owns and controls them and what vetting procedures are in place before they offer staff to clients for hire or appoint employees. External workers such as cleaners or night guards are often forgotten because they are not seen during the working day. Yet it is exactly among these 'invisible' people, with access to company premises when the employees are not around – the 'snooping office cleaner' episode in the film *Wall Street* will be recalled – that corporate spies have found cover for their snooping.

An amazing number of companies seem to believe that information security merely merits the signing of an agreement and a paragraph in the operating manual. Given that leaks are more likely to occur through ignorance than malice this is woefully inadequate. If those working in the company are not explicitly and emphatically told about the importance of keeping corporate secrets safe and what this entails they can hardly be expected to avoid accidental compromises of security. They need to feel its significance emotionally instead of just logging it as another set of facts (in psychological terms possessing an affective rather than merely a cognitive understanding of the issue). Every new employee – and every temporary worker or external contractor – should be given a face-to-face briefing on the significance of preserving information security before being allowed to commence work. The purpose of this meeting is two-fold: to raise awareness (something that is rarely done to a satisfactory degree) and to provide guidelines as to what should not be done and what has to be done. Priorities for safeguarding different categories of information should be spelt out, so that everyone knows there are some things about the company that must never be discussed with outsiders. Given the frequent uncertainty as to the status of certain information the staff must be encouraged to always check with appropriate designated colleagues if they are at all unsure that disclosure is harmless.

Most companies are aware of the danger posed by employees who are disciplined, dismissed or made redundant and measures such as security audits of phone contacts and information stored on work computers and the prompt cancellation of physical and electronic access privileges are commonly used. All departing staff members should also receive an exit briefing in which they will be reminded of their legal and contractual obligations not to disclose trade secrets – and the potential consequences of breaching them.

External partners

Relations with suppliers, partners in the distribution channel, corporate allies, professional advisers and public bodies should include a security dimension. As with employees, the confidentiality clauses in agreements do not give enough protection. A firm should set boundaries on the types and extent of information it is going to give third parties and impress upon them that it expects any confidences imparted to be safeguarded. Helmer and colleagues[2] also recommend a quarterly security audit of these partners, including topics like how much business they do with your firm's competitors.

External activities and dissemination of information

Members of an organization need to maintain security sensitivity while away from the office. Released from the constraining influence of their corporate surroundings people are often astonishingly indiscreet. Any business traveller will have heard highly sensitive topics aired publicly by buffoons broadcasting to the world on their mobile phones and been able to read confidential papers or documents on laptop computers being used carelessly by a person near them. Sometimes a file on a plane or train is left unattended for a few minutes. A rapid, unobserved flick through this by the anonymous competitor representative sitting in an adjacent seat can result in a major breach of security. One of the easiest and most common ways of obtaining CI is to visit a bar or club frequented by the staff of a rival. Relaxing at the end of the week, with tongues loosened by alcohol, numerous indiscretions can be overheard. The same considerations apply at events like conferences and trade shows.

During the Second World War the British government had a striking slogan: 'Careless talk costs lives'. The stakes are not so great in business, but there is no doubt that careless talk costs money. Everyone in the firm needs to realize the danger and be educated into maintaining appropriate discretion.

SHOULD THIS ENTER THE PUBLIC DOMAIN?

Before a company releases information into the public domain it should have been checked to see that sensitive data is not being unnecessarily revealed and that the benefits of disclosure outweigh the risks. This applies to corporate brochures, the firm's website, news releases, journal articles, technical papers and advertisements (perhaps especially those for job vacancies which are often placed without prior scrutiny from a security angle). Nor should documents circulated among company staff be sent to outsiders without an explicit endorsement that this is harmless. Websites are often extraordinarily indiscreet because those mounting them have a natural tendency to be as informative as possible and pages are not vetted for their security implications before being added.[3] Although many organizations have grown more cautious with greater experience, international CI expert Arthur Weiss[4] has demonstrated that many confidential documents can be accessed with ease from the Internet (without any illegal hacking being involved). These include

2   Helmes, M., Ettkin, L. and Morris. D.J. (2000), 'The risk of information compromise and approaches to prevention', *Journal of Strategic Information Systems* (9), 5–13.
3   Aaron, R. (1997), 'Giving away the store? Tell people about your company on your website – but don't overdo it', *Competitive Intelligence Review*, 8(2), 80–82.
4   Weiss' firm AWARE has some excellent CI resources (www.marketing-intelligence.co.uk).

remarkably sensitive items intended for purely internal use such data on sales, new product test results, ranked lists of customers and business plans.

Media interviews present special problems because the company lacks editorial control over how they are reported, while too much may be given away under the pressure of live interviews (as was noted in the case of John Egan on page 117). CEOs need to be as alert and careful in what they say in public as their subordinates – indeed, more so. When Gerald Ratner got carried away at a conference and described some of his chain of jewellery store's products as 'crap' and likely to last 'about as long as a Marks and Spencer prawn sandwich', he managed to wreck a successful business he had built up over many years in the space of a couple of minutes. Although this example relates more directly to good public relations practice than information security, it is still a dramatic instance of the need for discretion in making public pronouncements.[5]

EXTERNAL RESEARCHERS

Requests to participate in surveys or academic research projects demand considered judgements, not hasty acceptances. The identity of the person making the request should be corroborated, the purpose of the exercise clearly understood (the vaguer this is the more suspicious one should be) and membership of a relevant professional body confirmed (reputable market research firms, for example, will subscribe to its code of conduct for undertaking surveys and using the results). It is also sensible to ascertain if a faculty member acts as a consultant to a trade rival or a competitor is sponsoring a student. Having made these precautionary checks the business advantages of taking part can be weighed against the risk of excessive disclosure. This principle applies with special force in the case of trade shows. Hence Compaq withdrew from attending the Comdex trade convention because participating was 'giving more information to competitors than to potential customers'.

INTELLIGENCE DANGERS OF LITIGATION

Damaging disclosure is one of the factors that should be taken into account before commencing litigation. Once a case is before the courts more harm may be done to the company's interests through what has to be revealed than is gained by winning it. Certain public filings are unavoidable to comply with legal obligations. However, only the minimum information to meet the requirements of the law should be filed.

KEEPING THE CORPORATE GUARD UP

The acuteness of information security awareness decays badly over time, so there has to be a ceaseless fight against complacency. Security consciousness must be reinforced through frequent reminders and prompt warnings of new threats, while the effectiveness of defences should be probed. The latter may involve using an in-house team or hiring consultants to simulate attacks aimed at uncovering weaknesses. Because a rival may not be too fussy about the way they obtain their CI this is the only situation where those hired to play a hostile role can legitimately employ unethical methods such as misrepresenting their identity.

---

5   A more recent example was the interview granted to *Playboy* magazine by the founders of the Google internet search engine company just before its flotation in 2004, a rash act which risked breaching US securities trading law.

PERILS OF PREDICTABLE BEHAVIOUR

Firms that act in a predictable way are presenting a larger target for CI activity than they should. Bristol-Myers were planning to produce a new drug and habitually used the same two locations for their test marketing. Their rivals Johnson & Johnson were able to uncover their strategy for the market launch and its probable date in a perfectly ethical way simply by sending observers to these cities. While Bristol-Myers could not keep the testing secret they could at least have made their competitor's task more difficult by switching their sample cities.

No suite of countersteps can ever totally guard against other parties learning something about our own organization. That is no reason for making it easy for them. As John McGonagle and Carolyn Vella say in their fine textbook *Protecting Your Company Against Competitive Intelligence*:[6] 'If you cannot prevent disclosure, conceal some of it. If you cannot conceal it, make it harder or more costly to acquire.'

Conclusions

- Absolute information security is unattainable, but far better standards of protecting corporate secrets can and should be achieved.
- A high level of security consciousness is nonetheless compatible with openness and a willingness to communicate where the benefits of this outweigh the risks.
- Safeguarding corporate secrets depends upon cultivating an awareness of their importance and the threats posed to them and adopting practices which help in shielding them.
- An Operational Security system based on the OPSEC model needs to be put in place and revised in the light of new threats and conditions.
- Defensive measures must be taken to reinforce areas of intelligence exposure identified through the OPSEC process.
- Complacency insidiously erodes security awareness and good practice. It must be combated through frequent consciousness raising, a continuous monitoring of threats and periodic simulated assaults.

---

6   McGonagle, J. and Vella, C.M. (1998), *Protecting Your Company Against Competitive Intelligence*, Quorum Books.

PART IV Appendices

▌ *CI Resources*

The CI profession, both in its collective manifestation as the Society of Competitive Intelligence Professionals (SCIP) and through the endeavours of individual practitioners and firms, can congratulate itself on having assembled a cornucopia of superb resources for further learning and undertaking business research. Both tyros wishing to get acquainted with the discipline and those seeking to broaden and deepen their existing knowledge of any of its myriad facets are well served thanks to the profession's passion for communication and education. I do not describe these richly informative (and continuously evolving) resources in any detail, but would urge readers to explore them – they are sure to find plenty to interest, enlighten, stimulate and assist them within their pages. It should also be noted that this is a selection of some of the best resources – not an attempt at anything approaching an exhaustive catalogue.

1   *SCIP*. A natural starting point for discovering what CI is about and its potential value to anyone in business. The society's website (www.scip.org) has a helpful section 'Getting Started in CI', while it also publishes three periodicals for its subscription-paying members:

   – *SCIP.online* – a fortnightly e-newsletter with the emphasis on the latest happenings in the world of CI.
   – *Competitive Intelligence Magazine* – appears six times a year and contains feature articles by leading practitioners.
   – *Journal of Competitive Intelligence and Management* – a quarterly collection of essays aimed at the more seasoned CI professional.

2   *Fuld and Company*. Leonard Fuld is one of the profession's pillars. His book, *The New Competitive Intelligence* (latest edition 1995, John Wiley & Sons) was the first book I found to read on CI as a specific subject. Both a great starting point and a reference guide worth frequently consulting, it is elegantly and clearly written. This classic combines a robust theoretical underpinning with a wealth of practical advice and numerous instructive 'war-stories' from his firm's long involvement in the field.

   The Fuld website contains many good things, particularly the pithy descriptions of 'What Competitive Intelligence is and What it is not' (an admirable rejoinder to those 'it's unlawful spying' slurs and widespread fallacies such as 'it's a recent invention' or 'it predicts the future'). An extensive section of Fuld resources and links to other ones is contained in the section: 'Intelligence Index and CI tools' (www.fuld.com).

3 *AWARE.* Another doyen of the global CI profession is AWARE's managing partner Arthur Weiss. His regular 'Ask Arthur' column in SCIP's *Competitive Intelligence Magazine*, where he tackles significant issues raised by readers, is always a very rewarding read.

The firm's website includes, in its 'Resources' section, 'A Brief Guide to Competitive Intelligence' which is an excellent overview of the discipline, and a superb set of links to 'CI Resources on the Internet'. One of AWARE's most valuable services to students and practitioners of CI is its extensive 'Recommendations for Further Reading', which lists, describes and assesses a large number of relevant books (www.marketing-intelligence.co.uk).

4 *Competia* is a global community of practitioners involved in CI and strategic planning. Most of its products such as *Competia Magazine* are only available to subscribers (who additionally gain access to the Competia Library with links to over one thousand online articles on CI and business strategy), but it also publishes three free monthly e-newsletters:

   – *CompetiaNews* – covering the latest developments in the CI sector
   – *CompetiaTools* – dealing with the newest tools for business information retrieval and dissemination
   – *Competia Government News* – primarily directed at public servants, but of interest to the wider CI community.

A very useful collection of links to industry bodies in a wide range of sectors is offered in 'Competia Express' and a section on its website (www.competia.com) lists suggested books to read.

5 *London Business School*'s award-winning 'BestofBiz' site contains many good things. These include briefings on topics such as corporate alliances and strategic pricing, research guides (one of which is devoted to competitive intelligence), a resource finder, book reviews and details of new articles on business subjects (www.bestofbiz.com).

6 *The CI Resources Index* contain numerous links to relevant associations, books and training programmes (www.bidigital.com/ci).

7 *Association of Former Intelligence Officers.* Catering for ex-government and military intelligence personnel, the association's site is also of interest to those interested in business intelligence (www.afio.com).

Books

A major drawback of being an enthusiastic practitioner of CI is the demand its literature makes upon one's shelf space! It might be thought – given so many first-class tomes devoted to the discipline are in print – that the last word had been said on the subject. My own experience as a book buyer refutes this view. I have found that each writer on CI worth reading approaches their task from a different angle and succeeds in delivering fresh insights. Hence every decent new CI text has something illuminating, stimulating and educative to offer to even the most experience practitioner.

I have already mentioned a great many authors, books and articles, but shall now recommend a few not referred to earlier:

- Ben Gilad's *Early Warning: Using competitive intelligence to anticipate market shifts, control risk, and create powerful strategies* published by AMACOM in 2003. Written with Gilad's customary brio and wit, this is a worthy successor to his influential *Business Blindspots*, Infonortics edition, 1996.
- *Strategic and Competitive Analysis: Methods and techniques for analyzing business competition* by Craig S. Fleisher and Babette Bensoussan, Prentice Hall, 2002. This book discusses over 20 analytical tools and illustrates their application with examples.
- *Super Searchers on Competitive Intelligence: The online and offline secrets of top CI researchers,* edited by Margaret Metcalf Carr and Reva Basch, Cyberage Books/Information Today, 2003. This contains interviews with leading researchers revealing the tactics they use to gather information.

A principle I strongly advocate is that a good CI analyst must 'think like a CEO'. Apart from reading business periodicals there are several fine monographs that will help develop this quality. Michael Porter's seminal *Competitive Strategy: Techniques for analyzing industries and competitors* (Free Press, 1988) and its sequel, *Competitive Advantage: Creating and sustaining superior performance* (1998) are obvious examples. Two other impressive texts are:

- *Modern Competitive Analysis* by Sharon Oster, now in its third edition (Oxford University Press, 1999), which combines sound theory with many real-world illustrations.

- *Exploring Corporate Strategy* by Gerry Johnson, Kevan Scholes and Richard Whittington (Pearson Education, 2004) is a massive, comprehensive textbook for teachers and MBA students. The latest revision is the seventh edition and is published in two forms by Pearson Higher Education – 'text only' and 'text and cases'.

CI software

Numerous packages are offered to support CI work. I have not discussed them in the course of this work because choosing between them depends so heavily on the particular circumstances the analyst is operating within and the array of offerings changes very rapidly.

General advice on how to compare and select CI software is given in: Chamberlain, R. and Davies, H. (2003), 'A framework for evaluating CI technologies', *Competitive Intelligence Magazine*, 6(2), March/April, 28–32, and Bouthillier, F. and Shearer, K. (2003), *Assessing Competitive Intelligence Software: A guide to evaluating CI technology*, Information Today.

The most comprehensive listing and review of specific packages is Fuld & Company's periodic *Intelligence Software Report*. Competia's CI Directory has links to CI/BI Software providers, as does the *CI Resources Index*.

Business information portals and communities of practice

1 Karen Blakeman's first-rate business information portal RBA Company Limited has been referred to in several chapters. She also produces a free monthly newsletter on new services and developments in BI called *Tales from the Terminal Room* (www.rba.co.uk).

2 William Hann's *Freepint* is an award-winning free twice-monthly e-newsletter with tips on using the Internet for research. Its site includes 'The Bar', an electronic forum of over 70 000 researchers throughout the world. Research queries can be submitted through this facility and its formidable range of expertise tapped to provide answers or referrals to other sources (www.freepint.com).

Two subscription-based services are also offered:

- *VIP* is a monthly publication devoted to business information products and people
- *VIP Eye* is a twice-monthly e-newsletter focussing on announcements of new business information services and products (www.vivavip.com).

3 BUSLIB-L is a network of business librarians (http://listserv.boisestate.edu/archives/buslib-l.html).

4 ResearchBuzz covers business research on the Internet. There are two versions, one available free of charge, the more extensive one on a subscription basis (www.researchbuzz.com).

5 UKeIG is a community of those involved with electronic information resources. It is a Special Interest Group of Britain's Chartered Institute of Library and Information Professionals (www.ukolug.org.uk).

6 Special Libraries Association. Includes a Competitive Intelligence Division (www.sla.org).

▮▮ CI Terminology

Every academic discipline and vocation has its own specialized jargon and acronyms. These serve as a convenient shortcut for communication between practitioners. Alas they also act as a barrier to understanding for outsiders. This is particularly so in the fields of management, finance and information, which lack the systematic, clearly defined nomenclatures available in the natural sciences. Indeed, the addiction to arcane acronyms, opaque phrases and fashionable buzz words are a deplorable aspect of too much management and business literature.

Competitive intelligence has its own 'terms of art', which can sometimes puzzle or confuse those coming to them for the first time. The index to this book will direct readers to explanations of the most commonly encountered of these. In addition, a couple of web-based resources have been mounted, available free of charge, which define and clarify CI terminology.

Thus the SCIP website contains Vernon Prior of Prior Knowledge's *The Language of Business Information* (www.scip.org/ci/languagebi.asp). This extensive dictionary ranges beyond CI to include helpful entries on terms used in information science and those relating to the Internet.

Fuld and Company also offer an *Intelligence Dictionary* covering over one hundred CI terms (www.fuld.com/Tindex.IntelDict.html).

▌▌▌ *Accounting Terminology*

Amortization   Depreciation of intangible fixed assets. Shown as a note in the accounts.

Assets   Any sums of money owed to the company or things that it owns that have a monetary value. Divided into:

- fixed assets (will be used beyond the coming company financial year)
- current assets (will be used up in the coming year).

Shown in the balance sheet.

Book value   The notional value of the company as shown in the balance sheet under 'shareholders' funds'. Also called its 'net assets' or 'net asset value (NAV)'.

Capital   A term with many meanings. In the context of the balance sheet it means the issued share capital of the company (that is, the value of shares sold to investors). Can also be described as 'called-up share capital'.

Capital employed   Usually defined as fixed assets plus working capital ('net current assets'). Both items shown in the balance sheet.

Cash   Includes actual notes and coins in the company's tills and safes plus whatever is in the company's bank accounts. Shown in the balance sheet.

Cost of sales   The *direct* costs incurred in achieving the company's sales, items such as wages and raw materials. Often reported separately from company's overheads. Also called 'COS' or 'COGS' (cost of goods sold). Shown in the profit and loss account.

Creditors   Those to whom the company owes money. Divided into:

- short-term creditors (must be repaid in the coming company financial year)
- long-term creditors (do not have to be repaid until after the coming year). Shown in the balance sheet.

Current assets   Assets that will be used up in the course of the coming company financial year. Comprise stocks, debtors and cash. Shown in the balance sheet.

Debtors   A party which owes the company money and is due to settle the debt within the coming company financial year. Shown in the balance sheet as a category of current asset.

Depreciation   When fixed assets are bought their cost is shown in the cash flow statement. However, this only relates to cash spent in one particular year. A fixed asset such as a vehicle will be used over several years. To spread its cost over the period of its useful life (that is, until it wears out or becomes obsolete) a charge will be made against the profit and loss. Shown as a note to the accounts.

Distribution and administrative costs   Also called 'overheads'. Expenses incurred by the company not directly related to sales achieved (for example, the cost of the sales force, accounting function and legal fees). Shown in the profit and loss account.

Dividends   Payments usually made in cash (but sometimes in the form of additional shares) to shareholders formally approved by them, but in practice at the discretion of the directors.

EBIT (also called PBIT)   Earnings before interest and tax. The profit the company has made before it pays interest and tax. Provides a measure of company performance disregarding how it is financed and the taxes imposed upon it. Shown in the profit and loss account.

Employees   The average number of employees working for the company is shown as a note to the accounts.

Equity   Either:

- the book value of the company, in other words, 'shareholders' funds' as shown in the balance sheet
- ordinary shares as opposed to preference shares. Details of ordinary shares are shown in a note to the accounts.

Exceptional or extraordinary items   'One-off' profits or losses, that is, a profit made from the sale of a building by a company which is not in the property business. Shown separately from the normal 'operational profit' arising from the firm's usual activities in the profit and loss account.

Face value   see *Nominal value of shares*

Fixed assets   Assets that will be used for a period longer than the coming company financial year, comprising both tangible assets such as buildings, plant and machinery, vehicles, computers, furniture and intangible ones like patents, other forms of intellectual property and licences. Shown in the balance sheet.

Interest   The net interest paid by the company is shown in the profit and loss account.

Intangible fixed assets   Something the company owes that has monetary value although lacking a physical existence such as patents, copyrights, brands, licences and concessions. Shown in the balance sheet.

Inventories see *Stocks*

Issued share capital Nominal value of shares multiplied by the total number of shares in issue. Shown in the balance sheet as part of shareholders' funds.

Liabilities Any sums of money owed by the company to other parties. Divided into:

• short-term liabilities (must be paid within the coming company financial year)
• long-term liabilities (do not have to be paid within the coming year).

Shown in the balance sheet.

NAV Net Asset Value – see *Net assets*

Net assets Total assets minus total current and long-term liabilities = net assets. In British accounts net assets are called 'shareholders' funds'. Also called the company's 'net worth', 'net asset value' or 'book value'. Shown in the balance sheet.

Net current assets Current assets minus current liabilities. Also called 'working capital'. Shown in the balance sheet.

Nominal value of shares Arbitrary value assigned to them when issued which represents the extent of their holder's liability should the company fail. The market value will nearly always be different. Also known as face or par value. Shown in the note relating to issued share capital.

Operating profit Profit achieved after taking all expenses into account except for interest and tax. Measures the profitability of the company's underlying operations, so a critical yardstick. Will equal EBIT and PBIT if there are no extraordinary or exceptional revenues or expenses. Shown in the profit and loss account.

Par value see *Nominal value of shares*

PBIT Profit before interest and tax. Equals EBIT. Shown in the profit and loss account.

Post-tax profit Profit achieved after all expenses, including interest and tax, have been deducted. Shown in the profit and loss account.

Preference shares Dividends on these must be paid before equity shareholders receive any dividend. Detail shown in a note to the accounts.

Provision Sum set aside in the accounts to provide for an expected or possible expense. Examples include doubtful debts (where management are not fully confident they will be paid), redundancy costs or court cases where the company is being sued and will have to pay damages if it loses. Shown as a note to the accounts.

Retained profit Profit not distributed to shareholders, but reinvested in the company. Shown in the profit and loss account.

Reserves   Amounts retained within the company which may or not be allowed to be distributed as dividends to shareholders. Most common is retained profit, which draw upon to pay dividends, but there are other types (revaluation and share premium account, for example) which cannot be used for this purpose. Shown in the balance sheet as part of shareholders' funds.

Revaluation reserve   If the fixed assets (typically land and buildings) of the company are revalued, their appreciation in value over the figure shown in the balance sheet is treated as a category of reserve. Shown in the balance sheet.

Segmental analysis   If a company has several distinct lines of business or operates extensively overseas, the accounts should provide details of revenues and profits derived from each line of business or geographical area. Shown as the first note to the accounts.

Share premium account   If a company's shares are sold to investors for more than their nominal value, the premium over nominal value paid by investors is transferred to this reserve. Shown in the balance sheet.

Shareholders' funds   The notional value of the company as shown in the balance sheet. Also called 'net assets' or 'net asset value' (NAV). It is the sum that would be theoretically left if all assets were turned into cash and all liabilities paid off.

Stocks   Also called 'inventories'. Consist of:

1) stocks of raw materials
2) work in progress (that is, partially completed work)
3) finished goods or services that have not yet been sold.

Shown in the balance sheet as a category of current asset.

Tax   The Corporation Tax charge imposed upon the company is shown in the profit and loss account. Other taxes are treated as operating expenses, while Value Added Tax (VAT) is deducted from the figure quoted for turnover.

Tangible asset   A physical asset such as a desk, a van or a computer. Shown in the balance sheet.

Turnover   Sales or revenue achieved (excluding VAT) by the company. Shown in the profit and loss account.

Working capital   Current assets minus current liabilities. Shown in the balance sheet as 'net current assets'.

IV *US/UK Accounting Terms*

US

Balance sheet

Property, plant and equipment

Inventories

Accounts receivable ('receivables')

Accounts payable

Stockholders' (or shareholders') equity

Common stock

Equity (excluding common stock)

Statement of income

Sales

Cost of sales

Selling, general and administrative costs (SGA)

Income before taxes

Net income

UK

Balance sheet

Fixed assets

Stocks

Debtors

Creditors

Shareholders' funds

Ordinary or equity shares

Reserves

Profit and loss account

Turnover

Cost of sales

Distribution and administrative costs

Pre-tax profit or profit before tax

Earnings (or profit) – attributable to equity shareholders

Index

About the Author

Christopher Murphy is a director of business consultancy Ravensbourne Research Limited and been engaged in competitive intelligence assignments ranging across the whole span of the discipline for the past 15 years. Clients he has worked with encompass businesses of every size from start-ups through to multinational giants, as well as many public sector and not-for-profit organizations. His sectoral experience is correspondingly diverse, embracing professional services, financial institutions, manufacturing, retailing, consumer goods, together with national and local governmental bodies and charities.

He has been one of the editorial team on Jordan Publishing's flagship encyclopaedia: *International Corporate Procedures*, which deals with legal, accounting and disclosure requirements for over 50 jurisdictions since 1992. He has also contributed many articles to an extensive variety of journals, reference works and conference proceedings in the business, financial, information and other fields.

Chris has presented numerous training courses and workshops on competitive intelligence, the interpretation of accounts, corporate finance, economics, statistics, company law and other topics in a great diversity of public and in-house settings. As well as delivering courses at the London, Manchester and INSEAD business schools, he has trained on behalf of corporate clients in the USA, Germany and the Netherlands.

He studied economics, history and political science at the University of Hull, Birkbeck College, London and the London School of Economics. He is a member of the Society of Competitive Intelligence Professionals, the Society of Business Economists and the World Futures Society and is a Fellow of the Royal Statistical Society.

You can contact Chris via any of the following means:

Ravensbourne Research Limited
4, Croxted Mews
Croxted Road
Dulwich
SE24 9DA

Tel: 020 8658 0487
Mobile: 0780 3507753
Fax: 020 8460 8842
Email: Chrismurphy1999@yahoo.co.uk